MW00811194

TRAGEDY AND THE MODERNIST NOVEL

This study of tragic fiction in European modernism brings together novelists who espoused, in their view, a Greek vision of tragedy and a Darwinian vision of nature. To their minds, both tragedy and natural history disclosed unwarranted suffering at the center of life. Thomas Hardy, Virginia Woolf, Albert Camus, and Samuel Beckett broke with entrenched philosophical and scientific traditions that sought to exclude chance and undeserved pains from tragedy and evolutionary biology. *Tragedy and the Modernist Novel* uncovers a temporality central to tragic novels' structure and ethics: that of the moment. These authors made novelistic plot the delivery system for lethal natural and historical forces, and then countered such plot with moments of protest – characters' fleeting dissent against unjustifiable harms.

MANYA LEMPERT is Assistant Professor of English at the University of Arizona. She specializes in the nineteenth- and twentieth-century novel, ancient and modern tragedy and philosophy, and theories of evolution.

TRAGEDY AND THE MODERNIST NOVEL

MANYA LEMPERT

University of Arizona

CAMBRIDGE
UNIVERSITY PRESS

CAMBRIDGE
UNIVERSITY PRESS

University Printing House, Cambridge CB2 8BS, United Kingdom

One Liberty Plaza, 20th Floor, New York, NY 10006, USA

477 Williamstown Road, Port Melbourne, VIC 3207, Australia

314–321, 3rd Floor, Plot 3, Splendor Forum, Jasola District Centre, New Delhi – 110025, India

79 Anson Road, #06–04/06, Singapore 079906

Cambridge University Press is part of the University of Cambridge.

It furthers the University's mission by disseminating knowledge in the pursuit of education, learning, and research at the highest international levels of excellence.

www.cambridge.org
Information on this title: www.cambridge.org/9781108496025
DOI: 10.1017/9781108865616

First published 2020

A catalogue record for this publication is available from the British Library.

Library of Congress Cataloging-in-Publication Data
NAMES: Lempert, Manya, 1984– author.
TITLE: Tragedy and the modernist novel / Manya Lempert.
DESCRIPTION: New York : Cambridge University Press, 2020. | Includes bibliographical references and index.
IDENTIFIERS: LCCN 2020016619 (print) | LCCN 2020016620 (ebook) | ISBN 9781108496025 (hardback) | ISBN 9781108811484 (paperback) | ISBN 9781108865616 (epub)
SUBJECTS: LCSH: Modernism (Literature) | Fiction–20th century–History and criticism. | Tragic, The, in literature. | Nature in literature. | Tragedy–History and criticism. | Greek drama (Tragedy)–Influence. | Darwin, Charles, 1809-1882–Influence.
CLASSIFICATION: LCC PN56.M54 L46 2020 (print) | LCC PN56.M54 (ebook) | DDC 809.3/9112–DC23
LC record available at https://lccn.loc.gov/2020016619
LC ebook record available at https://lccn.loc.gov/2020016620

ISBN 978-1-108-49602-5 Hardback

For my mother

Contents

vii

Acknowledgments

With their incomparable support, Dorothy Hale, Ann Banfield, and Catherine Gallagher have made this book possible. Dori, exemplar and mentor, has been my lodestar. Virtuosic and giving, Ann has shown me the way. Cathy has been the finest interlocutor and ally.

At Stanford, Brett Bourbon and Josh Landy kindled my interest in modernism and philosophy early on. At the University of California, Berkeley, Debarati Sanyal and Chenxi Tang crystallized my thinking in their French and German seminars. Juliana Chow, Spencer Engler-Coldren, Seulghee Lee, Rosa Martinez, Rasheed Tazudeen, and Sunny Xiang have been my muses and confidants. I am grateful to the Mabelle McLeod Lewis Memorial Fund for affording me the time to finish my dissertation. Ian Duncan has fostered this work with his sparkling conversation and unstinting generosity. Maura Nolan has been an unparalleled advisor on tragedy.

At Tilburg Philosophy Summer School, Simon Critchley inspired and encouraged me. At the University of Arizona, Laura Berry championed this work. David Sterling Brown, trusted comrade, wrote with me. Paul Hurh and Lynda Zwinger were crucial readers in departmental review. Homer Pettey commented on drafts shrewdly and indefatigably. For their invaluable guidance, I also relied on Dan Blanton, Jennifer Jenkins, Doug Mao, Ander Monson, Trudy Obi, and Johanna Skibsrud. Ronan McDonald and Ato Quayson were vital and indispensable manuscript readers. Catherine Flynn and Cindy Weinstein gave pivotal advice, and Arum Park and Sarah Weinstein provided decisive assistance with manuscript preparation. Carolyn Vega at the New York Public Library's Berg Collection helped me a great deal. I would also like to recognize the labor of Stephanie Sakson, and that of Edgar Mendez at Cambridge University Press. Earlier versions of parts of Chapters 2 and 3 have appeared as "Virginia Woolf, Charles Darwin, and the Rebirth of Tragedy," *Twentieth-Century Literature* 64, no. 4 (2018): 449–82, and as "Thomas Hardy's Theory of Tragic

Character," *Studies in the Novel* 49, no. 4 (2017): 470–92. I owe much to these journals' editors; I appreciate their permission to incorporate that material here.

Craig Hoyt at the University of California, San Francisco, has been my lifelong proponent. I am indebted to Jeff Deutsch and David Lewis for their friendship and collaboration. Charlotte Goodwin, Maria Robinson, and Miriam Rosenfeld have buoyed me up since childhood. From college to Cal to the desert, Peter Nilson has been my sine qua non. He is the sustaining force behind this work.

To Ray Ryan, who endorsed and welcomed me at Cambridge University Press, and who saw this book to completion, I owe every thanks.

CHAPTER I

Introduction
Modernist Tragedy

Attic Novelists

Why did modern European novelists value ancient tragedy? I find that they turned to the Greeks to rebel against ossified, lethal thought in their own time. Tragedy was, for them, a diagnostic tool. With it, they traced present-day sufferings to their political and existential sources. In their view, tragedy fostered exposé. For a cadre of modern writers, tragedy lent itself to depicting and responding to recurrent crises and their aftermaths. Tragedy allowed writers to think about senseless chance and violence in the natural world; it allowed them to think about political violence, intergenerational trauma, and cyclical calamity. Tragedy was a refutation of Western chauvinism, with its Panglossian defenses of the capitalist and colonialist status quo; Voltaire's Dr. Pangloss maintained that all was for the best in the best of all possible worlds. Tragic fictions thought otherwise. Tragic novels acknowledged grief, rage, and irredeemable loss. They represented wanting justice, absent consent, and limited agency. These writers formulated an ethics of tragedy as well, which involved collective resistance to atrocity, in straitened circumstances. Their tragedies presented characters beset by amoral or immoral forces, and such works modeled the defiance of structures of harm – neither their denial nor their reproduction.

Thomas Hardy, Virginia Woolf, Albert Camus, and Samuel Beckett contested a cultural tendency to defend undue and unequal suffering. They recognized a different impetus in Greek tragedy: to expose and excoriate suffering and to interrogate its provenance. For this reason, Greek tragedy appealed to them. Refusing to justify suffering, their own fiction was tragic. In their modern milieus, in the context of secularizing science, they recast the whims of the gods as the accidents of natural history. Their shared belief in a Darwinian account of creation, heedless of creatures' pains, underwrote their representations of uncaring natural phenomena, of the ill luck of birth and circumstance, and of historical actors who emulated and compounded the callousness of natural processes.

The aim of this book is not to suggest that a murky tragic sense in art and life was one symptom of an amorphous modern angst. Instead, I would like to illustrate a specific model of living that this set of authors who affiliated themselves with the genre advanced in their novels. Along the way, I would like to distinguish these novelistic conceptions of tragedy – implicit in these authors' fiction and explicit in their writings on ancient Greek thought and drama – from other influential theories of the art form (Aristotle's and Nietzsche's, for instance). Such contrasting of novelists with giants of philosophy shows just how new and iconoclastic these authors' return to a very old genre was. Their rethinking of tragedy was a serious acknowledgment of – and response to – a life suffused with contingency: the contingency of individual histories, of history, and of humanity's existing at all.

I find a pronounced disjunction between literary tragedies and philosophical theories of tragedy. Philosophies of tragedy aim to redeem suffering; this is their raison d'être. Literary tragedies just as forcibly and constitutively do not. Modernist critic F. L. Lucas makes this point persuasively in *Tragedy in Relation to Aristotle's "Poetics,"* which Virginia and Leonard Woolf published in 1927:

> It is easy enough to talk glibly of reconciliation and harmony over the dead bodies on the tragic stage. It may be true that the cry of the blood of Agamemnon is satisfied at last with revenge, that Oedipus comes to rest in a glorious grave in quiet Colonus, that Heracles ascends to sit on the right hand of Zeus; but can we suppose that to Cassandra, to Jocasta, to Dejanira all seemed to end so pleasantly in a pink sunset of satisfaction? Does the world of tragedy or the tragedy of the world really bear any relation to this Universe squirted with philosophic rose-water? It is an astonishing conception. Many another Dr. Pangloss has endeavored to make mankind swallow the world like a pill by coating it with sugar.[1]

Lucas is referring to Hegel in this last line. Simon Critchley echoes Lucas's sentiment: "In the *Philosophy of Right*, Hegel writes, 'No people ever suffered wrong. What it suffered, it merited.' This is wrong."[2]

For the writers in this study, tragedy is not suffering's apologist. In their hands, tragedy evinces a different ethics. This ethical program entails, first, representation of undeserved pain. Pursuant to this representation is a spirit of protest, which generates short-lived glimpses of more salutary living. This is the tragic ethics that Woolf encapsulates in saying: "The moment was all; the moment was enough."[3] These transformative moments are not cure-alls, but they suffice to hold despair at bay. What I find so wrenching in modern tragic fiction is how evanescent, how tenuous these moments are. But they are also so essential. Visionary and liberatory, they bespeak rival modes of experience and rival social relations. Tragedy, in this modernist vein, confronts imperiled communities with "all" they can do, rather than All, but ventures that "all" might be "enough."

These authors refuse to assign compensatory value to suffering, which is the modus operandi of much interpretation of tragedy. It is also the modus operandi of much imperialist political theory, Christian religious thought, and natural history both before and after Darwin. Darwin's explanation of evolution, as I argue in Chapter 2, introduces a tragic conception of natural history into modern thought. In the mid-nineteenth century, Darwin recognized chance, not design, as the engine of all life. Darwin heretically argued that random variation among creatures – the unpredictable, good or ill luck – underwrote the existence of species. A core tenet of tragedy, long resisted, became a core tenet of the modern life sciences: chance, the contingent, the unforeseeable, what the Greeks called *tuchē*. Greek tragedies depicted externally wrought, fortuitous necessity, divorced from mercy, from justice, from theodicy. Darwinian natural selection likewise preserved and destroyed creatures – retaining traits that happened to be adaptive and jettisoning those that did not – with no conscious volition and no further end in mind, only because of chance differences among creatures. In both Greek tragic drama and Darwinian evolutionary biology, no moral Mind allocated fate to individual beings. As a result, tragedy and evolutionary theory faced analogous interpretive distortion; a preponderance of theorists sought to banish the unplanned, the aleatory, from fiction's and science's narratives of individual and species-wide destiny. By contrast, the strain of literary modernism that I treat conceives of nature in a manner distinct from redemptive or teleological discourse. The writers in this study admitted chance into their fictional worlds. Their revival of what they understood to be a Greek tragic worldview constituted a literary backlash against comforting, anthropocentric accounts of human origins and human futures. These authors saw the fickleness of the Greek gods in Darwin's godless nature. In the Greek plays, too, the inhumanity of men matched the indifference of divinity; similarly, in tragic novels, indefensible cultural logics ape the pitiless material world. Tragic antagonists, ancient and modern, prove double: for these writers, the larger universe's insensibility too often finds its analogue in lethal social and political norms.

Like Darwin, these novelists convey the paucity of meaning, the dearth of sufficient reason, that attaches to suffering. In their tragic framings of life, these writers animate characters who find themselves compelled to accept a restricted compass for action, and who commit to act nonetheless. These novelists also gravitate toward lyrical, time-dilating moments in their fiction, which serve as ballasts in the tragic tide, temporary stays to tragic inevitability. In Hardy's case, these brief interludes exist primarily in imagination. Hardy's final two tragedies, *Tess of the d'Urbervilles* and *Jude the Obscure*, privilege characters' and narrators' momentary conjurations of a present that stands apart from and in insoluble conflict with brutal culture. What was a rhetorical fixture of Greek tragedy – disputing the irrevocable plot at hand – is a prominent facet of Hardy's tragedies as well. It is characters' should-have-been lives, fleetingly evoked, that Hardy's tragedies exhort readers to make reality. Hardy's hypothetical moments of reprieve then emerge as full-fledged, realized moments of safety and satiety in Woolf. Woolf takes Hardy's message of unforgiving temporality to heart, but where his moments were yearning and abortive, hers become tragedy's pièce de résistance. Woolf juxtaposes these moments against the timelessness of abstract concepts and the deep time of evolution. Given these metrics, human joys and cataclysms measure as naught. Still, Woolf devotes the lion's share of her fiction to these rare intervals of security and solidarity, precisely because they do such outsized work to sustain characters in the face of inhuman timescales. Across both Woolf's and Camus's oeuvres, these signatures of modernism – "moments of being," Woolf calls them – function as bulwarks against ruthless natural forces and the viciousness of modern history. Mirroring Woolf, Camus abandons traditional plot structure in favor of ephemeral, rapturous moments, set in the shadow of natural and historical menace. Beckett's characters also contend with ambient conditions both inscrutable and agonizing; they respond with denial (doubt, disbelief) as a mode of pain management. But Beckett's late novella *Company* brings resuscitating moments into an otherwise devastated fictional world. Although these moments are still epistemologically and emotionally suspect – not apogees of happiness – they attest to surroundings that might allow for pleasure, amelioration, or company.

In various ways, then, these authors pit vulnerable people and their fragile moments of respite against encircling, inhuman forces that warp and extinguish personhood. Such fiction admits ineradicable constraints on people's freedom and flourishing, yet envisions small-scale dissent, momentary resistance to annihilation. Equally in their oeuvres, however, these writers picture characters who are drawn to not being – to ceasing to be, ceasing to ruminate and to feel – and such character studies in negation, I argue, operate as cautionary tales. Modern fiction becomes a site of counterpoised ethical experiments: in tragic ethics, on the one hand, and in nihilism, on the other. Juxtaposing fleeting "yeses" against suicidal "nos," these writers work to counteract ethical paralysis, what critics of tragedy from Plato onward feared to be the genre's issue. The abdication of moral and political action was also what literary critic György Lukács held to be the message of the modernist novel in particular.[4] But the literature in this study maintains that although the natural processes that produced our human senses, language, and cognition appear, in Camus's parlance, absurd – devoid of intention and unconcerned with humankind – our creation of meaning is precisely what such absurdity galvanizes. Modernist tragedy envisions a model of sociality based not on transcendent design but on its absence: shared defiance of the amoral and inhumane.

These authors' readings of Greek tragedy and their own tragic fictions mark, in the late nineteenth and twentieth centuries, a concerted departure from much of the genre's reception history. From the Middle Ages forward, a dominant objective in philosophy and literary theory was to decipher metaphysical order in Greek tragic drama and to testify to such unity in modern instantiations of the genre. Hardy's tragedies, by contrast, denounce this recasting of mortal luck and the cruelties of men as the victim's wrongdoing in a providential universe. Woolf calls Hardy "the greatest tragic writer among English novelists" and lauds his daring to represent "that human beings are the sport of forces outside themselves," forces that participate in no salutary plan.[5] Woolf finds Hardy ground-breaking in his novelistic communiqué that "no symbol of caprice and unreason [is] too extreme to represent the astonishing circumstances of our existence."[6] Woolf comments extensively on the insurrectionary truth-telling of Hardy's tragic predecessors as well: "it is to the Greeks that we turn when we are sick ... of the Christianity and its consolations, of our own age."[7] Camus, too, who is strikingly Woolfian in his ethics and aesthetics, turns to tragedy to emphasize the lamentable passage from natural peril to manmade atrocity. He contends that European "history has put on the mask of destiny"; this history behaves as the divine or natural fatality that it claimed to supersede.[8] What Horkheimer and Adorno called enlightenment's delusion – its pretension to banish fear with reason – modernist tragedy also exposes.[9] Beckett, too, identifies no consoling antidote to mortal fear in natural or social history. Instead, he scathingly defines tragedy as "the original and eternal sin" of having been born.[10] Deriving such wording from Anaximander and Schopenhauer,

Beckett has in mind a chronic and congenital suffering, punishment for the transgression one has committed at birth – even as there is no reason for individual existence to be so cardinal a wrong. He has in mind a crime that cannot be expiated, in a world that cannot be set right.[11] Beckett anticipates Anne Carson's account of tragedy; in her introduction to her translation of four plays by Euripides, she writes: "Why does tragedy exist? Because you are full of rage. Why are you full of rage? Because you are full of grief."[12] Beckett, too, associates tragedy with a grief that cannot be remedied. Even if we were to succeed in expelling noxious cultural narratives from our midst, such that "[n]othing will remain of all the lies they have glutted [us] with," Beckett suggests that we would still be subject to wrenching embodiment: "Tears gush from [the eye] practically without ceasing, why is not known, nothing is known, whether it's with rage, or whether it's with grief, the fact is there."[13] Beckett's indignant narrator in *The Unnamable* labels this reasonless, ineliminable torture "getting humanized."[14]

This strain of European "modernism" is distinct from European "modernity" insofar as it disputes European modernity's imperialist premises: its insistence on progressivist history, on unassailable subjects who are self-determining.[15] Tragedy is one of the strongest expressions of modernism's critique of modernity. The novelty of this modernist rapport with an ancient art form lies in its refusal to grant that European science and history render people ever more invulnerable to loss, in a world that makes underlying sense. It is true that in complex and varying ways, other spokesmen of the period – Eliot, Pound, Joyce, or Auden – engage in anti-metaphysical thinking, recur to ancient genres, and seek to depict fresh and unprecedented approaches to living. But their endeavors to shore up even partial and provisional order in the face of historical and epistemological uncertainty strike a more major key, possess a more sanguine and hopeful orientation, than does tragedy. More committed to epic, as C. D. Blanton argues, these other modernists still pursue "the claim to totality from which the form [epic] originates."[16] Blanton understands such totality, in Hegelian and Marxist terms, to be that of history, and shows us modernists who recognize that they cannot directly represent this totality in their work, but who endeavor to approach it obliquely, via a metonymic method that supplies shards of the whole as proof of its reality. Such authors, in this reading, manage to evoke precisely the fullness that their poetry cannot house within its bounds: "Conceived in this way, the epic remains *necessary* whether it is possible or not, the simple name of a need to conceive the present *as* historical, to think totality."[17]

I would say that what modernist tragedy indexes is the want of sense that inheres in the environments people inhabit. As postcolonial, feminist, and Marxist critics have shown, exposure to harm is not equally shared. Racial capitalism protects its beneficiaries and redistributes harm to internal and external Others. It displaces fault onto them. Crucially, racial capitalism exacerbates danger and consigns its victims to extreme risk. Both Hardy's and Beckett's characters resist induction into this order of violence. They balk at recruitment into the normative role of "man." Woolf shares this concern, that even dissidents will be compelled to think as their oppressors do. Camus is also focused on complicity in state violence. "All I maintain," says his character in *The Plague*, "is that on this earth there are pestilences and there are victims, and it's up to us, so far as possible, not to join forces with the pestilences."[18] Camus imagines opposition to pestilential ideology and he imagines characters who perpetrate colonialist terror and try to defend enslavement. These authors, that is, depict an array of characters: from culpable insiders to demonized and defiant outsiders. When their writings, then, evoke a common humanity and shared precarity, this is not to deny or to elide political injustice. Instead, from their tragic perspective, the horror of mortal suffering per se only emphasizes the fact that eugenic, genocidal Western politics – the gratuitous horrors of white supremacy, patriarchy, colonialism, and fascism – are indefensible.

Such tragedy does not subscribe to a dialectical logic either: the divisions that these authors represent between persons and injurious forms of power are not precursors to reconciliation. Paul Saint-Amour, leery of too stringent a definition of modernism, offers the following rule of thumb: "the term 'modernism' functions as nonexclusive shorthand for works that display, even speculatively or intermittently, an anticontemporary or counterconventional temper."[19] What is anticontemporary and counterconventional in modernist tragedy is characters' piecing together that there is no lasting safety to be derived from their surroundings. The plots in which they are inscribed are crushing – and these plots are binding, some for now, some forever. As Jay Clayton has argued, this merciless logic of plot characterized fin-de-siècle naturalism and twentieth-century dystopian fiction as well.[20] But naturalist and dystopian narrative arcs primarily referenced social ills, whereas these authors drawn to Greek tragedy explicitly paired violent social practices with representations of a natural world bereft of directive, meaningful structure. Foreign to the tragic novel, then, is experience of the Kantian sublime, in which vulnerable subjects come to realize that they do hold pride of place in an intelligible cosmos and that reason protects them from harm even as their bodily senses are overwhelmed by the might or enormity of inhuman forces. While modernist literary critics like Lukács and Joseph Wood Krutch stipulated precisely this – that tragedy qua genre goes hand in hand with a transcendence of pain and of incoherence – the tragic novelists in this study detect, as Woolf puts it, "no such kindly meaning" in "the huge blackness of what is outside us, of what we are not."[21]

I defend in such modernism a "mortalist humanism" that holds collective susceptibility to loss to be the basis for tragedy and for ethics – an idea that Miriam Leonard and Bonnie Honig criticize in Judith Butler's work.[22] I do not think, to answer Honig and Leonard, that this ethical turn to "mortalism" evacuates tragedies of their specific historical content or ushers in apolitical inaction. Honig argues, too, that there must be more to tragedy than solidarity in grief, and points to a feast that mourning Priam and Achilles share in the *Iliad* and to an invitation to dance even in *Antigone*.[23] And here I fully agree. I have found solidarity in enjoyment to be the defining ethical yield of modernism's tragedies. Those imagined or impermanent possibilities of happiness, manifestations of some alternate world, are enshrined in these tragedies' pages. Where literary critic Cristopher Watkin sees impoverished ethics and "ascetic atheism" in this period, I see the tragic sociality that keeps characters afloat in the face of disaster and structural violence.[24] Watkin contends that a modern eschewal of religion leaves only "meagre crumbs of . . . happiness."[25] But what Watkin labels "scraps of immanence" in the wake of faith, I find rehabilitated and prized in modernist fiction.[26] Watkin illuminates philosophical endeavors today, in Nancy, Badiou, and Meillassoux, to counter a perceived starvation diet after metaphysics, but I find that modernism's pared-down moments of precarious meaning already nourish a new and tragic ethics that sustains its characters. Modernism's tragic authors show us that to lament mortal finitude is not to pine for religion. These authors do not yearn for what they do not believe in, spiritual or political eschatology. These writers' tragic stances, on the contrary, commit them to beauty and justice, but without hope of deliverance.

Tragedy versus Philosophy

A certain strain of philosophy has long been antipathetic to the tragic conception of nature and history that these authors embrace; such philosophy has been hostile to depictions of irremediably fragile persons besieged by amoral and immoral forces. Plato roundly disparaged tragedy in the

Republic precisely because, in his apt assessment of it, it bore witness to human grief at gutting and unwarranted misfortune. To use Aristotle's terms, tragedy as Plato saw it lacked efficient and final causes for human suffering; it evoked a cosmos in which there was no clear origin of our keenest pains, and no higher purpose for them. The gods subjected mortals to *tuchē*, not *eikos*; the latter refers to rational odds we can calculate, the likely or probable. For the Greeks, *tuchē* and *eikos* were ontologically distinct categories. We might think of *tuchē* as stochastic: impossible to predict in advance. Not surprisingly, then, Aristotle's defense of tragedy consisted in ascribing an intelligible source to tragic fates. Aristotle bound tragedy to *eikos*. In Aristotle's *Poetics*, tragedy was ideally to stem from knowable causes, from characters' own inadvertent mistakes; these were not culpable but pitiable. The causal logic of tragic plot, then, was to have little connection with divine whim, curse, or prophecy that sullied mortal happiness. A man was his own causal nexus of suffering; neither gods nor others persecuted him. Further responding to Plato's contention that tragedy upended a stoic regimen of the soul, Aristotle also assigned the genre a productive social *telos*: that of catharsis. However we understand this much-debated term, catharsis is of benefit to audiences.[27] It is productive, not destructive. So Terry Eagleton, in his twenty-first-century investigation of the genre, can gaze backward and say that "tragic art for conservative theorists is a supremely affirmative affair."[28] Affirmative tragedy may seem like a contradiction in terms, but it is true that for a majority of thinkers, tragedy must dramatize suffering that is morally justified, socially useful, or aesthetically gratifying. Aristotle, Hegel, Nietzsche, and Lukács subscribed to versions of this view. But as I show in Chapters 2 and 3, Hardy squarely departs from Aristotle, and Woolf from Nietzsche; in Chapter 4, I explain Camus's rejection of the counter-tragic philosophy of Sartre. And the philosophers whom Beckett preferred – early Greek thinkers apart from Plato and Aristotle, as well as Geulincx, Schopenhauer, Mauthner, and Wittgenstein, among others – also broke ranks with Plato and his descendants and with existentialist humanism, and pictured life at odds with intelligible, consolatory, or anthropocentric design.

Here is one illustrative example, however, of the prevailing philosophical impulse to neutralize suffering, especially in connection with tragedy. In three separate ways, Nietzsche over the course of his career sought to interpret tragedy as a recipe for redemption from pain. First, he contended that it proffered narratives of individual heroism so beautiful they rendered life's torments bearable for us. Second, he suggested that tragedy hinted at the possibility of mystical self-dissolution and recovery of unindividuated

being, the ultimate salvation from mortal grief. Third, he determined that
tragedy pointed the way to an endorsement of our mortal sufferings
themselves. Nietzsche offered the first two readings in *The Birth of Tragedy*
(1872, revised 1886). Here he suggested that tragedy's salves are supplied
by the two generative drives in Greek drama: the Apolline and the
Dionysiac. Both serve to soothe individuals (tragedy's characters and
audiences), who are aghast at *tuchē*: "the terrors and horrors of existence,"
"the Titanic forces of nature," the "unpitying" "cosmic stupidity."[29] Well-
wrought Apolline illusion affords the individual hero succor: "the Apolline
quality of the mask [is] the necessary result of gazing into the inner, terrible
depths of nature – radiant patches, as it were, to heal a gaze seared by
gruesome night."[30] Tragedy's terrifying truth – figured as a glimpse of
nature in all its chaotic and inhuman chanciness – is "overcome by the
Greeks, or at least veiled and withdrawn from view" by these Apolline
ministrations, in order "to seduce us into continuing to live."[31] Every
sighting of nature must be alleviated by Apolline fiction: "Here, at this
moment of supreme danger for the will, *art* approaches as a saving
sorceress with the power to heal. Art alone can re-direct those repulsive
thoughts about the terrible or absurd nature of existence into representations with which man can live."[32] Art produces a trompe l'oeil vindication
or relaxation of our suffering.

The truth of nature that so daunts the individual is, for Nietzsche, the
Dionysiac – the destructive, fecund, uncaring wellspring of life. And
Nietzsche's key argument in *The Birth of Tragedy* is that although such
nature nauseates individual men and women, their suffering does not stem
from nature itself but from the singular evil of individuation. Our primary
misfortune is *being individuated in the first place*. If we could rejoin the
Dionysiac stream of life, we would be released from mortal terrors.
Precisely the loss of personal identity that sickens individual consciousness
is the mystical homecoming we need. This for Nietzsche is the message of
the pre-Classical, springtime rituals of the fertility spirit Dionysus, who
was dismembered only to be reimmersed in the whole. With this rite, the
entirety of the community, in Nietzsche's view, rejoined nature as well:

> Not only is the bond between human beings renewed by the magic of the
> Dionysiac, but nature, alienated, inimical, or subjugated, celebrates once
> more her festival of reconciliation with her lost son, humankind. Freely the
> earth offers up her gifts, and the beasts of prey from mountain and desert
> approach in peace.... Now the slave is freeman, now all the rigid, hostile
> barriers, which necessity, caprice, or "impudent fashion" have established
> between human beings, break asunder. Now, hearing this gospel of

universal harmony, each person feels himself to be not simply united, reconciled or merged with his neighbour, but quite literally one with him, as if the veil of maya had been torn apart, so that mere shreds of it flutter before the mysterious primordial unity.[33]

For brief moments we are truly the primordial being itself and we feel its unbounded greed and lust for being; the struggle, the agony, the destruction of appearances, all this now seems to us to be necessary, given the uncountable excess of forms of existence thrusting and pushing themselves into life, given the exuberant fertility of the world-Will; we are pierced by the furious sting of these pains at the very moment when, as it were, we become one with the immeasurable, primordial delight in existence and receive an intimation, in Dionysiac ecstasy, that this delight is indestructible and eternal. Despite fear and pity, we are happily alive, not as individuals, but as the *one* living being, with whose procreative lust we have become one.[34]

Nietzsche proposes that all tragic heroes and heroines are Dionysus' doubles: encased in individual form but destined to return to the whole. This is what the ecstatic, intoxicated, carousing band of satyrs – Nietzsche's envisioning of the early tragic chorus – signifies. Nietzsche does not practice archeology or anthropology, but the extraction of a formula for mystical return to nature, supposedly encoded in Greek drama: *"the doctrine of the Mysteries taught by tragedy*: the fundamental recognition that everything which exists is unity; the view that individuation is the primal source of all evil; and art as the joyous hope that the spell of individuation can be broken, a premonition of unity restored."[35]

Late Nietzsche proceeds to develop one final cure for mortal fear: even as individuals we might delight in the Dionysiac. Nietzsche comes to deem desire for the dangers and accidents of the Dionysiac the very marker of a healthy psyche. The painfulness of individuation becomes the preferred experiential register of those with sufficient strength of character to relish all aspects of their fate, as Nietzsche writes in *The Will to Power* (1901):

"How much truth can a spirit *endure*, how much truth does a spirit *dare*?" – this became for me the real standard of value . . . a Dionysian affirmation of the world as it is, without subtraction, exception, or selection. . . . The highest state a philosopher can attain: to stand in a Dionysian relationship to existence – my formula for this is *amor fati*.

It is part of this state to perceive not merely the necessity of those sides of existence hitherto denied, but their desirability; and not their desirability merely in relation to the sides hitherto affirmed (perhaps as their complement or precondition), but for their own sake, as the more powerful, more fruitful, *truer* sides of existence, in which its will finds clearer expression.[36]

All three of Nietzsche's approaches to tragedy aim for life's wholesale affirmation; in this instance, the heroic will to power seeks the truth, whereas formerly Apolline loveliness had hidden it from view or choral Dionysiac "unity" had promised liberation from all self-consciousness.

Whichever model of tragedy Nietzsche espouses, however, his theories align him more with modernism's nontragic "mythical method" than with the Greeks. T. S. Eliot's elaboration of this mythical method specifies narrative forms and mental archetypes – patterns of sacrifice and rebirth – that can be marshaled to counteract, even to vanquish, catastrophe and sorrow. Indebted to James Frazer's *The Golden Bough*, Eliot warms in particular to the new anthropology's notion of primal rites in which suffering is a source of renewal. Eliot sees anthropology's rituals as the newly disclosed blueprints of culture. He finds such enduring structures to lie at the heart of his own poetry, W. B. Yeats's, and James Joyce's *Ulysses*.[37]

As we will see, however, precisely what tragedy means to Hardy, Woolf, Camus, and Beckett is the refusal of regenerative, stabilizing plot structure (*mythos*). Just as Hardy's tragic novels contest nineteenth-century anthropology's romance of the sacrificial victim, Woolf's fiction challenges the twentieth century's recourse to consolatory rereadings and redeployments of ancient ritual and myth. In the first decades of the twentieth century, anthropologist Jane Ellen Harrison, for instance, championed a Dionysiac temporality that in her view privileged matrifocal interconnection over individualist and hero-worshipping patriarchy. Harrison praised the modern recovery of such ancient temporality in Henri Bergson's work: "Dionysos, with every other mystery-god, was an instinctive attempt to express what Professor Bergson calls *durée*, that life which is one, indivisible, and yet ceaselessly changing."[38] Modernist writers, then, are associated with this recuperative Dionysiac-Bergsonian temporality, or with anthropology's cyclical time of ritual. Yet the march of the hours in tragedy is inimical to such fusion of loss and resurrection; signally, modernist tragedy cannot break the spell of individuation. There is a tragic perspective separate from Nietzsche's solutions to suffering and from anthropological, mystical, or mythical methods: characters brave incurable fates, mutinously achieving moments of reprieve in the face of their intractable antagonists. These moments constitute resistance to fate; characters oppose the compounding, the exacerbating of fate. Nietzsche's *amor fati*, love of the perilous status quo, is not their way. Here we see the difference between loving the totality of fate, believing it to possess, in its entirety, benefit or justification, and the affirmation of rare intervals of peace that irradiate an otherwise lamentable condition.

This book therefore departs from studies of modernism and modernity that take nineteenth-century philosophy's invention of "the tragic" to represent the cultural zeitgeist and to be the incitement to a literary return to tragedy. A study like K. M. Newton's *Modern Literature and the Tragic* makes this case for the philosophical roots of modernist tragedy. Newton reads modern novels as illustrations of the philosophy of the tragic; such philosophy, as we have seen, assumes broken totality to be the source of suffering, just as late nineteenth-century and early twentieth-century anthropology assumed discord to be the precursor to rapprochement. In Newton's readings, then, tragic literature stages dialectical rupture, warring parts of an underlying whole. Newton understands tragedy to be delivering a reminder to "respect" both sides: subject and object in Schelling, colliding ethical principles in Hegel, "undecidable" plans of action in Derrida.[39] In this vein, recent criticism has also revisited philosophies of the tragic themselves. Miriam Leonard's *Tragic Modernities*, for instance, follows in the footsteps of Peter Szondi's foundational *An Essay on the Tragic* and presents philosophers and political theorists – from Hölderlin and Hegel to Schmitt, Arendt, and Žižek – for whom the conflicts involved in metaphysics, revolution, gender, and subjectivity are "tragic" yet emancipatory, paving the way for future reconciliation and progress. This book is instead interested in tragedy as the literary probe of communities' and persons' irremediable, Icarus-like falls.[40] Indeed, a groundswell of contemporary classicists and philosophers – Stephen Halliwell, Anthony Cascardi, Jonathan Lear, George Harris, Michael Lurie, Martha Nussbaum, and Simon Critchley – have argued in recent decades that philosophical accounts of tragedy from Plato to Nietzsche and beyond have sought to foreclose the grief and lamentation, chanciness and vulnerability, that pervaded the Greek original.[41] Tragedy has in fact been philosophy's Other, ripe for extirpation. This book contends that it is in modernist tragedy that philosophy's sanguine figurations of modernity are discarded.

Tragic Nature

The renegade premise of the fiction in this book is that nature cannot redeem us. Its might and magnitude are neither a Kantian spur to transcend our bodily fragility nor a Romantic or mystical refuge for besieged and bounded bodies, a reprieve from mechanization or mortal finitude. Nonetheless, from Hegel's and Nietzsche's readings of tragedy to the American pragmatism of Charles Sanders Peirce to the French vitalism of Henri Bergson and the English process philosophy of Alfred North

Whitehead, we find the anti-Darwinian conviction that nature is inspirited with some governing mental or vital principle. While the cofounder of natural selection, Alfred Russel Wallace, and its American popularizer, Asa Gray, maintained that theistic design must guide evolution (Wallace in the sphere of man, Gray in every particular), Nietzsche, Bergson, Peirce, and Whitehead commuted this promise of theistic oversight into varying assurances of an immanent force in nature that directed its progress. For Nietzsche, it was the will to power, that physiological craving for flux that leads us to love all that befalls us. For Bergson, it was the *élan vital*, a vital impetus responsible for evolution that comprised various tendencies; these forked into so many tributaries, disseminating and developing themselves as life flowed on. Consciousness, for Bergson, was one such tendency, and in humanity it reached its fullest potential. As Donna Jones writes of Bergson's vitalism:

> Man was to become once again one with the universe through intuition.... Through the philosophical elaboration of the conception of intuition, Bergson, working in the idealist tradition of *Naturphilosophie*, had hoped to provide a connection between man and the natural world so that the individual need not regard herself as living in, on the whole, an alien natural environment but rather as having arisen out of and thus being one with nature, every bit of which is now imbued with cosmic significance.[42]

For Peirce, similarly, it was love that pervaded all matter and governed evolution. The law of love, Peirce stated explicitly, was a corrective to the heartless Darwinian law of natural selection. Peirce posited his "agapastic theory of evolution" in *The Monist* in 1893, arguing that sympathy in response to chance occurrences drove evolution; Peirce accepted chance, rejecting determinism, but insisted that love fed on accident.[43] Peirce proposed "the formula of an evolutionary philosophy, which teaches that growth comes only from love" and theorized "a love which embraces hatred as an imperfect stage of it" – a love strengthened by encounters with less developed forms of itself.[44] Its healing operation, Peirce determined, "discloses for the problem of evil its everlasting solution."[45] For Whitehead, too, nature was nowhere blind mechanism or aimless spontaneity, but a purposeful "structure of evolving processes. The reality is the process."[46] Whitehead claimed in *Science and the Modern World* (1925) that "Fate in Greek Tragedy becomes the order of nature in modern thought," stipulating that both tragedy and nature manifest cosmic design.[47] Their necessities are inalterable, but they are not divorced from a directive sentience; necessity and panpsychist consciousness go hand in hand. The "remorseless inevitability" of the "decrees of fate" in Greek tragedy and of the "laws of physics" in Einsteinian theory are, for Whitehead, inseparable from all-pervading Mind and "moral order."[48] Like Samuel Alexander in *Time, Space, and Deity* (1920) and C. Lloyd Morgan in *Emergent Evolution* (1923), Whitehead suggested that human mental states arise on the world stage as a necessary level of evolutionary complexity. Both Whitehead and Peirce shared the conviction that even before human life developed, all matter possessed mind, to varying degrees, and could therefore transform the world purposefully – making nature's history one of striving consciousness rather than unconscious mechanism. On such a reading of life, the future is indeterminate, because of chance, but "evolutionary love" (Peirce) or panpsychist "process" (Whitehead) guides the movements of existence. Fellow process philosopher Charles Hartshorne commented that "[o]ne can well imagine Plato or Leibniz being greatly impressed by the arguments of Peirce and Whitehead for an evolutionary version of idealism."[49]

It was this species of anthropocentric belief that Darwin could not countenance – he abjured the many proposals in earlier evolutionary theory that excised chance or insentience from their explanatory frames.[50] He stood firm in perilous waters, never departing from the sentiment he expressed to Asa Gray in 1860: "But I own that I cannot see, as plainly as others do, & as I sh[oul]d wish to do, evidence of design & beneficence on all sides of us. There seems to me too much misery in the world. I cannot persuade myself that a beneficent & omnipotent God would have design-edly created the *Ichneumonidæ* with the express intention of their feeding within the living bodies of caterpillars, or that a cat should play with mice."[51] Hardy adopted this loveless conception of nature, whose anti-idealist postulates seemed clear, as K. M. Newton elaborates:

> [N]atural selection was irreconcilable with purpose or meaning and ... species which survived did so largely through mutations produced by chance.... Darwin had referred to "the clumsy, wasteful, blundering low and horridly cruel works of nature" and his contemporary Ernst Haeckel proclaimed that natural selection destroyed all basis for belief in a moral order: "the 'moral ordering of the world' is evidently a beautiful poem which is proved to be false by the actual facts ... It exists neither in nature nor in human life."[52]

No wonder this metaphysical corollary of Darwin's otherwise compelling history of life met with such resistance. Despite the widespread public approval that Darwin enjoyed in the decade following his 1859 publication of *On the Origin of Species*, his work was increasingly challenged. Peter Bowler calls the period 1875–1925 "the eclipse of Darwinism," adopting

Julian Huxley's phrase.[53] Peter Morton labels it "Darwinism on the Deathbed."[54] In Darwin's own lifetime, engineer Fleeming Jenkin mistakenly maintained that variation could not survive the merging of inherited traits that Darwin proposed. Devout physicist William Thomson (Lord Kelvin) concluded that the ages of the sun and the Earth – which he vastly underestimated, working prior to the turn-of-the-century discovery of radioactive isotopes and atomic energy – could not allow sufficient time for the descent with modification that Darwin envisioned. The early Mendelians, in the first quarter of the twentieth century, believed that gradual Darwinian change was incompatible with particulate inheritance. William Provine writes that in "the early 1910s ... England had no experimental geneticist who was a Darwinian, and no Darwinian naturalist who incorporated the new science of heredity into his work."[55] An abiding aversion to chance also stoked counter-theories from every corner: Social Darwinist and eugenicist teleologies, neo-Lamarckisms that insisted on use inheritance, and theories of orthogenesis that maintained that evolution advances arrow-like toward a particular end, thanks to inner directives, not chance and natural selection. In Germany in 1932, Richard Woltereck characteristically surmised that "[c]hance plus selection as creator of the diversity and the well-planned order of organisms ... will be recorded in the future as one of the strangest errors of the human propensity for causal explanations."[56] Ernest Boesiger reminds us that influential anti-Darwinist Bergson "said it was unthinkable that a series of accidents, maintained by selection if they were advantageous, could produce in two different evolutionary lines the construction of identical structures."[57] As late as 1941, French geneticist Lucien Cuénot, as Boesiger details, found that "[l]iving matter is certainly regulated by physicochemical laws – but it also requires for its evolution an anti-chance factor. The Cartesian machine needs an inventor, a conductor, some 'obscure' profound and unknown cause of the biological finality."[58] Like so many, Cuénot felt obliged to "admit a transcendental force, a will, an intelligence that guided nature."[59] This tenacious sentiment had already led Hardy to lament in his 1922 preface to *Late Lyrics and Earlier* that "belief in witches of Endor" – belief in machinating spirit of whatever stripe, possessed of a plan for man – "is displacing the Darwinian theory."[60]

   When Hardy passed away in 1928, the modern evolutionary synthesis of genetics and Darwinism was just beginning. Those at its vanguard in England were part of the extended Bloomsbury circle. Woolf's field of acquaintance included the exceedingly evolutionarily literate Aldous Huxley; his brother, renowned evolutionary biologist and science popularizer

Julian Huxley; and groundbreaking evolutionary geneticist J. B. S. Haldane. Woolf signed her name to a personal copy of H. G. Wells, Julian Huxley, and G. P. Wells's nine-volume collaborative chef d'oeuvre, *The Science of Life* (1929–31). Bertrand Russell also brought a preference for Darwinism and a scorn for its detractors to Bloomsbury. In Russell's words, humanity was doubtless "the product of causes which had no prevision of the end they were achieving."[61] Woolf, too, shared this disposition, which Jay Clayton describes:

> Haldane and Julian Huxley had no patience with metaphysical, religious, or pseudo-scientific theories that attempted to mitigate the materialist foundation of the evolutionary synthesis. Haldane's demonstration that the natural selection of purely random mutations was the basis of all evolution, human and otherwise, made no compromise with mystical or idealist notions that postulated a guiding purpose to evolution. He inveighed against the folly of Henri Bergson's concept of *"élan vital,* or vital force, which pushed organisms forward along the path of evolution.". . . Russell, too, rejected fuzzy-minded ideas in the 1920s such as Arthur Eddington's postulation of a "mind-stuff" directing evolution or Lloyd Morgan's "emergent evolution" that suggested a "Divine Purpose underlying the course of evolution."[62]

Camus, too, knew and admired French evolutionary biochemist Jacques Monod, who held that "[a]ll religions, nearly all philosophies, and even a part of science testify to the unwearying, heroic effort of mankind desperately denying its own contingency."[63] Monod's treatise *Chance and Necessity: An Essay on the Natural Philosophy of Modern Biology* showed how organisms can, by chance, come to be structured to reliably reproduce themselves. *Chance and Necessity* took its epigraph from Camus's parable of tragic lucidity, "The Myth of Sisyphus."

Kirsten E. Shepherd-Barr calls Beckett "the post–New Synthesis playwright *par excellence.*"[64] She contends that "Lucky's speech [in *Waiting for Godot*] gives Beckett's Darwinian view in a nutshell: there is no God; humanity is moving toward extinction; and the universe is succumbing to entropy."[65] Dirk Van Hulle likewise explains that Beckett's reading of Austrian language philosopher Fritz Mauthner exposed him to "Darwin's notion of contingency" – to Maunther's own conviction that Darwin had demolished anthropocentric ideas of purpose and progress and had instead revealed to us the "contingent history of the world, or 'Zufalls-geschichte.'"[66] Maunther argued for the aleatory development of sense perception and reasoning. Van Hulle draws our attention to this passage from Maunther's *Contributions to a Critique of Language* that Beckett transcribed in his "Whoroscope" notebook of the 1930s:

that reason is therefore not a superhuman gift bestowed on humanity, that it is not an unchanging and eternal deity, that reason evolved in humanity and evolved into what it is, but that it also, however, could have evolved differently; when we recognise with a twitch as that of a wriggling worm that we are, not only in every step in our miserable existence, but also in what we hold to be the eternal and unalterably fixed fundamental laws of our intellectual being, merely a game played by the coincidence that is the world.[67]

That our species-being is a product of chance is the fixed fact for these writers. Hardy and Woolf, Camus and Beckett aim to acknowledge non-human outsides and origins. They are not exclusively concerned with subjective experience, as modernism as "inward turn" might have it. Jessica Burstein calls modernism that steers clear of human perspectives "cold modernism": "the premise of cold modernism is that there is a world in which the mind does not exist, let alone matter ... Insofar as cold modernism engages a world without selves or psychology, it is not anti-humanism but ahumanism."[68] Burstein notes Russell's kindred conviction, presented at length in Ann Banfield's *The Phantom Table*.[69] In *The Problems of Philosophy* (1912), Russell maintains that the physical world exists whether we observe it or not.[70] But as Burstein notes, it is still *we* who register the world's independence of us.[71] Burstein labels modernist fiction that represents human feeling "hot"; even feelings about a world without us turn up the heat, whereas "[t]here are no laments in cold modernism, for there are no characters who would conceive of themselves as subjects."[72] Tragic modernism, then, is by turns cold and hot: it represents and laments the cold.

The authors in this study anticipate the concerns of Quintin Meillassoux's "speculative realism," outlined in *After Finitude: An Essay on the Necessity of Contingency*: that the world is indeed separable from our thinking it, exists before and beyond human cognition, and without reason. Ceding no turf, as Meillassoux refuses to do, to faith in a realm of designed, revelatory necessity that lies outside our understanding, modernism's characters instead treat a paucity of explanatory infrastructure in the world as an understood truth. They portray a universe indifferent to human needs and desires, in no way inspirited by panpsychist Mind or vital principles, in marked contrast to much contemporaneous philosophy of science (Nietzsche, Peirce, Bergson, Whitehead). In Meillassoux's reading, such philosophers recenter human experience as the only depth we can sound. Since the Enlightenment, Meillassoux argues, continental philosophy has been at war with scientific objectivity. Meillassoux maintains that starting with Kant, philosophical insistence upon our necessarily human point of view denies either our direct knowledge of a world independent of thought (what Meillassoux calls the trap of "correlationism") or such a world's very existence (the "subjectivism" of certain idealisms or vitalisms). Correlationism posits an undergirding reality we cannot apprehend directly, to which our perceptions are in some way fit; subjectivism posits that consciousness is the ineliminable basis of all reality. Meillassoux deems these philosophical positions incompatible with mathematics's, cosmology's, and paleontology's (to name a few) attestations to a time and space apart from consciousness. Because such philosophy positions the human subject as the ground of all knowledge, Meillassoux calls it "Ptolemy's revenge" against Galileo and Copernicus.[73]

Hardy, Woolf, and Camus, however, attempt to evoke a material world neither dependent on consciousness nor wholly unknown to it. Beckett, on the contrary, seeks to depict a world that does thwart our direct apprehension and communication of it: "Siege laid again to the impregnable without [*Siège remis devant le dehors imprenable*]. Eye and hand fevering after the unself.... Truce for a space and the marks of what it is to be and be in face of."[74] In his "Philosophy Notes" of the 1930s, Beckett copies from Wilhelm Windelband's and Heinz Heimsoeth's *The Handbook of Philosophy* this summary of the Kantian position that consciousness is inseparable from all scientific knowledge: "it puts a stop to naturalism with the demonstration of autonomous laws and the superior significance of the mental (as of the human consciousness with its spiritual-meaningful forms which has to be assumed in all science and scientific worldview)."[75] Beckett himself comments on Kant's stance that it is because of our a priori modes of understanding ("spiritual-meaningful forms") that we know the phenomenal world, understand objects within it, and can only think (not directly know) a noumenal world untouched by subjectivity: "Kant's proof that the conditions of the possibility of experience are also the conditions of the possibility of the objects of experience!!!"[76] But Beckett does not adopt Kant's view that it is fixed and preordained mental categories that present us with a world of objects. It is, rather, a happenstance language and embodiment that provide us with our human point of view. Beckett's thinking seems to dovetail with these remarks of Maunther's, which Beckett also transcribed in his notes of the 1930s: "Whatever the human may dare to do through superhuman strength in order to discover truth, he always finds only himself, a human truth, an anthropomorphic picture of the world."[77] For Maunther, our faculties have the effect of anthropomorphizing, organizing, and sanitizing the riotous nonhuman particulars of the world. Thus contra Meillassoux, Beckett understands the problem of the eighteenth century to be its claims to know more (not less) than human beings can: "The crisis started with the end of the 17th century, after Galileo.... The Encyclopedists wanted to know everything ... But that direct relation between the self and – as the Italians say – *lo scibile*, the knowable, was already broken."[78] Beckett, however, understands this debarment from unmediated knowledge to be a relentless reminder of nonhuman externality. He presumes that there is chaos, a conditioning mess, beyond our human prism. He neither believes in transcendental structures that are the preconditions of our cognition nor makes our limited aperture onto the world necessary to the world's existing.

For Hardy, Woolf, and Camus, then, art can and must speak of the "great outdoors," Meillassoux's shorthand for a world independent of us.[79] As Russell says of his dismissal of Kant and Hegel: "With a sense of escaping from prison, we allowed ourselves to think ... that the sun and stars would exist if no one was aware of them."[80] For Beckett, too, even if *le dehors* proves indescribable, it presses itself upon us as a locus void of existential answers ("I am not interested in the 'unification' of the historical chaos any more than I am in the 'clarification' of the individual chaos, & still less in the anthropomorphisation of the inhuman necessities that provoke the chaos").[81] Even from different angles, these authors butt up against – know – limits to what can be rationalized, to what reason can humanize. For these tragic writers, reason confronts characters with truths that bring little ease or safety. Reason opens characters' eyes to their impotence and insecurity. They come to know that justification is wanting for much that they must submit to in life. It is tragedy that constitutively begins with such paining lucidity. Of Sisyphus, Camus's paradigmatic tragic hero, Camus maintains "the lucidity that was to constitute his torture"; to know that he is consigned to inalterable and meaningless suffering is the root of his tragedy. In Camus's reading of Oedipus, too, "from the moment he knows, his tragedy begins."[82]

Joseph Conrad makes this point beautifully in letters to R. B. Cunninghame Graham of 1897 and 1898. Conrad captures modernism's Darwinian, chance-infused conception of tragic lucidity:

> There is a – let us say – a machine. It evolved itself (I am severely scientific) out of a chaos of scraps of iron and behold! – it knits. I am horrified at the horrible work and stand appalled.... And the most withering thought is that the infamous thing has made itself; made itself without thought, without conscience, without foresight, without eyes, without heart. It is a tragic accident – and it has happened.[83]

And the machine will run on all the same.... Of course reason is hateful – but why? Because it demonstrates (to those who have the courage) that we, living, are out of life – utterly out of it.[84]

What makes mankind tragic is not that they are the victims of nature, it is that they are conscious of it. To be part of the animal kingdom under the conditions of this earth is very well – but as soon as you know of your slavery the pain, the anger, the strife – the tragedy begins.[85]

Hardy's ten-year-old Jude comes to knowledge in this manner. He comes to awareness of the fact that "Nature's logic was too horrid for him to care for" and that he "did not want to be a man."[86] For Hardy's young astronomer in *Two on a Tower* (1882) it is the same: he finds that "[i]t is quite impossible to think at all adequately of the sky – of what the sky substantially is, without feeling it as a juxtaposed nightmare."[87] When Woolf's Bernard in *The Waves* glimpses "the world seen without a self," scientifically, he does not feel empowered; he feels obliterated.[88] Mrs. Ramsay in *To the Lighthouse* also decouples knowledge from solace: "With her mind she had always seized the fact that there is no reason, order, justice."[89] The ubiquitous pounding of the waves, which "remorselessly beat the measure of life" as quotidian sounds die away, makes her "look up with an impulse of terror."[90] This terror specifically accompanies the acquisition of knowledge and is the same that pervades the novel's middle section, "Time Passes." Flowers, we are told, are "eyeless, and so terrible."[91] "Eyeless" documents the flowers' inhuman alterity; they have no hint of human perceptual capacity. But exactly this insensate otherness, from a human vantage point, is "so terrible." This line of text passes from recognition of inhumanity to a human terror of it. This same view of imperturbable natural processes – that "as soon as you know ... the tragedy begins" – leads Miguel de Unamuno to conclude in *The Tragic Sense of Life* (1913) that for human beings "everything vital is anti-rational, not merely irrational, and ... everything rational is anti-vital. And this is the basis of the tragic sense of life."[92] Insights furnished by reason will be life-negating; all that is vital, or life-affirming, counteracts the torture of what we know.

Modernism versus Nihilism

In Conrad's apt formulation, reason stands appalled and demands some palliative; this study suggests that tragic authors supply "moments of being" as this vital cordial. But Conrad, like Plato and Unamuno, also detects a further peril in tragedy: the possibility that it will indeed impel us to relinquish life altogether. We see this abdication of self and society take a range of forms in modern fiction, from wanton destructiveness to political quietism to suicide. I would like to think of all of these as willed nihilism: the pursuit of not caring, the embrace of nothingness. Willed nihilism may be an active political program as well; Camus classifies state rationalizations of murder as nihilism. The fiction in this study both identifies and protects against this brand of nihilism. It dramatizes characters who actively resist such nihilism's encroachment and also those who seek it – who espouse nihilism as a numbing agent for pain or as a means of downplaying or denying the pains of others. These latter procedures, however, make for fictional minds so harried and distressed that it furnishes readers with *negative examples*: models of how not to live.

I distinguish willed nihilism from nihilism as a historical process, as Nietzsche defined it. In the 1880s, Nietzsche predicted the advent of a post-Christian nihilism in the decades to come: Western Europe would reach the culminating point in the history of belief when those reigning transcendent values it had thought indestructible would no longer seem credible. Should former believers resist a descent into ethical apathy, they would be obliged to fashion their values anew.[93] What Nietzsche pictured as imminent – the absence of grounding metaphysical meaning – would bring Europe nearer to the baseline postulates of ancient Greek schools of thought like Sophism and Atomism. In this sense, modern tragic fiction is a return to Greek nihilism, to a vantage point untethered to any superhuman authorship of moral absolutes. But neither these Greek philosophies nor modern tragic novels embrace the total meaninglessness and moral vacuity that Nietzsche foresaw in the wake of Christianity. Simon Critchley and Martha Nusbaum elaborate the ethical stakes of Nietzschean nihilism as follows:

> Nihilism is the breakdown of the order of meaning, where all that was posited as a transcendent source of value becomes null and void, where there are no skyhooks upon which to hang a meaning for life. All transcendent claims for a meaning to life have been reduced to mere values and those values have become incredible, standing in need of what Nietzsche calls "transvaluation" or "revaluation."[94]

> The threat of nihilism is the prospect of the collapse of the will, the refusal to continue ordering and valuing.[95]

Modernist philosopher Emil Cioran thinks of it, as Critchley writes in *Notes on Suicide*, as a demise particular to the modern optimist: it is optimists who cannot survive the loss of the ethical security they formerly enjoyed.[96] The optimist is too dependent on celestial hopes or their terrestrial substitutes and cannot endure disillusionment. Portuguese modernist Fernando Pessoa's suicidal narrator, the Baron of Teive, exemplifies this species of crisis. The Baron pens his suicide note, citing the failure of his literary endeavor.[97] He cannot stitch his lyrical fragments into a streamlined whole. This failure convinces him of the falsity of his governing worldview – he has been wrong to assume that life possesses coherence – and his disappointment is unendurable.

But for Nietzsche, such dissatisfaction should occasion a "revaluation" of values. In this spirit, Nietzsche advances the will to power (*amor fati*). In this spirit, the tragic modernist novel proffers a hatred of fate and of pain apologetics – paired with love for countervailing moments of care and solidarity ("the moment was all; the moment was enough"). But it is also true that tragedy's rescaled values, for some characters, do not suffice as counterweights to anguish. Here, significantly, we do not have the optimists' perhaps platitudinous despair, their pining for a credence they have lost. Instead, we have pessimists devastated by the precarity of all that they treasure in traditional faith's stead. Conrad describes this despondency as follows, directly after his remark that "as soon as you know . . . the tragedy begins": "We can't return to nature, since we can't change our place in it. Our refuge is in stupidity, in drunken[n]ess of all kinds, in lies, in beliefs, in murder, thieving, reforming – in negation, in contempt – each man according to the promptings of his particular devil."[98] A coterie of modernist characters does turn to frenetic distractions, whether prosocial or cruel or self-destructive, as routes to forgetfulness. Schopenhauer had also made this point about the seductions of negation, of willed nihilism, in response to tragedy:

> so in the tragic catastrophe we turn away from the will-to-live itself. Thus in the tragedy the terrible side of life is presented to us, the wailing and lamentation of mankind, the dominion of chance and error, the fall of the righteous, the triumph of the wicked; and so that aspect of the world is brought before our eyes which directly opposes our will. At this sight we feel ourselves urged to turn our will away from life, to give up willing and loving life.[99]

We turn on our accident-prone, precarious loves, wanting them to ebb away. Unamuno in *The Tragic Sense of Life* and Cioran in *On the Heights of Despair* (1934) also rehearse this life-negating train of thought:

> [M]an, by the very fact of being man, of possessing consciousness, is, in comparison with the ass or the crab, a diseased animal. Consciousness is a disease.[100]

> Is it not tragic to be man, that perpetually dissatisfied animal suspended between life and death? I'm weary of being a man. If I could, I would renounce my condition on the spot, but what would I become then, an animal? I cannot retrace my steps.... As far as I am concerned, I resign from humanity. I no longer want to be, nor can still be, a man.[101]

"We can't return to nature, since we can't change our place in it" – "I cannot retrace my steps" but "I no longer want to be ... a man." To "resign from humanity" is not, then, to resume instinctive function as crab or ass. This signature renunciation of species amounts to turning "our will away from life" entirely. In this vein, modernist characters imagine and glamorize devolution. They insistently envision becoming nonhuman animal or inorganic matter, in order to elude their condition.

This is not the mystical deliverance from reasoning and individuation that nontragic literature and philosophy rehearse. This is not, for instance, the mysticism that D. H. Lawrence's Birkin in *Women in Love* (1920) identifies:

> mindless ... mystic knowledge in disintegration and dissolution, knowledge such as the beetles have, which live purely within the world of corruption and cold dissolution ... "It is a desire for the reduction-process in oneself, a reducing back to the origin, a return along the Flux of Corruption, to the original rudimentary conditions of being –!" ... "going back to the savages for our sensations, – always seeking to *lose* ourselves in some ultimate black sensation, mindless and infinite – burning only with destructive fires, raging on with the hope of being burnt out utterly –"[102]

What I am describing is not modernist primitivism or any such revelation of self-abolishing Dionysiac ecstasy or infinite Begrsonian *durée*. It is not the mystical liberation that Clarice Lispector's heroine in *The Passion According to G.H.* uncovers: both terrified and tantalized, she exchanges "my life" for "Life."[103] She calls her individual form a superficial "accretion" of "civilization" and hungers to slough it off, in favor of "identity" – understood as sameness – with raw, primordial, prehuman and nonhuman matter.[104] To prove it she feasts on the innards of a cockroach. Nor is this book about Deleuze and Guattari's notion of the human and the nonhuman that become indistinguishable. Deleuze and Guattari understand characters to be absent from a landscape in fiction – ocean, moor, or town – only insofar as characters have *become* the sensations of ocean, moor, or town: "Ahab ... has entered into a relationship with Moby Dick that makes him a becoming-whale and forms a compound of sensations that no longer needs anyone: ocean. It is Mrs. Dalloway who perceives the town – but because she has passed into the town like 'a knife through everything' and becomes imperceptible herself. *Affects are precisely these nonhuman becomings of man.*"[105]

Rather than an entrée into oceanic being, however, nonhuman becoming in the fiction I treat carries the valence of suicide. This drive to extinguish consciousness is on display, for instance, in Beckett's narrator's recurrent fantasies in *The Unnamable*. He dreams of insensate ("all-nescient," unconscious) Worm who is spared all suffering.[106] Critics may point to modernism as privileging the animal, the nonhuman, the posthuman – Lawrence and Lispector make sense in this regard – but some among modernism's characters seek to cauterize their wounds by ceasing to be. Jean-Michel Rabaté treats the Beckettian distrust of personhood in *Think, Pig! Beckett at the Limit of the Human* as an invitation "to move beyond the human and try to think otherwise – like an animal, perhaps like a goat or a pig."[107] But modernism's tragic fiction is concerned with human experiences of creaturely suffering and with specifically anthropogenic forms of subjugation and systematized violence. Tragic fiction thinks the dynamics of harm – of finitude and chance, of manmade modes of oppression – and it thinks lament and resistance.

Such fiction is antihumanist in the sense that it rejects all images of a privileged people made in God's image, reigning over the earth. Beckett and Camus also share an eschewal of Sartrean humanism, with its promise that individuals direct their own fates (transcend their "facticity," displace necessity with freedom).[108] Beckett's characters clear away pretensions to a "higher," more-than-creaturely command of existence, with their corrosive invective and uncontrollable bodies. But they are still yoked to their condition as bounded and ruminating mammals, subject to grief and pain; this is part of their "form of life" (*Lebensform*), in Wittgenstein's terms.[109] The nonhuman perspective of instinct-driven and unconcerned goat, pig, or worm is not available to them.

In crisis, then, certain of modernism's characters choose between humanity and an imagining of that humanity negated, and find negation preferable. This is Rhoda's calculus in Woolf's *The Waves*, as she whispers to the passing star and spreading wave, "Consume me."[110] This is the yearning that Pessoa's nature poet Alberto Caeiro voices then resists in *The Keeper of Sheep* (1925). Caeiro maintains that "Nature is simply parts, nothing whole" and that "there's no one great All these things belong to."[111] Caeiro everywhere observes a difference between conscious and unconscious life: "But flowers wouldn't be flowers if they felt anything – / They'd be people," "Nature hasn't any inside; / It wouldn't be Nature otherwise."[112] He is a most cheerful connoisseur of outdoor scenes, except in those moods when he would

> give anything just to be the roadside dust
>
> . . .
>
> rather than go through life
> Looking behind and feeling sorrow . . .[113]

He composes four poems that express this longing and then interprets them as follows: these "Songs that deny me" "Give the lie to everything I feel, / They are the opposite of all I am . . . ."[114] During the composition of this life-negating series, he must have been "sick completely – ideas and everything."[115] Such poems represent, he concludes, "the landscape of my soul at night," its nihilistic face.[116] Caeiro captures a whole strain of modernist thought and feeling – the inclination not to be, the temptation of self-abnegation – in these brief verses. He names his condition soul-sickness, what Nietzsche called "time-sickness."[117] It is important to see that these modernist pleas to be stardust or roadside dust exemplify what Martin Hägglund in *Dying for Time* has called "chronophobia," fear in the face of oncoming moments that are, constitutively, pitched on the precipice of extinction. Textual excavation of the tragedies in this study, however, does not support Hägglund's conclusion that modernist novels depict, despite characters' protestations otherwise, that at base what we love about time (the source of "chronophilia") *is* this whisper of loss.

Instead, such tragedy shores up the more familiar critical picture of a modernism invested in arresting the grains' fall through the hourglass; tragedy stages this losing yet sustaining battle. This book's further contention is that modernist novelists accentuate characters' bleak, desperate, soul-sick maneuvers, only to have penned negative examples: proofs that such recourse to willed nihilism does more harm than good. Tragedy may beget a desire for insensibility; insensibility, in turn, may clear the way for the immoderate violence of tragedy. But tragedy and nihilism have anti-thetical *Weltanschauungs*: the latter is committed, as Lukács says, to antisocial negation and to the "disintegration of personality," while the former is committed to shared, Sisyphean defenses of personhood.[118] Camus is quick to stipulate that "we live in tragic times. But too many people confuse tragedy with despair."[119] Beckett is equally firm: "I simply cannot understand why some people call me a nihilist. There is no basis for that."[120] Instead, catastrophic history and the natural world's atheistic, inhuman scope and scale make for tragedy that nevertheless engenders characters' rebellious pursuit of moments of joy, beauty, passion, and intimacy, in lieu of a wish for nonbeing. Such an account of modernist fiction runs counter to (1) theories such as Garrett Stewart's and Jonathan Gottschall's that consider narrative itself (not climactic moments) to be the quintessential mechanism of character formation, (2) theories such as Alain Robbe-Grillet's that find that modernist novels continue to personify nature as deliberate savior or adversary (what he calls the novel's "tragic humanism"), and (3) theories such as Paul Sheehan's that contend, on the contrary, that so thorough is modernist fiction's departure from anthropocentrism and teleological narrative that it dissolves the differences between persons and their encircling environs.[121]

Tragic Sociality and Overview of Chapters

Chapter 2, "Hardy's Theory of Tragic Character," reads Hardy's late nineteenth-century tragic novels as part of an ascendant subgenre, uncompromising in its exposé of narratives that imprison us against our will and to our detriment. In moments of counter-narrative rebellion, both the impassioned narrator of *Tess of the d'Urbervilles* (1891) and the titular character of *Jude the Obscure* (1895) attack the logics of rape culture and internalized victim-blaming that, in Greek tragic fashion, descend on heroines from without and degrade them beyond recognition. This is, I argue, the antithesis of the Aristotelian model of tragedy in which protagonists themselves inadvertently cause their demises but are understood to be morally uncorrupted in the process. It is different, too, from the Christian interpretation of tragedy in which heroines fall because of their moral vices. Although Woolf, then, is sometimes viewed as a comedic author, I show in Chapter 3 that she not only praises Hardy's Greek sense of the tragic but also develops his vision of a modern tragedy that finds its generic home in the novel. In *To the Lighthouse* (1927) and *The Waves* (1931), Woolf perfects a novelistic structure that accentuates rebellious communities at odds with an affectless nature and an inhumane culture. Rather than an ethics of conquest and domination, this tragic form carries with it an ethics of human limitation and interdependence. In Chapter 3, titled "Woolf and Darwin: Tragic Time Scales and Chances," I also demonstrate that Woolf shares a vision of natural history with Darwin and Bertrand Russell and offers an alternative to much contemporary anthropological thought (Harrison, Murray) and philosophical thought (Nietzsche, Bergson).

Reaching beyond England in my ensuing chapters, I turn more explicitly to a form of contrast – between momentary affirmation and blanket negation – that emerges within the novels of Hardy and Woolf and is essential to the oeuvres of Camus and Beckett. These two authors dramatize a nihilistic aversion to caring (about others or oneself) that is so inhospitable to human survival that it concertedly galvanizes in readers what I have named the "ethics of recoil": a commitment to avoiding these characters' modes of thought. In Chapter 4, "Camus's Modernist Forms and the Ethics of Tragedy," we see that Camus's rich formulations of tragedy rebut what he takes to be Marxism's predetermined, utopian future and Sartrean existentialism's open and self-authored futures. In this chapter, I show that Camus depicts a bedrock of tragic subjectivity that cannot be eliminated. I proceed to show that, across Camus's work, this painful substrate of existence may lead characters to reject life, may stimulate the desire for nothingness-as-reprieve that Lukács located at the heart of modernism. I illustrate this vacuousness (this ethical and political nihilism) in Camus's *The Stranger* (1942) and its failed cultivation, in response to tragedy, in Camus's *The Fall* (1956). I argue that it is precisely this representation of benumbed and wanting humanity that may kindle its opposite in readers, desire for its reverse face – that of renewed existing and feeling, even tragically. Chapter 5, "Beckett: Against Nihilism," again identifies a confrontation between tragic pain and nihilistic insensibility, staged in Beckett's novels. I contrast this rivalry with one further artistic instantiation of an ethics: the joyful, mystical, Nietzschean model of self-dissolution on display in Lispector's novel *The Passion According to G.H.* (1964). G.H.'s pursuit of wordlessness and inhumanity – in her view, the truth behind human verbosity and craftsmanship – is what Beckett's character in *The Unnamable* (1953) claims to pursue also. Beckett himself is then read as a language skeptic in search of this emancipating silence. I counter this judgment of Beckett and his character. *The Unnamable*'s narrator finds that there is no such access to a liberating beyond. The more he struggles against embodiment and language, in pursuit of a superior mode of being, the more he severs himself from his attachments to the world. My argument relies on both textual analysis and the wealth of recent work in the Beckett archive, which has illuminated Beckett's drafts, readings, journals, and letters. I conclude that the logic of *The Unnamable* is revisited and refuted in Beckett's late *Company* (1979), whose narrator admits the attraction of a suicidal narrative strategy yet opts to resuscitate bonds with others by way of lyrical moments of memory.

For the authors in this study, solitude is proximate to suicide. Tragic sociality – the idea that we are more ecstatic, more defiant together – is therefore a value that runs throughout this book. Such tragic sociality does not make for invulnerability. A chorus of dissenting Trojan women in Euripides' *Hekabe* is still bound for enslavement. Becoming choral is not protection against harm. But it is a route to greater mutinies and to more lasting and insubordinate joys. Even the chimera of company in Beckett's *Company* enlivens its narrator. To form "common cause against that fluidity out there" is Woolf's formulation for this tragic sociality in *To the Lighthouse*.[122] Modernism's tragic characters do not ingest all alterity as Lispector's majestic, mystic G.H. does. But when the All is not forthcoming, social ties are paramount.

As Wai Chee Dimock argues, individuals were never the mainstay of tragedy: "the doom here descends on masses and masses of people, with no blame attachable. These people suffer not because they deserve it, not because they are fitly chastised, not because there is any proportionality between who they are and what is coming to them."[123] For Page duBois, similarly, tragedy is less concerned with individual actors, however calamitous their acts or universal their predicaments. Tragedy is concerned with the systemic conditions that render individual agency impossible, that visit misery on communities and make for commiseration:

> To read Greek tragedy, tragedy, the tragic, as a discourse on the individual, even one conceived within the narrative of absolute spirt or split by incestuous desire, is to reveal perhaps a nostalgic desire for a sovereign, individual, heroic subject, one who can still make choices, even catastrophic ones, that determine his or her fate.[124]

Greek tragedy, modernist tragedy, and tragedy today signal that collectively we are "in face of" superior and deleterious force. Who, in such straits, can go it alone?

CHAPTER 2

Hardy's Theory of Tragic Character

Neo-Greek Modernism

The *Diagnostic and Statistical Manual of Mental Disorders* (*DSM*) answers the question, "What is wrong with you?" Because it lists symptoms that are meant to describe individuals, this diagnostic encyclopedia risks pathologizing social and familial inequities as personal illness. As Australian psychotherapist Michael White has argued in *Maps of Narrative Practice* and elsewhere, the better question is, "What has happened to you?"[1] This rival formulation acknowledges structural forces that wreak havoc on individuals. What I am contending is that literary tragedies concertedly draw our attention to such externally wrought stigma that individuals are made to internalize. What the *DSM* may occlude – disordering social and historical contexts – and what it does as a result – blame the victim – are the defining features of Hardy's late tragedies.

Ancient Greek tragedians likewise staged overwhelming and unjustifiable engines of suffering (sheer ill luck as well as environments pervaded by sexism, racism, classism, xenophobia, war, and slavery) that eviscerated people precisely by causing them to suffer and then characterizing them (and not their circumstances) as flawed. Tragedy, that is, presents us with injurious conditions borne as personal fault. Like Michael White, I find that in attending to narratives of character formation, we can unearth the social construction of much that otherwise passes for personal deficiency. Hardy ensconces these punitive judgments within natural and cosmological histories that offer no extrahuman safety nets. Where social supports fail, Hardy suggests, there is no fallback, no cosmic redress for injustice.

Tess of the d'Urbervilles (1891) and *Jude the Obscure* (1895) picture forward-moving narrative as corrosive to character and plot's interruption – in Fredric Jameson's term, its antimony, or moments of "affect" – as constructive of character.[2] While Hardy's fiction might seem to fit Jameson's definition of realism because it maintains "destiny" and "affect" in conflict, these novels' objection to fate and preference for the counter-vailing moment signal their departure from Jamesonian realism. No won-der Virginia Woolf, who decries the novelist's bondage to conventional story lines, praises "the violence and convolution of Hardy's plots" and his nonnarrative "moments of vision."[3] Too little noticed in Hardy criticism is the fact that these novels' insistence on plot coincides with their indict-ment of it; that Hardy represents, qua tragedy, narratives that constitute characters despite themselves, in brutal and coercive ways. Such is Hardy's modernist contestation of modernity's own pretensions to self-mastery and world-mastering. What today draws a groundswell of literary critics to tragedy drew Hardy then: its uncompromising exposé of the extent to which we do *not* author ourselves and are imprisoned within story lines not of our choosing.

Hardy disposes of plot as the purveyor of social and existential comfort – as a template for *Bildung* that would enjoin readers to believe in "the world-as-homeland," in Franco Moretti's phrase.[4] Instead, Hardy's tragic trajectories communicate the "transcendental homelessness" that György Lukács considered the signature of the novel.[5] Such was Lukács's 1916 assessment in his *Theory of the Novel.* Following his Marxist matu-ration, however, Lukács reserved this definition for the *modernist* novel only. Hardy's fiction embodies, then, all that Lukács associates with "'modernist' anti-realism" and "anti-humanism": the "denial of history, of development," the absence of faith in an objective, ameliorative narra-tive of history that structures the world and that realism discloses.[6] For Hardy, however, any such master plot is unrealistic and false, what later tragedian Albert Camus would call modernity's melodrama, what critic David Scott has lately called modernity's romance.[7] Thus in Hardy's incipiently modernist fiction, no celestial or terrestrial script assures the salvation of his leading men and women. Such "failure" of plot under-mines – casts doubt upon – theories of human and social perfectibility and of autonomous, all-conquering subjectivity. Instead, tragedy's narratives prove the enemy of wish-fulfillment: the very marker of reality in these works is plot's negation of characters' wishes.

Only pauses in narrative, those fleeting or imagined moments in which characters flourish, contest plot's hegemony. These vanishing or yearning interludes, which erupt and expire against the backdrop of plot, engender Hardy's tragic multiverse – the alternate worlds in which plot might have flowed or meant differently, in which events transpired or were understood otherwise. While Tess and Sue, then, are doomed to inscription within a dominant narrative, Hardy's novels as a whole exhort readers to make this narrative's "mere" fictions – its counterfactuals, its profusion of momentary interpretive and experiential anomalies – reality. Hardy's tragedies, like their Greek predecessors, give voice to myriad interpretations of the plot twists at hand, insisting that multiple readings of them are possible. In good Sophist fashion, Hardy's tragedies deliver not only irrevocable destiny but embattled perspectives on it: the prosecution and defense of varying accounts of the fate in question. In a space of optative desire, that is, we see the origin and meaning of events contested and reframed, their relation to external and internal compulsion reconstrued. Just as Sophist philosopher Gorgias composed his "Encomium of Helen," a plurality of interpretations that exonerated the most castigated of women – Helen was overpowered by Aphrodite, by Paris's abduction and rape, by language, more victim than villain – so Tess's narrator raises an "Encomium of Tess" and Jude an "Encomium of Sue," in moments of counter-narrative rebellion.

These moments mark the unjust condemnation of these characters, what plot only furthers; tragedy, here, consists in Tess's and Sue's undue conscription into guilt. Tragedy consists in their being damned from one perspective, defended from another. To bridge the ancient and the modern: if it is tragic that culpability attaches to Sophocles' Oedipus through no fault of his own, simply because he is destined to fulfill Apollo's prophecy, then it is equally tragic that Tess and Sue, innocent victims, are consigned to guilt by certain Christian interpretations of their histories. Ironically, these Christian readings, casting each woman's adversity as evidence of her moral corruption, prove the irascible oracle – bereft of reason and justice – that neither can escape. Attic bad fortune subjects Tess to rape and Sue to the deaths of her children, but it is a Christian interpretive schema, in which these unjustifiable events are taken to be judgments against Tess and Sue, that destroys these women. "Dead; dead; dead," sleeping-walking Angel pronounces Tess, having learned of her past; he proves a seer whose newfound conviction that her soul is tainted, her purity a masquerade, conjures his lethal vision into being.[8] It is *Tess*'s narrator and Jude who hew to a rival conception of personhood: that all that transpires without one's consent should not be held against one. Indeed, as Jean-Pierre Vernant argues, both fifth-century legal and tragic vocabularies themselves began to contest the notion of character revealed and determined from without. This archaic Greek conception of religious guilt – in which divine curses attach to generations, constitute individuals, and impart defilement to them – still pervaded tragedy, but characters increasingly lamented and questioned it. In Vernant's words, an unforeseen action could render one de facto and insuperably guilty from the religious perspective. Such an "action does not emanate from the agent as from its source; rather, it envelops him and carries him away, swallowing him up in a power that must perforce be beyond him since it extends, both spatially and temporally, far beyond his own person."[9] But precisely these conditions come to seem the basis of one's innocence from a legal and psychological perspective. According to the ancient religious model, guilt depends on superhuman exercises of power, on externally dictated transformations in character, on all that "envelops ... and carries away" one's former identity; on the ancient secular model, human motivations are determinative. In the latter case, persons are blameless for all they do involuntarily, under constraint or in ignorance, while blame may attach to all they do voluntarily. In representative fashion, Oedipus first espouses the religious view, taking himself to be synonymous with abomination in *Oedipus Tyrannus*; his identity appears to him forever changed, inseparable from "my guilt, horrendous guilt," his unveiled "sickness to the core."[10] But he voices an emended self-image in *Oedipus at Colonus*. He maintains that his person ("deep inside me") is distinct from the miseries visited upon it:

> But no, no –
> how could you call me guilty, how by nature?
> . . .
> But in fact,
> knowing nothing, no, I went ... the way I went –
> but the ones who made me suffer, they knew full well,
> they wanted to destroy me.[11]
>
> I am innocent! Pure in the eyes of the law,
> blind, unknowing, I, I came to this![12]
>
> I have suffered it all, and all against my will!
> Such was the pleasure of the gods, raging,
> perhaps, against our race from ages past.
> But as for me alone –
> say my unwilling crimes against myself
> and against my own were payments from the gods
> for something criminal deep inside me ... no, look hard,
> you'll find no guilt to accuse me of – I am innocent![13]

In similar fashion, powers external to Hardy's women conspire to "destroy" them, and succeed in besmirching their characters, yet others protest their innocence, their abiding goodness, adopting Oedipus' line of reasoning: that they suffer against their wills and that there is nothing "criminal deep inside" them for which such suffering is "payment."

Tess's narrator and Jude, however, do not view Tess and Sue as divinely singled out for pain; instead, "man and senseless circumstance" supplant the "pleasure of the gods, raging" against them.[14] Secular "power that must perforce be beyond [them] since it extends, both spatially and temporally, far beyond [their own persons]" insists on the degradation of their good character, which they varyingly accept and refuse. As fateful as the Olympians, human convictions, religious or otherwise, foist guilt on these heroines who have done nothing wrong; like Greek dramas, Hardy's works both stage and indict this phenomenon. Thus Tess's narrator and Jude do not see these women as the authors of their own misfortunes. To hold these heroines accountable for what has occurred is the Aristotelian move that makes tragic figures themselves – not divine whim or other people – causally, inadvertently responsible for their own unhappiness, even as their intentions are blameless and their goodness remains intact. On Aristotle's reading, instead of external force that takes aim at good character, internal force inaugurates one's suffering, even as one's moral quotient is undisturbed. In Aristotle's view, the world does not, fundamentally, seek to undercut one's identity, to undermine heroines' good natures – or others' perception of their good natures. Certainly, Tess's and Sue's apologists also maintain their undiminished virtue, but in so doing they *contest* the prevailing wisdom that such women have become "bad"; they dissent from the dominant view that these women are morally debased. And they cannot concur with Aristotle that a heroine's pain is self-inflicted. Finally, these novels abjure the Christian interpretation of tragedy that excludes not only outside influences that are bent on disrupting noble character but also tragic heroines' initial goodness. In this strain of Christianized tragedy, foundational moral failings beget such figures' punishments. This latter mode of analysis treats plot itself as the outcome of *hamartia*, understood as an ethical flaw that earns heroines their chastisement; it is precisely this model of inner iniquity that Oedipus denounces. Such moralizing of the tragic fall, then, is not Greek literature's creation. Plato envisions such a moral universe as the antithesis of tragedy, and it is Aristotle who considers tragic characters to be the unwitting source of their fates. Full moralization of the genre, in which personal vice is the root of suffering, comes with medieval and early modern reimaginings of tragedy.[15] But even contemporary readings of Hardy's tragic novels that remove *hamartia*'s moral valence – assigning Tess a character flaw that is simply her heredity, her deterministic, biological inheritance – make her person the engine of her fate.[16] Yet Greek tragic destiny descends on characters from without and engulfs them. Greek tragic characters are not their fates' sole site of origin.

Characters, in the Greeks and in Hardy, are not responsible – in a causal or moral sense – for the entirety of what befalls them.

When critics then argue that Hardy's concentration on externally wrought demises is a fault in his novelistic craftsmanship, a ponderous over-plottedness, they fail to see that crushing outside forces are the signature of his Greek tragedy – and that in incorporating such destructive power into his fiction, Hardy lays the foundation for indicting the assimilation of such menaces into justificatory narratives.[17] Combining tragedy and the novel, Hardy fiercely accentuates the fragility and innocence of characters: the victims of tragic plot twists, blamed for their victimhood. If, as Woolf says, it is true that "all novels . . . deal with character, and that it is to express character – not to preach doctrines, sing songs, or celebrate the glories of the British Empire, that the form of the novel, so clumsy, verbose, and undramatic, so rich, elastic, and alive, has been evolved," then Hardy's novelistic tragedy does target what comes to the fore in modernist fiction, characters' inimitable, feeling natures, and mercilessly pits both plot and its construal against them.[18] The inhumanity of the invulnerable gods becomes, in Hardy and in modernism more broadly, the inhumanity of natural and cultural environments.

Only Tess's narrator consistently recognizes and champions the guiltless and thriving character that it is not Tess's fate to secure in the eyes of the world.[19] Only he suggests that she can leave her rape and its pains behind her – or that, if she cannot, her past might be viewed as wholly without shame or, indeed, advantageous to her. If every detail of her experience must contribute to her character – like innumerable drops of coloring that tint a clear liquid – he opts for accounts of that coloring that are salutary to Tess. Such, indeed, is Nietzsche's recommendation in *The Gay Science*: to be "poets of our lives" who "see what is necessary in things as what is beautiful in them."[20] Tess's narrator, therefore, distinguishes between the Tess driven to extremity by Angel's and Alec's appraisals of her and the Tess who might have been, who should have been – who fought to be. His rightful Tess is pulled from her "natural" course, which bends toward happiness, and forced down a fatal track: casualty of rape and of the meanings Angel and Alec assign to it.

When Jude and Sue then come closer to finding what Tess's narrator regrets that she will not –"the two halves of a perfect whole that confronted each other at the perfect moment" – they do appear to judge one another aright and to vibrate at the same affective frequency.[21] Their tenor of feeling, which *Jude* delimits as properly human and humane, contrasts with that of affectless natural processes and with their fellows' excessively

animalistic or devout dispositions. Yet their union comes "fifty years too
soon": their finely developed sympathy for all living creatures is precocious.[22] Their love is also belated in that each has already married wrongly.
And for all that each locates in the other the "right and desired one," they
travel opposite trajectories, backward or forward in time, away from one
another: Jude moves from his modern-day spirituality to pre-Christian
belief in a tragic universe of unearned suffering, whereas Sue begins
irreverently pagan and ends mired in Christian views of transgression.[23]
Their prized moments of intersubjective intimacy – when they are most
themselves – have no staying power. Plot and their divergent accounts of it
debilitate both and drive them asunder.

In *Jude*, Sue's misassumption of culpability, following the deaths of her
and Jude's children, allows Hardy to depict how the moralization of tragic
events is a strategy to survive them, to assign them an explanation in order
to bear them – yet also how excruciating such moralizing logic, which
makes character wholly responsible for fate, can be. Hardy's fiction as a
whole, however, does not blame Sue for blaming herself and does not
present her grief-stricken worldview as the final revelation of her character.
Given the extent to which the novel laments what she has become – the
pain her transformation causes both her and Jude – it suggests that tragic
circumstances, beyond Sue's control, have destroyed rather than clarified
her character. Just as Tess never has the chance to pass from grief to
prosperity, because others do not take her side in time, Sue's "mental
volte-face" signifies that affliction has obliterated her former identity – she
whom Jude considers the true Sue.[24]

Hardy's fiction undertakes a delicate feat of representation: to separate
the emergence and consolidation of character from character's distortion at
the hands of both unforeseen events and pernicious belief systems. Hardy's
tragic novels attempt to differentiate flourishing Tess and Sue, on the one
hand, from what occasions their "ruins," and from their ruined selves, on
the other.

Hardy versus Plato and Aristotle

Hardy's Sue in fact acts out Plato's counter-tragic dream of moralization.
As Stephen Halliwell argues, in the myth of Er that closes *Republic* X Plato
is at pains "to translate potential tragic material into the substance of a
moralistic fable" in which man "is taken to bring his own fate on himself;
the cause of it lies in his own soul. His sufferings will be a punishment, and
Platonic punishment is good for its subject."[25] Aristotle, however, delivers

a subtler transformation of tragedy in his *Poetics*. While he does not convert it to moral fable, he does hold its characters causally responsible for their fates. Although this might seem a less substantial revolution in thinking – Aristotle does not, after all, seek to eliminate the very category of innocent suffering – what is so eliminative about his interpretive model is that while tragic characters are not morally at fault for their pains, neither are extrahuman forces or other human beings. Whereas Oedipus contrasts his inner guiltlessness with a supernatural determination to persecute him, Aristotle lodges both the innocent victim and the architect of his doom in one and the same person.

Aristotle resists any external cause – divine or human, opaque or intelligible – as the source of a character's fall or flourishing. The events of the play ideally issue from *him*. When Aristotle objects to the irrationality of the deus ex machina, for instance, he refuses a narrative development that does not follow necessarily from a hero's own deed. Aristotle rejects the gods' obscure ends as causes of the plot's unfurling; he rejects how unexpectedly fortunes can change in their hands. If chance must make an appearance in tragedy, Aristotle asserts that "even chance events make the greatest impact of wonder when they *appear* to have a purpose (as in the case where Mitys's statue at Argos fell on Mitys's murderer and killed him, while he was looking at it: such things do not *seem* to happen without reason)."[26] In this instance of an occurrence that gives the impression, at least, of possessing a clear explanation, its reason is also a moral one: the murderous villain has brought this fall (this tumbling statue) upon himself. Thus it is Aristotle's commitment to excluding the Greek gods' unreason – their inscrutable and unpredictable behaviors – from the tragic stage that constitutes his "secularization" of tragedy.[27] Aristotle asserts that what lies beyond characters' doing is extraneous to plot: "Plots should not consist of parts which are irrational. So far as possible, there should be no irrational component; otherwise, it should lie outside the plot-structure."[28] Aristotle pictures personal ignorance or powerlessness as a complete etiology of suffering; he paints human vulnerability to unsolicited eventualities as an imperfection native to persons themselves. Although such figures elicit pity because they are not actively to blame for their woes, their passive accrual of guilt can be traced to them alone.

In his own ethical writings, Aristotle is likewise committed to delineating the sources of excusable and culpable action. In keeping with legal developments of the fifth century BCE, he determines that the threshold for guilt depends on the individual himself. That which he does under external compulsion or in ignorance is not his fault. But he is responsible for all that he does knowingly and intentionally. As Martha Nussbaum concludes, Aristotle would judge Oedipus morally responsible for homicide only and not for parricide.[29] And as Vernant explains, Aristotelian actors do not have free will in the Christian sense; instead, they are bound by internal compulsion to behave as they do.[30] Character, once formed, cannot do other than it does. But when such inner mandate is wanting, as in tragedy, Aristotle concludes that characters are driven not by the divine (prophecy, curse) or by the social (war, enslavement, rape, revenge) but by their own limited knowledge. Instead of brute power that wreaks havoc on persons and communities who can react – lament, persuade, even defy certain of their oppressors – characters are their own worst enemies. Jonathan Lear captures Aristotle's deft interpretive maneuver as follows: "In Aristotle's conception of tragedy, the individual actor takes on the burden of badness, the world as a whole is absolved."[31] To dramatize the "badness" of the world is indeed, for Aristotle, bad form. Aristotle's poetics, his aesthetic prohibitions against "impossibilities, irrationalities, morally harmful elements, contradictions, and offences against the true standards of the art," carry an ethics: keep evocations of senseless external threat to a minimum.[32]

It could seem that Aristotle in fact paves the way for Hardy, by seeing that tragedy can be secular – that characters' ignorance of past and future need not be divinely produced and that divinely orchestrated plots are not the only means of communicating the divergence between laudable characters and their desired outcomes. But Aristotle does more than reconceive tragic suffering as terrestrial in origin. He does more than understand divine irrationalities as so many metaphors for fearful and pitiable mortal luck in the world. Granting that Aristotle believes a rational sequence of events to be more fear-inspiring than a capricious one, because comprehensible misfortune impresses audiences more with its likelihood, he still derives some additional benefit from making unwitting characters the source of their ills, rather than others who plague them. As Nussbaum writes: "The unanswered question ... is why Aristotle insists that the causal mechanism must be an act of the hero's, rather than a (casually intelligible) network of events that bears down on him from outside."[33] Perhaps the answer is that heroes who unknowingly engender their own doom (or risk doing so, catching themselves in the last instant) are not, for Aristotle, the starkest dramatization of a pitiless cosmos that governs and sports with mortals. Aristotle instead delimits and minimizes the sphere from which menace comes, steering clear of the chancy divine agency and its secular substitutes that remain the paradigmatic signifiers, in Attic drama, of a universal human vulnerability to loss.

Modernist literary critic F. L. Lucas rightly remarks that "Aristotle himself . . . felt that the misfortunes of absolutely righteous characters were too shocking for the tragic stage"; the hero must have some causal part to play in his own destruction.[34] Yet Lucas remarks that Aristotle was also misread: "not studied in the Greek spirit, but rather as if he had been a Hebrew prophet," as if his tragic actors were morally corrupt from the start.[35] This is an apt critique of Aristotle's reception. Nonetheless, Aristotle's own partial implication of tragic persons in their falls already serves to quash further inquiry into the limits of agency, into the extent to which others yoke us to identities we internalize, conscript us into damning systems of meaning we cannot dismantle. Halliwell concludes that Aristotle practices the "denial of tragedy's deepest level," "more of an attempt to woo it over to philosophy's side than to meet it on its own terms."[36] Anthony Cascardi diagnoses in the philosophical tradition as a whole a defining need for tragedy to be "overcome," "defeated," or "averted."[37] Aristotle's very commentary on the genre begins to contain and to sanitize it: it requires that characters generate the fullness of plot. In Aristotle, the moment of *anagnorisis* (recognition, self-knowledge) ideally coincides with the *peripeteia*, the reversal of fortune contrary to expectation – and it is one's own unintended deeds, their meaning come fully to light, that effect the narrative shift from well-being to sorrow. There is no further antagonist to discern or denounce.

For numerous contemporary philosophers, literary critics, and classicists, then, Aristotle envisions a rational, even benign universe in a way that the ancient tragedians do not.[38] That is, undeserved, often inexplicable upheavals of fortune (*tuchē*, luck, the allotment of the gods) await and deform virtuous heroes and heroines in Athenian plays; in Aristotle, however, it is characters' susceptibility to error that determines their fates. And while Aristotle recognizes that what is "deep inside" one is no protection against disaster, he fails to mark that this is particularly true when outside forces target mortals' virtue and dignity. Unlike Aristotle, Hardy's Angel takes the ancient religious view that undeserved events, once transpired, undercut one's good character and refashion it in the image of the abominations that have taken place – they damage it or abolish it entirely. Here, intention is in no way an exculpatory or self-preservatory lifeline; for Angel, no gap exists between scandalous fate and goodness of character, as eventually it does for Oedipus, and as it does for Aristotle and Tess's narrator. For the majority of the novel, Angel is convinced that Tess's involuntary action necessitates the reappraisal of her identity. Discovering her past, Angel feels that he has not loved the real Tess, but a counterfeit, "[a]nother woman in your shape," even as Tess protests that "I am the same woman, Angel, as you fell in love with."[39] Angel's change of opinion comes too late; too late does he conclude that the "beauty or ugliness of a character lay not only in its achievements, but in its aims and impulses; its true history lay not among things done, but among things willed."[40] And even more condemnatory than the Greek religious perspective – that recasts character in light of fate, regardless of personal volition – is the Christian perspective in *Jude* that holds persons' outcomes and intentions to be congruent. To end badly, Sue concludes, one must have begun bad. Sue re-sees Aristotle's pitiable and unintended fall – of the hero who is morally sound both before and after – as the fully deserved consequence of her own sinfulness.

Hardy's novels, however, maintain that character is not always coincident with its endpoint. Tess is not equivalent to her destiny; she is not, to her narrator, the product of her cumulative circumstances because she has not initiated them and they should not, in his view, be permitted to define her. Contra Aristotle, Tess's narrator finds that it is the very mischance of malign human agency bent on harming Tess that issues in her "fallenness," while in accordance with Aristotle, Tess's narrator deems her virtue unwavering – precisely what Angel fails to recognize until the novel's close. Even Sue, whose character is eclipsed in the end, who embraces self-slander where Tess attempts to resist it, is not reducible to her final posture, in Jude's estimation. Sue promotes the Aristotelian premise that the sufferer alone is responsible for her doom. Sue supplements this view with a model of Christian tragic causation in which it is not Aristotle's ignorant misstep that accounts for her suffering, but her own moral depravity. Hardy's fiction as a whole, however, pictures "pure" character at war with circumstances that curb and criminalize it: "the inherent will to enjoy" menaced by "the circumstantial will against enjoyment."[41] In contradistinction to Angel and to Sue, Tess's narrator and Jude view tragic suffering as Tess's mother does: "as a thing which had come upon them irrespective of desert or folly; a chance external impingement to be borne with; not a lesson."[42] Hardy's fiction, that is, trains its readers in a new mode of decryption, asking us to reject the notion that a heroine's final outcome presents the consolidation of her character. Hardy's protagonists do travel a single, unitary course, but Hardy's novels suggest that plot and its interpretation can warp and obscure personhood, rather than bring it fully to light.

Two Tesses

From the moment we meet Alec, Tess's narrator establishes, contra Aristotle, that Alec is the instigator, the seed of this tragic plot, not Tess. Hardy's narrator positions Alec as "the 'tragic mischief' of her drama – one who stood fair to be the blood-red ray in the spectrum of her young life," a fact that she "[does] not divine, as she innocently" beholds him.[43] During Alec's rape of Tess, Hardy's narrator maintains this grammar of over-powering fate and powerless character: upon her "tissue" Alec "traced such a coarse pattern as it was doomed to receive."[44] In Hardy's anti-Aristotelian view of tragedy, "practically blank" Tess is branded, tattooed, stenciled in suddenly – her life plot marked by an agency not her own. No philosophical or theological attempts to rationalize this occurrence, the narrator asserts, will satisfy our "sense of order" or "mend the matter":

> Darkness and silence ruled everywhere around. Above them rose the primeval yews and oaks of The Chase, in which were poised gentle roosting birds in their last nap; and about them stole the hopping rabbits and hares. But, might some say, where was Tess's guardian angel? where was the Providence of her simple faith? Perhaps, like that other god of whom the ironical Tishbite spoke, he was talking, or he was pursuing, or he was in a journey, or he was sleeping and not to be awaked.
>
> Why it was that upon this beautiful feminine tissue, sensitive as gossa-mer, and practically blank as snow as yet, there should have been traced such a coarse pattern as it was doomed to receive; why so often the coarse appropriates the finer thus, the wrong man the woman, the wrong woman the man, many thousand years of analytical philosophy have failed to explain to our sense of order. One may, indeed, admit the possibility of a retribution lurking in the present catastrophe. Doubtless some of Tess d'Urberville's mailed ancestors rollicking home from a fray had dealt the same measure even more ruthlessly towards peasant girls of their time. But though to visit the sins of the fathers upon the children may be a morality good enough for divinities, it is scorned by average human nature; and it therefore does not mend the matter.[45]

"Why," he repeats twice, the insoluble question that haunts this tragic formation of character. It is against such a "coarse pattern" and the Tess it forges – hounded by her past – that Hardy's narrator rails, imagining the open future that ought to be hers.

In this scene, too, Hardy's narrator renders Christianity as unresponsive and impotent as the supreme pagan divinity, Baal, of whom Elijah ("the ironical Tishbite") speaks with contempt. Elijah reports that Baal's proph-ets beseech their god to display his power, but "there was neither voice, nor any to answer, nor any that regarded."[46] For Hardy's narrator, this "primeval" indifference *is* the enduring condition of the natural world. The Greek gods who look aside in much Attic drama as human beings wreak havoc upon one another are now the "purblind Doomsters" of Hardy's "Hap."[47] Now the countenance of the mist is "eyeless," as Hardy writes in his anti-theistic poem "A Sign-Seeker."[48] For the nonhuman world not to look, not to care, is for Hardy both a tenet of Darwinian science and a tenet of tragic fiction.

Hardy's narrator also makes this episode the occasion to indict the Attic logic of inherited familial curses. These Greek precursors to the Christian "sins of the fathers" are demonic miasmas that infect innocent youth, inevitably. Like biological agents, they do not mete out warranted punishment. Hardy's narrator objects to the spurious notion that Alec's rape of Tess is retribution for those rapes that her male ancestors have perpetrated against their social and sexual inferiors. This is precisely the structure of violence that Aeschylus dramatizes and challenges: crime begets crime begets crime. The vileness of one act is expunged by the commission of that same act against the previous wrongdoer. Aeschylus himself is at pains to break this cycle, to envision a new form of juridical practice that does not visit wrong upon wrong. And Hardy's narrator's tirelessly mounted defenses of Tess, as we will see, show his own loathing for a logic in which the viciousness of the fathers is paid for with the life of the daughter. Here, Hardy's tragedy recovers from the ancients the indictment of such models – Iphigenia slaughtered by Agamemnon, her father, for wind to Troy, and Cassandra raped by him, or Hekabe's daughter, Polyxena, sacrificed by the Greek host so that Achilles's ghost can have her. In the company of the Greek tragedians, *Tess* reprises and reproves the very idea of sacrifice: beginning with the May Day celebration, a descendant of pagan fertility rites in which the death of the maiden, initiated into sex, ensures the vigor of the harvest, and clothing Tess in the same ceremonial white frock to meet Alec.[49]

The gods of pagan and Christian mythology slumber while Alec invades Tess's sleep. It is Tess, however, who sees writ large on the boards of a stile, "THY, DAMNATION, SLUMBERETH, NOT."[50] Her own impulse is to challenge this credo, that bad fortune is proof of bad character: "'But,' said she tremulously, 'suppose your sin was not of your own seeking?'"[51] He who paints the words replies, "I leave their application to the hearts of the people who read 'em," and Tess boldly counters: "I think they are horrible . . . Crushing! Killing!"[52] She goes further: "'Pooh – I don't believe God said such things!' she murmured contemptuously."[53] But it is precisely her fellows' insistence on her impurity that casts the fatal pall over her life.

Hardy's narrator, however, reiterates that while her rape changes her, it spells her undoing in this moralizing universe only. His commentary works to establish how singular, how anomalously reproving is her particular social milieu: "Most of the misery had been generated by her conventional aspect, and not by her innate sensations."[54] He imagines other worlds in which she would thrive, where no one would require her to be Angel's immaculate, neopagan goddess, the vestal proto-Christian of the vale, in order to survive and to flourish. Specifically, he imagines places in which she would have no past, ensuring that no life-negating interpretation of it could prevail:

> Moreover, alone in a desert island would she have been wretched at what had happened to her? Not greatly.[55]

> [B]ut just created, to discover herself as a spouseless mother, with no experience of life except as the parent of a nameless child, would the position have caused her to despair? No, she would have taken it calmly, and found pleasure therein.[56]

> Let the truth be told – women do as a rule live through such humiliations, and regain their spirits, and again look about them with an interested eye. While there's life there's hope is a conviction not so entirely unknown to the "betrayed" as some amiable theorists would have us believe.[57]

Tess's narrator's fictions and truths, however, contradict those of his story world. Tess is consigned to surroundings in which these "amiable" theorists of damnation have their way, a world in which her narrator's imagined scenarios do not win out. Yet it is his signature practice to improvise alternatives to her fate and to denounce the fact that she is made to feel guilt and shame for her tragic ill luck. He devises three more retellings of her story, incompatible with one another, but each in her defense. Hardy's narrator suggests that Nature's own morality clears Tess of guilt vis-à-vis her past, that amoral Nature purifies Tess of her past entirely, and that her past enhances rather than impeaches her character.

In his first gambit, Hardy's narrator allows that Tess's internalization of guilt is real to *her*, but also, editorializing heavily, asserts that hers is an inaccurate self-assessment. Because she personifies nature such that its harsh weather seems a commentary on her culpable soul, he rejoins that nature bespeaks her innocence. He pivots away from the tragic, unseeing Nature that has eyelessly countenanced her rape and imagines a Nature whose own moral tenets refute society's "moral hobgoblins":

The midnight airs and gusts, moaning amongst the tightly-wrapped buds and bark of the winter twigs, were formulae of bitter reproach. A wet day was the expression of irremediable grief at her weakness in the mind of some vague ethical being whom she could not class definitely as the God of her childhood, and could not comprehend as any other.

But this encompassment of her own characterization, based on shreds of convention, peopled by phantoms and voices antipathetic to her, was a sorry and mistaken creation of Tess's fancy – a cloud of moral hobgoblins by which she was terrified without reason. It was they that were out of harmony with the actual world, not she. Walking among the sleeping birds in the hedges, watching the skipping rabbits on a moonlit warren, or standing under a pheasant-laden bough, she looked upon herself as a figure of Guilt intruding into the haunts of Innocence. But all the while she was making a distinction where there was no difference. Feeling herself in antagonism she was quite in accord. She had been made to break an accepted social law, but no law known to the environment in which she fancied herself such an anomaly.[58]

Hardy's narrator wishes to imply that by the standards of "Nature," by the laws "known to the environment," Tess has committed no crime, that these "haunts of Innocence" are indeed her asylum and vindication, refuting her self-indictment. Hardy's narrator would himself exonerate her, and seeks in this view of nature his keenest ally and her most invincible apologist: she is "no different" from, "in accord" with her natural surroundings, and therefore as blameless as they. He confirms that for all her "conventional" shame, "[e]very see-saw of her breath, every wave of her blood, every pulse singing in her ears was a voice that joined with Nature in revolt against her scrupulousness."[59] It would seem that the "natural side of her which knew no social law" is proof of her truest character.[60]

"Nature," now the faultless external realm of tree and pheasant, and the manifold of seen and unseen laws that govern all life, travels inward – is her nature too. "Every wave of her blood" denies the very categories in which condemnation of her might be framed, the terms in which she, too, castigates herself. Her "natural side" has its own commandments that countermand the artificial charges brought against her. Her narrator's description of her child, too, presupposes the misattribution of sin to a stainless being: "So passed away Sorrow the Undesired – that intrusive creature, that bastard gift of shameless Nature who respects not the social law."[61] Tess's narrator bitingly evokes the perversions to which he bears witness: rendering a child a "sorrow," the creaturely "intrusive," a gift a "bastard," Nature herself culpable. He plays on the opposing meanings of "shameless" – wanting proper shame, from society's condemnatory perspective, and exempt from needless shame, under nature's law.

But is there no shame in the forced act of procreation that begot Sorrow? Because Tess is young, fecund, and luxuriantly attractive, is her rape, too, harmless, lawful, even salutary? Furthermore, are the "moral hobgoblins" of religion, classism, and sexism really Tess's own "fancies"? This well-intentioned shielding of Tess from censure is riven with contradiction. She has every practical reason to be concerned for her future, even if the causes of her fear and regret, namely, her feelings of shame, sin, taint, and culpability, should be dismissed. If her persecutors are "out of harmony with the actual world," what actual world does Hardy's narrator mean? The so-called natural world, whose "ethics" absolves her of guilt by licensing her rape? The world of society as it should be, the counterfactual, just, and humane world that the entire novel coaxes its readers to desire? Just as Hardy's narrator's "real" Tess is not the recipient of punitive, sham "justice," his "actual world" does not dole out such punishments. Meanwhile, the actual world in which Tess dwells denies her a lifetime of love and kills her without remorse. It shoots these pheasants from whom, in her narrator's reverie, she is no different.

Invoking Nature's laws to acquit Tess, to decriminalize her biology, her person, and her past, her narrator risks justifying all that has befallen her under Nature's ostensible supervision. He must, then, to protect his heroine, retreat from claims of Nature's justice, reserving the sphere of compassion, of the ethical, for the very human society that elects her ruin; and that society's thoughtlessness, its failure to care for Tess, must be criminal in a way that Nature's is not. Her narrator must communicate that no laws of Nature have protected Tess from an indefensible and not innocuous rape; no bough or pheasant has interceded on her behalf. Tess's very exemption from guilt must be a matter of human discrimination, not of resemblance to the unfeeling haunts of forest and vale. Even as Hardy's narrator intermittently brandishes Nature's immunity from shame as a strategy to afford Tess relief from her anguishing "scrupulousness," he also registers that this shamelessness, this imperviousness to sentiment, is Nature's keenest deficiency. Nature cannot differentiate between shameful and unshameful acts as narrator or reader can. Nature cannot preclude the former or condone the latter. Tess, unaware of her supporters, can only lament that God's blameless sun shines "on the just and the unjust alike."[62]

Acknowledging that Tess's environment cannot, after all, serve as her character witness or sympathetic companion – for the "familiar surroundings had not darkened because of her grief, nor sickened because of her pain" – Tess's narrator embarks upon his second mode of defense, suggesting a new analogy between his heroine and her environment that promotes her recovery and flourishing.[63] Allowing that her surroundings, however rich in their "oozing fatness and warm ferments," are alien to human feeling and judgment, he proceeds to emphasize that this fertile vegetation and Tess are still wont to rejuvenate, to rise phoenix-like from the ashes of their literal or metaphorical winters: "Yet even now Tess felt the pulse of hopeful life still warm within her."[64] Morality aside, the biosphere in its lush plenitude still objects to her tragic end: a "particularly fine spring came round, and the stir of germination was almost audible in the buds; it moved her as it moved the wild animals," and "some spirit within her rose automatically as the sap in the twigs. It was unexpected youth, surging up anew after its temporary check."[65] Knowing full well that Tess's life will be permanently and prematurely checked, her narrator nonetheless paints her encounter with Alec as he thinks it ought to be, as a "temporary check" only:

> The irresistible, universal, automatic tendency to find sweet pleasure some-where, which pervades all life, from the meanest to the highest, had at length mastered Tess. Being even now only a young woman of twenty, one who mentally and sentimentally had not finished growing, it was impossible that any event should have left upon her an impression that was not in time capable of transmutation.[66]

He militates for Tess's resilience and adaptability – her developing character – in lieu of a character ossified and contracted in one fell swoop.

Whether Nature is Tess's moral advocate or her amoral partner in indomitable, resilient life, her narrator consistently suggests that her own "innate sensation," her oft-referenced life "pulse," proves her keenest source of resistance to crushing social scruples. Her human nature, like her narrator's, throbs with counter-scruples, counter-impulses. But at times her inborn sensations pain her, intrude on her well-being; her inner ecology, that is, is not unequivocally salubrious, the internal imprint of some external perfection. Within Tess's own body, her nature may either "sing" "revolt" or "thrust" "oppressiveness" upon her, and she must navigate these promptings and impediments to her happiness.[67] Hardy's narrator cannot derive an infallible code of ethics from any supernatural, extrahuman, or human source; human convictions, in Humean fashion, spring only from interrogations of fallible human practices.

Yet because of the profusion of perspectives that Tess's narrator vary-ingly adopts and abandons, readers accuse the novel of inconsistency.

In 1895 Lionel Johnson criticizes Hardy, in representative fashion, for embroiling readers in a morass of contradictory descriptions and pronouncements:

> Mr. Hardy is not content to frame his indictment, by the stern narration of sad facts: he inserts fragments of that reasoning, which has brought him to his dark conclusion. They are too many, too bitter, too passionate, to be but an overflow, as it were, from his narration: they are too sparse, too ironical, too declamatory, to be quite intelligible.... I want definitions of *nature*, *law*, *society*, and *justice*: the want is coarse, doubtless, and unimaginative; but I cannot suppress it.[68]

Johnson's is not a coarse or illegitimate want; Hardy's fiction provokes this ache for definition. It is Hardy's narrator's own, as he labors both to delineate and to refute those conceptions of "*nature, law, society*, and *justice*" that entrap his heroine. His array of declamatory statements is at once too sparse and too passionate to be fully intelligible, but this jostle of ardent, piecemeal viewpoints is still more intentional than haphazard. Hardy's narrator does not labor for absolute clarity and fail; rather, what his interwoven proclamations add to "stern narration" is the novel's aura of active, critical, ethical struggle. His "reasoning" does not simply rehearse, or justify, a "dark conclusion" to come. With consistency, he entertains rival stances in an endeavor to challenge dismal events and to determine (alongside his readers) those premises about Nature, human nature, and the distortion of character that either undo Tess or pose alternatives to her demise. It is entirely true that he is "not content" to narrate unobtrusively, but "overflows" into character himself, bitter and ironical: "'Justice' was done," he announces scathingly, "and the President of the Immortals (in Aeschylean phrase) had ended his sport with Tess."[69]

Tess's narrator, therefore, has one further counter-narrative that he brandishes both early and late: "But for the world's opinion, [Tess's] experiences would have been simply a liberal education."[70] He chooses to allude to Tess's past merely as a fortuitous eye-opener, a school-of-hard-knocks tutorial, amplifying her spirit. He adopts a seemingly myopic, even cold-hearted position of disregard – casts Tess's rape and loss of a child in unequivocally positive terms – precisely to counter in advance the gratuitous suffering that he foresees for her. If she is the teleological outcome of her past, he reasons, her character is the richer, the more loving and loyal, for her experience. In this particular judgment of her prior powerlessness and current knowledge, he cleaves only to the benefits of her suffering, excluding all else, intimating the potential brightness of the future that will be denied her. He celebrates her maturation, brushing aside at what cost she has achieved it. This "should have been" account, conditional given the facts of the fiction, is for Hardy's narrator much closer to the truth of the matter. He emphasizes, as no one else will, that the woman who attracts Angel possesses these prior experiences – they enrich her gaze, augment her beauty – experiences that Angel refuses to hear and cannot understand.

Hardy's narrator is not as fickle or as unreliable as Angel. Hardy's narrator adopts this contrarian position – "Tess's passing corporeal blight had been her mental harvest" – *because* her fate is the opposite of the scenarios he rehearses, her allotment the inverse of his hopes.[71] Angel's appreciation of Tess's mental harvest – Angel's awareness of her alluring gravitas, whose origin eludes him – is of passing duration, while a conviction of her lasting corporeal blight overtakes him. Although Hardy's narrator insists on nature's regenerative power, Tess will find herself insuperably "unregenerate" in the eyes of others.[72] Tess indeed tries to leave her past behind: "She dismissed the past; trod upon it and put it out, as one treads on a coal that is smouldering and dangerous."[73] Tess strives to keep at bay the "gloomy spectres" of a self-characterization that will break her, and yet "[s]he knew that they were waiting like wolves just outside the circumscribing light."[74] For all that Tess labors to banish the past (never daring to recast it as her narrator does), she comes to feel that she cannot evade a character imposed on her from without, which affords her the "almost physical sense of an implacable past which still engirdled her": "It intensified her consciousness of error to a practical despair; the break of continuity between her earlier and present existence, which she had hoped for, had not, after all, taken place. Bygones would never be complete bygones till she was a bygone herself."[75] In light of such imprisonment, Tess's confinement to an "earlier" character formation that she cannot transmute, Hardy's narrator seems driven to model an agitated intellect constantly at odds with the modes of thought, the "standard of judgment," the "sense of condemnation," that have led Tess to despair of getting by.[76] He resents all that conspires to transform his "pure" heroine (a character she never loses, in his view) into a heroine with blood on her hands.

From the beginning, he narrates a Tess who is cowed, intimidated, and compelled to intimacy in Alec's carriage, where Alec plants his "kiss of mastery" upon her.[77] Alec spies, hunts, and follows her, his predation sinister. When Alec then returns to reentrap her, seething with anger at his thwarted possession, he announces, "I was your master once; I will be your master again," and this ineluctable symmetry of abuses, which robs Tess of self-determination a second time, is what Hardy's narrator seems unable to bear in silence.[78] Similarly, if he must give voice to Angel's condemnatory thinking, he will classify it as a "hard logical deposit" and insert his tidbits of counter-logic.[79] If Angel dares to call Alec Tess's "husband in Nature" (and to suggest that "[i]f he were dead it might be different"), Hardy's narrator will evoke Tess's visceral revulsion to such a classification.[80] Tess is nonetheless forced to believe, to repeat those words, to argue that "this man alone was her husband."[81] It is a supposed truth so inimical to her feeling that, unable to voice or to legitimate an alternative conception of union or self (too late would Angel sanction it), she strikes down that which she has been compelled, time and again, to accept as a restraint to her every bodily impulse, and she dies for her resistance. The patriarchal state condemns her violence, not Alec's or its own.

Overcome with "mad grief" and lamentation – "Oh – oh – oh!" – Tess cannot bear that Alec has a second time "made me be what I prayed you in pity not to make me be again."[82] The "original Tess," whom Angel at long last recognizes, has for the second time lost sovereignty over her body: "allowing it to drift, like a corpse upon the current, in a direction dissociated from its living will."[83] Like Sue to follow, Tess's living will is broken, her body turned corpse under subjection and false belief. Only on killing Alec does Tess experience a short-lived, poetic beat of joy, but "[t]his happiness could not have lasted – it was too much – I have had enough."[84] As she knows, her moment of being will not arrest her narrative's merciless becoming. Her very self-assertion, her defense of personhood, saddles her with the charge of guilt, of culpable action, that she had sought to disprove. So Hardy's narrator, his own tale's counter-weight, constantly gestures toward a "great passionate pulse of existence, unwarped, uncontorted, untrammeled," hers in his imagining, as if he cannot tolerate the events he transcribes, and must conjure the pulse of her "might have been" life, playing devil's advocate to the "tragic machinery" he represents.[85]

Sue's Reversals

Whereas Tess falls prey to others' life-negating interpretations of her, Sue herself cannot bear a tragic universe in which suffering and death have no decipherable meaning and lie beyond her control; Sue moralizes her own fate. Attic calamity causes her to efface the very character that Jude comes to love: Sue's reversal of fortune leads her wholly to reenvision the world and herself. *Jude* pictures Sue's final penitence – the denial of her bodily impulses – as the negation of her character.

It is tragic loss, with its unbearable surfeit of sadness, that comes to divide them: "Sue and himself," Jude realizes, "had mentally travelled in opposite directions since the tragedy."[86] Sue comes to feel as Tess had, that "in inhabiting the fleshly tabernacle with which Nature had endowed her, she was somehow doing wrong."[87] Sue's unprecedented grief spawns her newfound conviction that "Arabella's child killing mine was a judgement – the right slaying the wrong"; it is a commentary on "my badness."[88] Even as this "despairing self-suppression" suffuses her conversation with Jude – their speech grows as racked and uncertain as his sickly gait – Sue calls her curtailed liberty of expression "self-mastery."[89]

When the very religious proscriptions that Jude has ceased to obey consume Sue's thought, he forswears them further. "It is no use fighting against God!" she cries in her reactionary desperation, following her announcement that she will return to her first husband, Phillotson, and Jude replies:

> It is only against man and senseless circumstance.... You make me hate Christianity, or mysticism, or Sacerdotalism, or whatever it may called, if it's that which has caused this deterioration in you. That a woman-poet, a woman seer, a woman whose soul shone like a diamond – whom all the wise of the world would have been proud of, if they could have known you – should degrade herself like this! I am glad I had nothing to do with Divinity – damn glad – if it's going to ruin you in this way!... How you argued that marriage was only a clumsy contract – which it is – how you showed all the objections to it – all the absurdities! If two and two made four when we were happy together, surely they make four now?... [C]an this be the girl who brought the Pagan deities into this most Christian city? – who ... quoted Gibbon, and Shelley, and Mill?... [Y]ou are *my* wife!... All wrong, all wrong!... Error – perversity! It drives me out of my senses. Do you care for him? Do you love him? You know you don't! It will be a fanatic prostitution – ![90]

Sue demonizes the very feelings that have justified her union with Jude. Now she opts for the ascetic, the self-flagellating suppression of her natural urges, opts for a "fanatic prostitution" of her body, because in her pain she blames her "unlicensed" pleasure and the heterodox convictions it sponsored for the deaths of her children.[91] She cannot accept "man and senseless circumstances," Hardy's own tragic antagonists, as her children's destroyers – for where is the reason, the redemptive power in that? She cries to Phillotson: "My children – are dead – and it is right that they should be! I am glad – almost. They were sin-begotten. They were sacrificed to teach me how to live! – their death was the first stage of my purification. That's why they have not died in vain!"[92] She must be the author of so agonizing a loss; she becomes a Christian theorist of tragedy.

Suffering of Attic proportion attaches Sue to those Christian scruples that she eschewed "in the independent days, when her intellect played like lambent lightning over conventions and formalities which [Jude] at that time respected, though he did not now."[93] She had been adamant that:

> It is none of the natural tragedies of love that's love's usual tragedy in civilized life, but a tragedy artificially manufactured for people who in a natural state would find relief in parting!... I am certain one ought to be allowed to undo what one has done so ignorantly! I daresay it happens to lots of women, only they submit, and I kick.... When people of a later age look back upon the barbarous customs and superstitions of the times that we have the unhappiness to live in, what *will* they say![94]

The "natural tragedies" of love involve unwanted partings, sincere losses: Sue's of her children, Jude's of her. But the "usual tragedy of civilized life" is gratuitous, "artificially manufactured," and consists in refusal of the "relief" of separation, of the "oughts" of free feeling. Thriving on forced couplings, manufactured tragedy drives asunder those who most desire togetherness. Sue has deemed the socially mandated strangulation of one's feelings, to the benefit of none, akin to the "amputation of a limb," and yet she now submits, stops kicking – because what she formerly designated "barbarous customs and superstitions" she re-sees as her atonement.[95]

Sue, who used to understand herself "[o]utside all laws except gravitation and germination," views Little Father Time's murder-suicide as an indicator of God's law.[96] Following a social excommunication based on "artificial compulsions" (Jude's term in Hardy's manuscript),[97] Sue is overtaken by "an awful conviction that her discourse with the boy [about the family's hardships] had been the main cause of the tragedy."[98] Yet for all that the child's act is read as Hardy's Malthusian interlude, in which Little Father Time determines to decrease the familial population ("Done because we are too menny"), it is social ostracism that leads him to feel that his life is unwanted.[99] This incident is itself a warning against the mis-assumption of personal fault. That *I* am to blame is the logic that destroys both mother and stepson. A certainty of her own sinfulness colonizes Sue's mind, and she submits her body to what most repels it on the notion that she now, rightly, subordinates sinful flesh to soulful faith in a proper and penitent manner. That it should feel so forced, so foul and punishing, she now takes as a sign of her perversity; Jude, of course, reads the pains of fanaticism as signs of *its* perversity and rejects the notion that a fault in her character has wrought her own misery. Sue, however, needs to believe in some moral *hamartia*, a tragic flaw in her nature, to erase from view the horrors of human cruelty and cosmic indifference.

Jude indicts a particular theory of tragedy: because "Fate has given us this stab in the back," as Sue rationalizes, we ourselves must have occasioned it.[100] Sue insists not only on her causal role in Little Father Time's act; she blames her heretical feelings for it. She then proposes a Christian solution to her initiatory crime of "self-delight," of making "a virtue of joy," that she and Jude have committed: "we should mortify the flesh – the terrible flesh."[101] For all that Jude resists her "creed-drunk" ethos, reiterating that "the letter killeth" and that "there's no evil woman in you," her conviction of their iniquity does pain him to death.[102] *Tess*, too, indicts this "crushing" narrative logic: "All was, alas, worse than vanity – injustice, punishment."[103] Tess also recognizes the lethal procedure by which unearned griefs are recast as religious fault. Angel's "view of her so deadened her," and so punishing is his conviction of her impurity that even he comes to suspect that his "conventional" thinking constitutes the indefensible cruelty of a forsaken and Greek tragic universe: "God's *not* in his heaven: all's *wrong* with the world," he conjectures irreverently.[104] It is Tess's narrator who vociferously reminds us that any number of alternative readings of Tess would have saved her. Similarly, when Sue determines that the stabs of Fate are a Christian commentary on her character, the widow Edlin recognizes that this interpretation is the real doom that overtakes her, that cuts her off from all human connection and sentences her to self-exile as the most defiled of women: now "[s]he's got nobody on her side. The one man who'd be her friend the obstinate creature won't allow to come near her."[105] Edlin regrets the further plot twist that issues from Sue's new philosophy: "the self-sacrifice of the woman on the altar of what she was pleased to call her principles."[106] Tragedy, the undeserved desecration of good character, forced into an impossible mold – that of poetic justice – announces the end of all joy for Tess, Sue, and Jude.

Scapegoating

Ancient Greek ritual and modern psychotherapy, we will see, practice this same defamation of character. Investigating ritual, Anne Carson details the archaic and classical Greek policing and disparagement of women and their voices. Women's "monstrous" cries were permissible only in funereal and ritual settings. Male sound, by contrast, was the province of reason: "Verbal continence is an essential feature of the masculine virtue of *sophrosyne* ('prudence, soundness of mind, moderation, temperance, self-control') that organizes most patriarchal thinking on ethical or emotional matters. Woman as a species is frequently said to lack the ordering

principle of *sophrosyne*."[107] Carson enumerates "a complex array of legis-
lation and convention in preclassical and classical Greece" that worked to
"clos[e] women's mouths":

> [T]he best documented examples are Solon's sumptuary laws and the core
> concept of Sophokles' blanket statement, "Silence is the *kosmos* [good order]
> of women." The sumptuary laws enacted by Solon in the 6th century BC
> had as their effect, Plutarch tells us, "to forbid all the disorderly and
> barbarous excesses of women in their festivals, processions, and funeral
> rites." The main responsibility for funeral lament had belonged to women
> from earliest Greek times. Already in Homer's *Iliad* we see the female
> Trojan captives in Achilles' camp compelled to wail over Patroklos. Yet
> lawgivers of the 6th and 5th centuries like Solon were at pains to restrict
> these female outpourings to a minimum of sound and emotional display.[108]

Tragedy, however, privileges personal, familial, and communal lament –
the expression of unbridled emotion. In this way, tragedy defies Solon's
laws and Sophocles' regulatory dictum. Women emote relentlessly, in
Sophocles, and men forgo controlled speech. Carson points to Sophocles'
Women of Trachis: "When a man lets his current emotions come up to his
mouth and out through his tongue he is thereby feminized, as Herakles at
the end of the *Trachiniai* agonizes to find himself 'sobbing like a girl,
whereas before I used to follow my difficult course without a groan but
now in pain I am discovered a woman.'"[109] It is the same fall from
sophrosyne that characterizes Sophocles' pitiable and debilitated Philoctetes.
The gods have consigned Philoctetes to an anguishing foot wound; his
fellow soldiers abandon him to an uninhabited island because his cries
disquiet and demoralize them.

Carson notes that "female sound is bad to hear *both* because the quality
of a woman's voice is objectionable *and* because woman uses her voice to
say what should not be said."[110] The whistleblower – in Greek life, if not
in Greek art – must be muzzled. Failing the sequestration of her voice,
choreographed rituals serve to quarantine and eliminate this "bad" sound
and social content: "Ancient society was happy to have women drain
off ... unpleasant tendencies and raw emotion into a leakproof ritual
container. The strategy involved here is a kathartic one."[111] To concen-
trate unwelcome sentiment in a base receptacle and to empty it was the
modus operandi of myriad cultural rites. These included "the Athenian
ritual called *Choes*":

> It featured a competition between celebrants to drain an oversize jug of
> wine and concluded with a symbolic (or perhaps not) act of sexual union
> between the god Dionysos and a representative woman of the community.

> It is this person to whom Demosthenes refers, saying, "She is the woman who discharges the unspeakable things on behalf of the city."[112]

The "unspeakable things" that *sophrosyne* compels men to repress – and to schedule women, on occasion, to discharge – are the revelations that would indict and endanger normative culture. If tragedies, too, were to possess this purgative function, their object would be to shore up *sophrosyne* and the status quo. This may be what readers of Aristotle's catharsis as purgation have in mind. But tragedy does not evince this mania for evacuation. It foregrounds pain to investigate its sources. It suggests that demonic curse and social opprobrium conspire, without warrant, to lodge iniquity in their victims. This procedure itself comes to seem immoral. When tragic characters and audiences cry out in grief and rage at their condition – precisely what Plato chastises as womanly or infantile lamentation – such feeling is the precursor to onlookers' outrage at characters' mistreatment.

Tragic subjects make visible their own persecution. That their woes are pinned on them as personal defects only accentuates the perversity of the gods, men, and women who weaponize shame and social exclusion to consolidate their power. Tragedy exposes this tactic, this displacement of blame onto the recipients of suffering. It is this logic, operative in social practice and ritual, that tragedy revisits and reproves. Consider, for instance, the fifth-century BCE political procedure of ostracism. Ostracism was the forcible exile of persons perceived to be threats to the political order.[113] Banishment maintained the inviolability of the political norm. It was the same thinking that licensed the fifth-century ritual of the *pharmakos*, the annual expulsion of a community member whose task it was to carry and cast out the evils of the city. Vernant writes of Sophocles' Oedipus in conjunction with this process, careful to indicate that Oedipus is reminiscent of – but not identical to – the *pharmakos*:

> [Oedipus] is a "savior" king who, at the beginning of the play, is the object of the prayers of an entire people as if he were a god holding the city's destiny in his hands; but he is also an abominable defilement, a monster of impurity concentrating within himself all the evil and sacrilege in the world, who must be ejected as a *pharmakos*, a scapegoat, so that the city can become pure once again and be saved.[114]

The difference, then, between *pharmakos* and tragic hero lies in ritual's and tragedy's divergent judgments of scapegoating. Assigning fault to the real-life *pharmakos* is socially sanctioned and celebrated; it is conceived as a means of collective absolution. The vilification of dramatic characters, on the contrary, raises the specter of vicious social and divine prerogative. It effects a lamentable transformation in personality or reputation. Whereas the eviction of the *pharmakos* is understood to cleanse the community – because he bears its misdeeds as his own – the tragic hero, also become a bearer of evils, seems to be the object of divine or social recriminations that do more harm than good. There is not a Christological structure to tragedy. Its sacrifices do not herald salvation.

Carson argues that this idea of salvific catharsis integral to Greek ritual – which I find that tragedy questions and censures – persists to the present day. Carson cites Freudian psychoanalysis as her example: "In Freud's theory the hysterical patients are women who have bad memories or ugly emotions trapped inside them like a pollution" that must be contained and expelled.[115] These women are sites of moral hazard, in need of decontamination. Carson extends this program of purgation to society at large: "As if the entire female gender were a kind of collective bad memory of unspeakable things, patriarchal order like a well-intentioned psychoanalyst seems to conceive its therapeutic responsibility as the channeling of this bad sound into politically appropriate containers."[116] Hardy's modern tragedies, then, contest this persistent inclination to quarantine women's suffering. Cleansing women of "bad sound" shades into cleansing society of them. This is the restoration of equilibrium that prefers to replace Tess with her unsullied sister in Angel's bed. If Tess cannot be relieved of her past and restored to health, she can be removed from the scene; the removal of evils proves eugenic.

Such an ethos of eradication seeks to confine "bad memories or ugly emotions" to discrete vessels and ignores the traumatic milieus responsible for them. Critics of today's fields of psychology and psychiatry level the same charge at the diagnosis of borderline personality disorder: "it locates the problem within the individual. 'BPD' hides disordered environments, misuse of power and perpetrators of abuse."[117] Bria Berger explains the designation: "The fifth edition of the *Diagnostic and Statistical Manual of Mental Disorders (DSM-5)* broadly defines personality disorders as 'enduring pattern[s] of inner experience and behavior that deviate markedly from the expectations of the individual's culture.'"[118] What is labeled out of cultural bounds is "memory of unspeakable things." What is deemed peripheral to the norm are its own deleterious effects. The "deviant" party is pronounced the anomaly. Once again, the ruling order (patriarchy, white supremacy) receives a clean bill of health at its victims' expense. As Berger notes, the majority of BPD's sufferers are women and "[i]n Foucault's (1982) sense, the client may therefore internalize the problem discourse and come to understand themselves as deficient and that deficiency as a fundamental quality" of their person.[119] Patients internalize their "sickness at the core" (Oedipus' phrase); encircling culture, with canny hypocrisy, persuades its victims that their failings and none of its own are at the root of their ailments. This is why, Berger writes, "[f]eminist critics of BPD offer an alternative perspective, generally viewing the diagnosis of BPD as pathologizing the ways that women respond to gendered abuse and oppression."[120] Clare Shaw and Gillian Proctor develop this position: "BPD – which is defined with no reference to trauma – effectively decontextualizes the experience of distress from its social causes, paying occasional lip service to the prevalence of histories of abuse among the diagnosed population before going on to locate distress and difficulty firmly within the individual."[121] The procedure these authors seek to name and to remedy – casting anger and "distress as symptoms of psychiatric illness and disorder rather than as a 'realistic response to an unacceptable reality'" – is the procedure that tragedy in its own way arraigns.[122] In both instances, the stigmatized behaviors of "disordered" persons are indices of noxious environments. But even as Aristotle encourages us to engage in amnesia, to overlook the past and to forget Apollo's prophecy, Sophocles' tragedy is intimately concerned with Apollo's mandate. While Aristotle gaslights Oedipus, tragedies themselves do not normalize the denial of invidious circumstances. In ancient and modern tragedies, classifying victims as the sui generis locus of corruption appears a reprehensible sleight of hand.

Euripides' *Hekabe* might be read in this light, as an exposé of hegemonic norms whose ills tragic characters internalize, sealing their fates. As Martha Nussbaum argues in *The Fragility of Goodness*, Hekabe herself contends that it is manmade custom, human law – *nomos* – that undergirds "necessity" and that communities call on the gods to sacralize:

> Well I am a slave and perhaps I'm weak.
> But the gods are strong. So is the law [*nomos*] that rules the gods.
> By reason of this law we believe in gods
> and live our lives distinguishing right from wrong.[123]

"Necessity defines us," asserts the chorus of enslaved Trojan women.[124] Odysseus announces to Hekabe:

> The Greeks are resolved to slaughter your [daughter] Polyxena
> . . .
> Don't make me tear her away by force,
> don't fight me.
> Realize your strength, realize your condition.
> You're smart. Think *necessity*.[125]

Odysseus has argued that a Greek reluctance to kill to sate Achilles' lust would be poor politicking. If the soldier is not compensated, how do kings warmonger in future? Polyxena accedes to her sentence "[b]ecause it is necessary / And because I want to die."[126] Foreseeing a "raw-minded master," she finds herself "preferring death to degradation."[127] But it is more than the insupportability of enslavement that decides her. Her noble station, she believes, requires this martyrdom. Greek might, in her assessment, makes right; to the victors go human spoils. She accepts that birth and power mandate her execution, and she resists ignominy, not its underlying social construction. To prove her virtue and valor, she will not buck, shriek, accuse, or supplicate. Polyxena will not resemble intemperate woman or desperate animal. She bares her own neck and chest for her captors. The Greek army is overawed by her unexpected *sophrosyne*. The Greek host hails her as a monument to courage: she "[e]xposed her breasts beautiful as a statue. / Set her knee on the ground and spoke to all a word of absolute nerve."[128] Polyxena pairs unemotional reasoning (male) with obedience and modesty (female); her final act is to fall so that her privates remain covered. According to Polyxena, her equanimity and assent to death constitute a reclamation of dignity, a last stand before the enemy.

But Polyxena's exemplary comportment facilitates her own murder. If she has escaped the degradation that usually attends tragic victims, she has not escaped their ejection from the community. She upholds the legitimacy of this ritual even as Hekabe challenges it: "What necessity drew them on to human slaughter / at a tomb where killing oxen is more suitable?"[129] Polyxena complies with every hierarchy that sustains Greek authority. She holds manly sangfroid to be superior to clamorous female dissent. Seeking to number herself among the privileged, she adheres to the values that cast her as disposable. To sidle up to power, in this play, is to license its depredations. Polyxena has proven herself on Greek terms; her prize is death.

Hekabe, by contrast, appears to grieve mutinously. She curses, debates, and supplicates her captors. Still, she fares no better than her daughter and she adopts the epithets addressed to her. A dethroned queen, she is derided qua slave and widow. She is demeaned for her age and infirmity. She is "barbarian," foreign and racialized.[130] She is called animal.[131] "Woman!" is the first word that a Greek (Odysseus) addresses to her, a slur.[132] She repeats these aspersions: "Wretch! – myself I mean."[133] She is now, in her own words, "nothing."[134] Nussbaum contends that when Hekabe's environment deteriorates further – from hellscape of rape and enslavement to moral anarchy, because a *friend* has murdered her one remaining son – Hekabe remakes herself in the image of this friend's craven inhumanity. Hekabe sings a new tune – *nomos*, homonym for melody and set of cultural mores – the tune that her faithless comrade has sung.[135] He has been a brute; she plots to brutalize him in turn. He crawls on all fours like a dog and prophesizes that it is her fate, too, to become a dog. She sops up his traitorous violence like a sponge. It is all the identity that she now has, but she alone is pronounced the bitch. "Those polluted bitches" is her foe's description of the women who wound him.[136] Hekabe is treated as the anomalous bitchy excrescence on the world's virtue. Even as male precedent informs her rebellion, she is blamed for its violence.

The Trojan women, that is, challenge Agamemnon's belief that only men can engage in armed revolt, but they model their action on the male aggression that surrounds and subjugates them. Their unexpected mutiny, coalescing as unified female militia – weaponizing domestic accoutrements (brooches) and trading on their supposed docility to lure their enemy into their ranks, their tents, and to disarm and violate him – seems to be a continuation of the destruction that the Greeks have wrought. Hekabe's army of women blinds (debases, debilitates, feminizes) the Thracian king who has murdered Hekabe's son. They murder his two boys in turn. He wails while they stand unmoved. Killing this traitor's children makes for a symmetry of abuses. Even as the Trojan women punish their neighbor's malfeasance, they follow a Greek example. They, too, present the sacrifice of innocents as wartime "necessity." They, too, conform to patriarchy's condemnatory and repressive norms, consigning their adversary to an outpouring of grief that renders him womanly and execrable. His noisiness places him in the wrong.

Tragedy – as Euripides and Hardy practice it – calls into question the rationality and morality of these cultural standards. Both tragedians show blameless women conscripted into their tormentors' ways of thinking. Flickers of hope, for these women, are short-lived. Sue's claim to irreverence, Tess's to love, Polyxena's to autonomy, and Hekabe's to righteous collective action are compromised. For tragedy's women, patriarchy's chokehold constrains their powers of dissent. Tess feels that she must return to Alec, Sue to Phillotson; Polyxena feels that she must die. Even Little Father Time internalizes the notion that he ought not to exist. Stamping out iconoclasm, intimacy, agency, and justice, these tragedies incite onlookers' desire for such content. It is this desire that Jude and Tess's narrator express, albeit fleetingly. In Hardy as in Euripides, the powerful harbor no pity for their victims. In Hardy as in Euripides, victims subscribe to the depraved beliefs that defame them. Hardy, however, meets these inevitabilities with evanescent protest. To the bleakness of Euripides, Hardy adds the imagined dismantling of hard necessity.

Nightmare Skies

Hardy takes pains, too, to convey that extrahuman arbiters of fate, whether divine or natural, will not work to counteract or to repair an immoral social world. In Hardy's tragedies, extrahuman processes lose their veneer of rationality as well; they prove insuperably pitiless and hard. They cannot act as savior. Such an understanding assails Jude at the beginning of *Jude the Obscure*. Farmer Troutham beats Jude for the crime of feeding the birds: "The birds and Jude started up simultaneously, and the dazed eyes of the latter beheld the farmer in person, the great Troutham himself, his red face glaring down upon Jude's cowering frame, the clacker swinging in his hand."[137] Abused, Jude reflects on his supposed transgression and concludes that "[e]vents did not rhyme quite as he had thought":

> Nature's logic was too horrid for him to care for. That mercy towards one set of creatures was cruelty towards another sickened his sense of harmony. As you got older, and felt yourself to be at the center of your time, and not at a point in its circumference, as you had felt when you were little, you were seized with a sort of shuddering, he perceived. All around you there seemed to be something glaring, garish, rattling, and the noises and glares hit upon the little cell called your life, and shook it, and warped it.
>
> If he could only prevent himself growing up! He did not want to be a man.[138]

Once again, Hardy's tragedy foregrounds entrenched authority (Troutham) curbing purportedly wayward behavior. Jude's brutal correction, however, reveals to him the violence of social mores, and of natural selection as well – of any ruthless logic.

Jude is "sickened" by the specter of interspecies warfare for finite resources. His surprise at Nature's disharmony grips and assaults him as Troutham does. Troutham strikes Jude with the same clacker that Jude pronounces a "mean and sordid instrument" with which to repel birds, and Jude appears to conflate Troutham's "punitive task" with the "horrid" prohibition on food-sharing.[139] Jude finds himself "weeping – not from the pain, though that was keen enough; not from the perception of the flaw in the terrestrial scheme, by which what was good for God's birds was bad for God's gardener; but with the awful sense that he had wholly disgraced himself."[140] Jude feels shame most of all. He is humiliated for his too capacious "fellow-feeling."[141] He comes to understand that adulthood means participation in violence (that is what it is "to be at the center of your time") and that endeavoring to opt out of it spells public "disgrace." Nature's logic does not protect its myriad creatures from injury, he realizes; nor do people protect them. Jude is made to cower before a "glaring" man who represents this "glaring, garish, rattling" condition, one that "seizes" him "with a sort of shuddering." Unlike Polyxena, Jude does not want to be a man, inducted into this society.

Aghast at nature's heartlessness and society modeled on it, Jude suffers from a defining compassion for defenseless, sap-bleeding trees and for helpless birds and earthworms:

> He could scarcely bear to see trees cut down or lopped from a fancy that it hurt them; and late pruning, when the sap was up and the tree bled profusely, had been a positive grief to him in his infancy. This weakness of character, as it may be called, suggested that he was the sort of man who was born to ache a good deal before the fall of the curtain upon his unnecessary life should signify that all was well with him again.[142]

He abhors human callousness toward animal and plant life and aches for slaughtered pigs and rabbits, with whom he identifies. Jude expects trees, too, to bleed in pain when men lay hands on them. Jude's readiness to extend sympathy to all persecuted beings destines him to prodigious vicarious suffering. He may be wrong about trees' misery. But this double "weakness" – this conspicuous concern for assaulted life and this instinctive conviction that plants feel pain – prepares him to recognize that the whole of the natural world does not share his objection to harm, his hatred of human ill usage. With biting irony, Hardy's narrator remarks that all will be "well with" Jude once again when he no longer aches, no longer feels. Hardy's narrator treats this wellness as pathetic fallacy; it ascribes sensation to an inanimate body, deprived forever of its chance for happiness. No solace awaits Jude: either he is a being in pain or he is insensate, having lost his feeling form. Trees may or may not suffer as Jude imagines, but his intuition that the entirety of life, the coexistence of its flora and fauna, does not rhyme as poetically as he would hope proves fully justified within this fictional world.

Across his oeuvre, Hardy conveys this absence of cosmic benevolence. Before *Jude*, Hardy's experimental *Two on a Tower* (1882) accentuates the uncaring alterity of the heavens. Hardy "[sets] the emotional history of two infinitesimal lives against the stupendous background of the stellar universe," as he writes in his preface to the novel.[143] This insentient expanse of sky leaves Swithin St. Cleeve, amateur astronomer, with a vertiginous sense of human precarity. St. Cleeve remarks that "the actual sky is a horror," crowded with "monsters to which those of the oceans bear no sort of comparison ... Such monsters are the voids and waste places of the sky."[144] Describing the sky's vacuity, St. Cleeve continues:

> And to add a new weirdness to what the sky possesses in its size and formlessness, there is involved the quality of decay. For all the wonder of these everlasting stars, eternal spheres, and what not, they are not everlasting, they are not eternal; they burn out like candles. You see that dying one in the body of the Greater Bear? Two centuries ago it was as bright as the others.[145]

Even this formless immensity of sky is short on time, rendering human consciousness, by comparison, a match lit and extinguished in a moment. This telescopic perspective dwarfs and chastens the human. It accentuates human transience, recommending against our own wanton destructiveness.

Hardy's *Two on a Tower* counterpoises the vastness of nonhuman spatial and temporal scales against the ephemeral lyricism of human loves:

> "[I]t [the night sky] overpowers me!" she replied, not without seriousness. "It makes me feel that it is not worth while to live; it quite annihilates me."[146]
>
> "So that, whatever the stars were made for, they were not made to please our eyes. It is just the same in everything; nothing is made for man."
>
> "Is it that notion which makes you so sad for your age?" she asked, with almost maternal solicitude. "I think astronomy is a bad study for you. It makes you feel human insignificance too plainly."
>
> "Perhaps it does. However," he added more cheerfully, "though I feel the study to be one almost tragic in its quality, I hope to be the new Copernicus."[147]
>
> [Looking through the telescope] [t]hey more and more felt the contrast between their own tiny magnitudes and those among which they had recklessly plunged, till they were oppressed with the presence of a vastness they could not cope with even as an idea, and which hung about them like a nightmare.[148]

An indifferent and indomitable sky – "it" – overpowers defenseless "me." The deep time of the stars has an enervating effect on viewers. The sky's spatial dimensions spark a feeling of "human insignificance." In opposition to Matthew Arnold's critical pronouncement that Sophocles' capacious perspective enabled him to grasp the entirety of life – "I have ventured to say of Sophocles, that he 'saw life steadily, and saw it whole'" – St. Cleeve and Lady Constantine think of tragedy in conjunction with human limits.[149] While for Arnold, Sophocles is "a man who has mastered the problem of human life, who knows its gravity, and is therefore serious, but who knows that he comprehends it, and is therefore cheerful," Hardy's characters admit that observation of nature, "almost tragic in its quality," may overwhelm them with a sense of personal annihilation.[150] Although St. Cleeve aspires to Copernicus's clarity, he distinguishes this cheering prospect from the sky's communiqué of human ignorance and impotence. As sanguine Victorian critic, Arnold contends that "the peculiar characteristic of the poetry of Sophocles is its consummate, its unrivalled *adequacy*," representing life in its totality. But St. Cleeve insists that "[i]t is quite impossible to think at all adequately of the sky – of what the sky substantially is, without feeling it as a juxtaposed nightmare."[151] In contrast to human affections, the fluctuations of the sky are comfortless, anathema to human "coping."

Hardy himself thinks of scientific knowledge as a bearer of grim and intractable realities, writing in 1902:

> Well: what we gain by science is, after all, sadness, as the Preacher saith. The more we know of the laws & nature of the Universe the more ghastly a business we perceive it all to be – & the non-necessity of it. As some philosopher says, if nothing at all existed, it would be a completely natural thing; but that the world exists is a fact absolutely logicless & senseless.[152]

Hardy doubts the validity of philosophies and theologies that claim to resolve "the great problem of the origin of evil."[153] Such treatments of undeserved suffering contrast a fallen, phenomenal, or imperfect world with a Paradise, painless Absolute, or pending utopia. Hardy likens Christianity to both Kant's idealism and Schopenhauer's pessimism because in his view all three intimate deliverance from pain in an alternate, extant reality: "The truth is that in ethics Kant, Schopr, &c. are nearer to Christianity than they are to Nsche."[154] But Hardy takes Nietzsche to task as well for his claims to eliminate pain here on Earth: "it seems to me that Nietzsche, Trietske, Cramb, & all of the school (if it can be called a school) insanely regard life as a thing improvable by force to immaculate gloriousness."[155] He finds Henri Bergson's *Creative Evolution*, published in English in 1911, likewise dubious in its insistence on an ameliorative tendency at the heart of life. Commenting on Bergson's evolutionism in 1914, Hardy observes that "if nature were creative she would have created painlessness, or be in process of creating it – pain being the first thing we instinctively fly from."[156] Hardy writes that unlike Bergson he cannot see "a sort of additional and spiritual force, beyond the merely unconscious push of life."[157] His 1896 poem "In Tenebris II" had already presented a figure ill at ease among his self-assured and optimistic contemporaries for whom "All's well with us: ruers have nought to rue!"[158] Hardy's lonesome dissenter determines, on the contrary, that "if way to the Better there be, it exacts a full look at the Worst."[159]

Assessing Hardy's fiction in 1914, D. H. Lawrence holds that the "terrific action of unfathomed nature," causally and morally unintelligible, must be the engine of tragedy – Greek, Shakespearean, and modern.[160] But Lawrence criticizes Hardy for depicting this nature, heedless of creatures' pain, "merely as being present in background, in scenery, not taking any active part, having no direct connection with the protagonist."[161] Lawrence argues that for "Oedipus, Hamlet, Macbeth ... out of this unfathomed force comes their death," whereas "Tess, Sue, and Jude find themselves up against the established system of human government and morality, they cannot detach themselves, and are brought down."[162] Virginia Woolf makes this same criticism of Hardy's *Jude*. While she lauds Hardy's evocations of extrahuman antagonists in his other novels, she regrets that "[h]ere we have revealed to us the petty cruelty of men, not the large injustice of the gods.... Jude carries on his miserable contest against the deans of colleges and the conventions of sophisticated society."[163] But the very ethical method that Hardy pursues leads him to set an immiserating social foreground against a vast and unresponsive background. Nature cannot rescue these characters, Hardy insists. That their vicious social milieu – its rape culture, its classism, its penchant for victim-blaming – undoes them is all the more unconscionable within this natural setting that makes no special provision for their survival.

Hardy's fictions do not, however, tip into despair and advocate the renunciation of life. Hardy's novels depart from Schopenhauerean resignation. In Schopenhauer's Catholic-inflected vision of the psyche, the will that pervades us is intrinsically self-defeating, sinful, and vain; the only pleasure we can know is negative, in the form of pain's cessation. Such pleasure devolves into boredom, and boredom spurs a fresh visitation of desire, that is, of pain that must be relieved. For Schopenhauer, "conscious life is an evolutionary mistake," to be corrected by death, and life constitutes an interminable, fruitless ride on the "wheel of Ixion," shuttling sentient beings between suffering and ennui.[164] Schopenhauer conceives of tragedy as a consummate parade of these torments, aesthetic distance from which underscores the necessity of resignation in real life, the forfeiture of desire, and the negation of the will to live. Hardy's novels, however, ascribe the pains of existence to fortuitous species being and injurious social norms that curtail positive pleasures, free from taint.

As Hardy remarks to interviewer William Archer in their "Real Conversation" of 1901: "Whatever may be the inherent good or evil of life, it is certain that men make it much worse than it need be. When we have got rid of a thousand remediable ills, it will be time enough to determine whether the ill that is irremediable outweighs the good."[165] Hardy endeavors to dramatize entrenched belief systems that make for lethal plot arcs. He demonstrates how social strictures that might be "got rid of" make for "killing" narrative trajectories in a universe that already heralds irremediable loss.[166]

Hardy's sense of inexorable mortal fate – immovable tragedy – sponsors his "meliorism."[167] His reckoning with a sky and earth that harbor no hint of anthropocentric design ignites his mutinous spirit, motivates his commitment to systemic transformation in realms that permit it. As he writes in his 1922 "Apology" to *Late Lyrics and Earlier*, if we confront the most forbidding facts of our destiny, we may cement our resolve to contest further horrors, to seek "the best consummation possible," a stance "so old as to ... permeate the Greek drama."[168] We will find ourselves impelled, in Hardy's imagining, to organize society so that "pain to all upon [the Earth], tongued or dumb, shall be kept down to a minimum by loving-kindness."[169] Hardy's novels call for this "loving-kindness" – ever-striving contestation of suffering – as an appropriate response to a universe teeming with both irreparable and reparable deficits in sympathy. "What are my books," he asks Archer, "but one plea against 'man's inhumanity to man' – to woman – and to the lower animals?"[170]

CHAPTER 3

Woolf and Darwin
Tragic Time Scales and Chances

Immitigable Trees

Virginia Woolf commits lavish attention to the representation of interiority. Far from suggesting that it is subjectivity, however, that pervades all of nature, she pointedly and poignantly confronts characters with radically nonhuman alterity. Whereas anti-Darwinian philosophers from Charles Sanders Peirce to Alfred North Whitehead refuted the notion of an amoral cosmos, attributing mind to the entirety of nature, Woolf's perspectivalism is set against a thoroughly anti-anthropocentric perspective. In depicting the natural world, Woolf finds her tragic antagonist: the expansive time of nature that does not "reflect the compass of the soul," but guarantees both the chanciness and finitude of human being.[1] Indeed, Woolf argues in "On Not Knowing Greek" (1925) that contemporary readers are drawn to the ancient characters of Homer and the Attic tragedians because "they are even more aware than we are of a ruthless fate. There is a sadness at the back of life which they do not attempt to mitigate."[2] Woolf herself animates characters who decipher a ruthless fate in the natural world around them.

In a paradigmatic scene from *The Waves* (1931), for instance, Woolf captures precocious young Neville's response to a murder in the apple orchard. Neville recounts freezing upon the staircase, paralyzed by the image of an "immitigable tree":

> I heard about the dead man through the swing-door last night when cook was shoving in and out the dampers. He was found with his throat cut. The apple-tree leaves became fixed in the sky; the moon glared; I was unable to lift my foot up the stair. He was found in the gutter. His blood gurgled down the gutter. His jowl was white as a dead codfish. I shall call this stricture, this rigidity, "death among the apple trees" for ever. There were the floating, pale-grey clouds; and the immitigable tree; the implacable tree with its greaved silver bark. The ripple of my life was unavailing. I was unable to pass by. There was an obstacle. "I cannot surmount this unintelligible obstacle,"

I said. And the others passed on. But we are doomed, all of us, by the apple trees, by the immitigable tree which we cannot pass.[3]

Woolf affords Neville this premonition of mortality, this epiphany of an obstacle both insuperable and inscrutable. Neville remembers halting upon the landing; he is "unable to pass by" once the revelation has come. That which arrests him remains "unintelligible" – no satisfactory explanation can be assigned to it – but a snapshot of the setting in question (as he saw it or imagined it) lodges itself in his consciousness "for ever." He names this visual tableau "death among the apple trees."

Neville's vision of the landscape is suffused with the terror of violent death, and of death per se. In the image he forms, "the moon glared" steadily and Neville himself is immobilized, while the leaves, too, are inflexible, and the dead man is rigid. Neville's picture, in fact, concentrates not so much on the dead man as on the fixity of objects in the scene – their petrification, which irrevocable destiny seems to effect. For Neville, this all-stilling and intractable obstacle is symbolized by the unyielding environment to which both he and a deceased fellow creature are exposed; "the immitigable tree, the implacable tree" occasions the brunt of Neville's displeasure. The tree's stark objectivity, its imperviousness to Neville's desires, is precisely what colors the events with horror. The tree stands unmoved while persons perish. Tellingly, the tree's bark is "greaved," encased in silver armor, a Greek warrior preparing for battle, greaved and not grieved. Eteocles, in Aeschylus' *The Seven against Thebes*, commands: "Bring my greaves to shield me from the lances and the stones."[4] It is now the greaved apple tree that acts as Neville's foe and he presages its victory: "we are doomed, all of us by the apple trees, by the immitigable tree we cannot pass." Rather than humanize the tree, Neville's militaristic metaphor attests to its paining otherness.[5]

This is precisely why Woolf praises Hardy as a neo-Greek tragedian, as "the greatest tragic writer among English novelists" – he, too, sets character consciousness against alien, unvanquishable powers.[6] Revealing her own commitments as well, Woolf argues in "The Novels of Thomas Hardy" (1928) that Hardy "makes us feel that we are backing human nature in an unequal contest."[7] Ours is an unequal contest, Woolf writes, against "Nature as a force" or, in Hardy's words, against the "eyeless countenance of the mist."[8] Hardy's phrase signals nature's want of foresight or special provision for humankind, and comes from his poem "A Sign-Seeker." In its verses, Hardy describes those who continue to believe "that Heaven inscrolls the wrong" of the malicious, those who

> rapt to heights of trancelike trust,
> These tokens claim to feel and see,
> Read radiant hints of times to be –
> Of heart to heart returning after dust to dust.[9]

But, Hardy writes, "Such scope is granted not to lives like mine."[10] Hardy's tragic novels instead recognize that it is only human "affliction [that] makes opposing forces loom anthropomorphous."[11] Like Hardy, Woolf sees that "we have time to open our minds wide to beauty and register on top of it the queer sensation – this beauty will continue, and this beauty will flourish whether we behold it or not."[12] Our minds open wide to loveliness and to pain, encountering them in the natural environment, and yet nature has no authorial intentions and exists apart from our human beholding.

Defending Hardy against criticisms of his fiction's godlessness and wild coincidences, Woolf asserts that he channels "that wild spirit of poetry which saw with intense irony and grimness that no reading of life can possibly outdo the strangeness of life itself, no symbol of caprice and unreason be too extreme to represent the astonishing circumstances of our existence."[13] It is Hardy's tragic *Weltanschauung*, Woolf writes, that shows us the extent to which "human beings are the sport of forces outside themselves," assailed by caprice and unreason.[14] Woolf herself expresses Hardy's anti-Christian and anti-Romantic sentiment in *To the Lighthouse*'s "Time Passes": "Did Nature supplement what man advanced? Did she complete what he began? With equal complacence she saw his misery, his meanness, and his torture."[15] Both Hardy's and Woolf's tragic intuitions center on a natural world that is, to human consciousness, as Woolf says echoing Hardy, "eyeless, and so terrible."[16] This is Diderot's, Hume's, Darwin's nature, not Wordsworth's, not deist Voltaire's. It is visionless and morally vacuous, communicating to characters that mortality and devastation have no transcendent purpose.

Friedrich Nietzsche, Jane Ellen Harrison, and Henri Bergson, on the contrary, conceive of nature both as a site of capricious change and as a safe haven for the human psyche. Nietzsche in *The Birth of Tragedy* (1872, revised 1886) and Harrison in *Themis: A Study of the Social Origins of Greek Religion* (1912) see the ancient Greek worship of Dionysus as an acknowledgment of nature's expansive time and perennial mutability, which make for human mortality; yet they understand this Heraclitean continuousness of all life, to which all creatures are returned, to be recuperative, more sustaining than menacing, within the context of Bacchic religion. Harrison writes that "Prof. Bergson has shown us that *durée*, true time, *is* ceaseless change, which is the very essence of life – which is in fact 'l'Évolution Créatrice,' and this is in its very essence one and indivisible."[17] In Nietzsche's and Harrison's thought, preclassical Dionysiac rituals show us the dissolution of the individual into this cyclical, communal, and continually renewing stream of life. Bergson himself is adamant that unpredictable ("creative") novelty is the principle of life. But Bergson, like Nietzsche and Harrison, sees this spontaneity as spiritually salutary, rendering evolution progressively grander, although not deterministically so. All life, all time, for Bergson, is bound together by the *élan vital*, "one and indivisible," an evolving set of tendencies that forms an everlasting whole to which human beings belong.

Woolf, in the midst of such thought, also accepts chance into her work – but joins the Attic tragedians, Darwin, Hardy, and Russell in holding such chance apart from vitalism and theism, and from consolatory ritual and myth. Woolf instead weds this new Darwinian chance to Socrates' idea of tragedy as the unforeseeable and wounding dice throw.[18] Woolf's fiction depicts nature's time not as a source of solace for her characters but as a harbinger of their doom: that which assures their lives' brevity and fateful contingencies. Increasingly, however, Woolf is read as expressing Harrisonian views of ritual, in which nature is maternal and reassuring, and fosters a sense of dynamic, shared, and lasting being. Woolf is presumed to reprise female-centered, communal rites of renewal within a restorative Dionysiac-Bergsonian temporality. Like Harrison, Woolf is said to critique Greek tragedy, on the contrary, as the genre of hero-worshipping and war-mongering masculinity, whose protagonists perpetrate familial and political violence. In this vein, Jean Mills reads Woolf as "the female Aeschylus" who exposes and censures such a mentality.[19] Mills describes *Jacob's Room*, *Mrs. Dalloway*, and *The Waves* as Woolf's feminist, "Aeschylean trilogy."[20] Sharon Marcus, Sandra D. Shattuck, and Rowena Fowler also explore Woolf's incorporation of a ritualistic collectivity, preserved in the choruses of Greek tragedy, into *Mrs. Dalloway*, *To the Lighthouse*, *The Waves*, *The Years*, and *Between the Acts*.

Not only, then, has Mrs. Ramsay been seen as a goddess of Greek myth, an incarnation of Demeter or Aphrodite, but she has been read as the guardian of the communal existence that Harrison described in her work on ritual.[21] Critics have contended that Mrs. Ramsay bears a likeness to Harrison's pre-Olympian archetypal mother, Themis, who stood for perennial life, the fabric of civilization, and the unity of the social body, animated by shared custom and emotion.[22] But does Woolf's view of tragedy really match Harrison's, so that it is only tragedy's retention of a

still Dionysiac chorus that Woolf can adopt approvingly? Does Woolf
share Harrison's sense that tragedies strive to promote individualism and
authorize patriarchal violence? Emily Dalgarno suggests instead that Woolf
associates this reading of the Greeks more with English education, reserved
for men, than with Greek literature itself; it was the university that
confused its own values with those of the classics. As Dalgarno uncovers
in *Virginia Woolf and the Visible World*, Woolf's notes on the life of
Euripides, which she made in 1923 and 1924 while reading the *Bacchae*
in Greek, contain this resonant remark about the playwright: "Mahaffy
aptly calls him 'the great outsider.'"[23] Perhaps Euripides, in Woolf's
assessment, was less a purveyor of Harrison's Dionysiac (ritual, collective)
ethos or Oxbridge's Apolline (mythic, heroizing) ethos, and more a
cultural skeptic suited to the Society of Outsiders Woolf would envision
in *Three Guineas* in 1937 and 1938. Members of this imagined Society
were to stand apart from the very institutional and educational norms that
took Greek tragedy to be an august paean to great men.

Woolf's thinking on tragedy might align her more with modernist
literary critic F. L. Lucas than with Harrison. Woolf affords Lucas her
lengthiest footnote in *A Room of One's Own* (1929), citing his *Tragedy in
Relation to Aristotle's "Poetics,"* which her own Hogarth Press had published
two years earlier. Woolf cites Lucas's remarks on the salient and perplexing
fact that so patriarchal a society as that of fifth-century imperial Athens
would so amplify the stature, the voice, the might of its female protagonists, that women, so muzzled and degraded in life, should so surpass men
in art. This phenomenon, Lucas observed, persisted in the tragedies of
Shakespeare, Racine, and Ibsen. Lucas, that is, epitomized a feminist and
pacifist reclamation of tragedy and of Euripides in particular, following the
First World War; the Woolfs held a review copy of Lucas's 1923 *Euripides
and His Influence* in their library, in which he maintained that "[n]ot
Ibsen, not Voltaire, not Tolstoi ever forged a keener weapon in defence
of womanhood, in defiance of superstition, in denunciation of war, than
the *Medea*, the *Ion*, the *Trojan Women*."[24] Woolf's longest-running Greek
tutor, Janet Case, likewise took a feminist view of Aeschylus, in "Women
in the Plays of Aeschylus."[25] Agreeing with Case in "On Not Knowing
Greek," Woolf notes Clytemnestra's strength of character and marks
Cassandra's "naked cry" of grief and grievance, directed at Apollo.[26]

That tragedy led its male characters, too, to unruly "crying out" was
among Plato's principal charges against it in the *Republic*.[27] Anne Carson's
"The Gender of Sound" attests to this Platonic impulse, across archaic and
classical Greece, to police vocalization, to rigidly segregate male and female

utterance. Measured, low-timbred speech was considered the province of men; female sound was its antithesis.[28] Women were to make noise in certain spaces only: those of exurban wildness, beyond the bounds of city and politics, or in funerary and ritualistic settings. The types of ejaculation assigned to women, Carson notes, were then treated as their natural inheritance and spurned as debased and horrifying.[29] Women's mouths were construed as monstrous, repugnant, and in need of bridling. Carson notes that in one ritual context, Demosthenes describes the female mouth as the site for "discharg[ing] the unspeakable," purging the community of its pollutants.[30] But the art form tragedy, as Plato recognized, went outside these social bounds: it lodged grief in the mouths of men as well as women. In Euripides' *Hekabe*, for instance, which Carson translates, the play's enslaved Trojan women open with customary cries of pain, "AIAI" and "OIMOI," but end tasting male power and brutalizing men in turn. Henceforth their exclamations are the male "PHEU." What Plato feared is the case – a blinded king wails "OIMOI," crawling on all fours. One reading of *Hekabe*, then, is that this veritable army of women (an inter-sectionally marginalized chorus) transiently bests men and is assimilated into their culture, adopting their language. Precisely this outcome is what Woolf's Society of Outsiders was to protect against: "emancipation" that amounts to mimicry of one's oppressors. But rather than this conscription into the system one had opposed, Woolf's tragic fiction dramatizes, in defiance of Plato, the universality of lament, the shared baring of grief. Woolf's tragedy gives voice to what her holograph of "Time Passes" calls "the anguish of life, its concealed pain, & the misery which is forbidden to cry out ♭ for comfort."[31]

Woolf lets her characters, male and female, cry out and procure what comforts they can. She revives the Greek tragedians' chanceful world of mortal fragility and presents her characters' resultant endeavors to take what stands they can against their own and others' destruction, to carve out brief, safe intervals in which they are released from fate's clutches. Albert Camus, as we will see in the next chapter, contends that this very practice – encountering inhuman conditions, facing and not denying them, and yet forging a means of going on – is "the highest lesson of the tragic universe."[32] In *To the Lighthouse*, Mrs. Ramsay finds such a "plat-form of stability" first as "a wedge-shaped core of darkness," then in associating herself with the perennial lighthouse beam.[33] For a moment, in imagination, she apportions more-than-human time to herself – without letting her personhood be swept away with it. It is the latter experience that threatens Bernard in *The Waves*, the disappearance of his

"I" into eyeless nature's larger life, and from which he recoils, seeking a literary language that neither denies the indomitability of onrushing nature nor is silenced by it. In this way, Bernard comes to cultivate the scaled-down staying power that moments of human communion afford him, as Mrs. Ramsay does also. Mrs. Ramsay disseminates "this peace, this rest" that she has achieved alone – a feeling of permanence, despite nature's reminders that human lives have little temporal duration – among family and friends.[34] Lily, too, finds herself "crediting the world with a power which she had not suspected – that one could walk away down that long gallery not alone any more but arm in arm with somebody."[35] Lily and Bernard then seek to memorialize such moments in their art, to "make of some scene, or meeting of people (all now gone and separate), one of those globed compacted things over which thought lingers, and love plays."[36] They celebrate and rely on these "moment[s] of friendship and liking – which survived, after all these years complete."[37] Woolf, too, evokes her indebtedness to such heightened interludes of feeling and writes of the aesthetic they foster:

> I find that scene making is my natural way of marking the past. A scene always comes to the top; arranged; representative. This confirms me in my instinctive notion – it is irrational; it will not stand argument – that we are sealed vessels afloat upon what it is convenient to call reality; at some moments, without a reason, without an effort, the sealing matter cracks; in floods reality; that is a scene.[38]

These most robust and memorable flashes of being, flares of cohesive and explicable reality, stand opposed to life's crushing misfortunes, those that mystify and overthrow consciousness. Between these extremes of fortified and extinguished life lies what Woolf describes as the enveloping "cotton wool" of "non-being," which makes for muted, leaden, diminished experience.[39] It is these momentary "shocks" of being that rouse us from an otherwise muffled state and that temporarily exorcise the specter of our not being at all.[40] Beyond this array of possibilities for the human, Woolf also represents a realm of entirely nonhuman existence. Woolf captures its myriad manifestations via renderings of the natural landscape – which itself delivers to characters shocks of beauty or affliction.

Emphasizing extrahuman time scales, Woolf signals the precariousness of even the most resplendent human scenes. Eric Levy writes that Woolf's "tragic time is a seething flux of generation and corruption, a formless 'chaos' of coming to be and passing away, with no purpose other than its own continuation."[41] Ann Banfield describes a complementary, non-Bergsonian tragic time, found in Bertrand Russell's idea of the irrevocable past, ossified into a sequence of earlier and later eventualities. Banfield associates this immobile time past with thinkers from Wittgenstein to Barthes, locating it, too, in Lucas's *Tragedy in Relation to Aristotle's "Poetics."*[42] Finally, Woolf's fiction evokes the fixity of Russell's logical universals – of abiding spatial and temporal relations, mathematical forms, and changeless abstractions. In these ways, Woolf sets the aleatory, the inalterable, and the timeless against fugitive moments of safety and solidarity.

Darwinian *Tuchē*

The novel allows Woolf to present the natural world as a locus of impersonal fatality. Whereas Aristotle, as we saw in the previous chapter, sought to banish Attic chance from the tragic stage, Darwin and Woolf render it inseparable from the theater of life. Darwin himself revives an Attic conception of fate, of humanity bound to unpredictable and morally blind chances. As Stephen Halliwell writes of such chance among the Greek tragedians:

> [Aristotle shows] his disregard for the theology of tragic myth, since within the world of this myth "chance" (τύχη) has a religious status. Traditional Greek ways of thinking, as Aristotle himself seems to acknowledge elsewhere, did not systematically distinguish between divine causation and the workings of τύχη. In this context τύχη is a word of varied usage, quite capable of subsuming the forces of gods and fate; it is perhaps the word most simply expressive of the fatalism of Greek tragedy and its mythic material, since it has the widest applicability to situations in which what happens is conceived to have been inescapable and externally determined.[43]

Chance names unforeseeable accidents and coincidences, inexplicable fluctuations in fortune.[44] *Tuchē* is the engine of tragedy, generating Necessity's irreversible fiats. Euripides' chorus in *Alkestis* paints this picture:

I find
nothing stronger than Necessity.
There is no cure –

. . .

Lady, I pray you, do not come at me.
For whenever Zeus nods yes
you bring it to pass.
Your will can crush iron.
And your spirit is a cliff that knows not shame.[45]

Neither goddess Necessity nor precipitous cliff knows moral compunction; nor is fickle, nodding Zeus more than a personification of chance. This image of Zeus indeed suggests two Greek associations with the chance involved in tragic fate: Zeus' nod may be (1) a unique occurrence, outside consistent, predictable causality, and (2) done without purpose or end in mind, or none we can discern. Thus chance events are allied with inscrutable motivation in two registers, that of cause and effect and that of right and wrong. It is this dual inexplicability, rational and moral, that attends the origins of tragic doom to which Sophocles' choruses allude also:

> You see how little compassion the Gods
> have shown in all that's happened; they
> who are called our fathers, who begot us,
> can look upon such suffering.
> No one can foresee what is to come.[46]

These "parental" deities wield incomprehensible and crushing authority. Euripides' irreverent characters insist, too, that "no one foresaw it" and that "[t]ime does not know how to keep our hopes safe."[47]

F. L. Lucas comments on such unexpected, unearned fortune as follows: "the problem of tragedy becomes one with the whole problem of evil. 'Poetic justice' – how hard the craving for it has died!"[48] In the natural sciences, it is Darwin who likewise finds the problem of evil insoluble. For Darwin, chance fates are one with the question of the "Origin of evil," as he says, of ill luck and undeserved suffering.[49] For all that Darwin emphasizes adaptation's clear benefits at the species level, his version of Necessity – the law of natural selection – appears to him too wasteful and too cruel, involves too many "injurious deviations of structure" to attest to a benevolent Creator.[50] The trouble with origins runs deeper still: not only is natural selection a morally dubious mechanism, but it acts on phenotypic fluctuations that give no sign of guiding the process. Variations follow no consistent causal logic and point toward no particular effects for which they arise (e.g., to serve the good of the organism). Darwin reasons that were the environment, creatures' own habits, or divinity itself directing evolution – the respective positions of Buffon and Erasmus Darwin, Lamarck, and Darwin's numerous critics – then variation should be more reliably adaptive. Because it is not, Darwin instead suggests that the environment must indirectly and unsystematically change the reproductive systems of all creatures, causing unforeseen alterations that appear only in offspring.[51] Darwin concludes *The Variation of Animals and Plants under Domestication* by stipulating that "no shadow of reason can be assigned" to the idea that variations "were intentionally and specially guided," no matter "the most perfectly adapted animals in the world, man included."[52]

It is this heretical vision of unplanned outcomes, however, that Darwin's American apologist Asa Gray seeks to correct in his reviews of the *Origin*. "We should advise Mr. Darwin to assume, in the philosophy of his hypothesis, that variation has been led along certain beneficial lines," Gray writes in *The Atlantic Monthly* in October 1860.[53] Gray's sentiment ruled the day: "we cannot think the Cosmos a series which began with chaos and ends with mind, or of which mind is a result"; there are no "events which mind does not order and shape to destined ends."[54] Thus while Darwin confided to T. H. Farrer in 1881 that he could not make sense of "the infinite sufferings of animals, not only those of the body, but those of the mind, as when a mother loses her offspring," Alfred Russel Wallace, codiscoverer of natural selection, insisted on the "directive agency" and "*organising* power" that we should unquestioningly understand as the causes of variation and the guides of evolution where man is concerned.[55] In *The World of Life*, Wallace reassures his readers that suffering is justified on both nonhuman and human fronts. He describes pain "as having been developed in the animal world for a *purpose*; as being strictly subordinated to the law of *utility*; and therefore never developed beyond what was strictly needed for the preservation of life."[56] Wallace extends this logic to human beings: we suffer only the minimum pain ("what is usually termed 'evil,'" Wallace concedes in *Darwinism*) requisite to the inciting of our own self-protective energies, as well as our moral and spiritual development.[57] Yet Darwin does not accept this rationale, and responds to Gray in letters of July and November 1860:

> To take a crucial example, you lead me to infer (p. 414) that you believe "that variation has been led along certain beneficial lines". – I cannot believe this.[58]

> One word more on "designed laws" & "undesigned results." I see a bird which I want for food, take my gun & kill it, I do this *designedly*. – An innocent & good man stands under tree & is killed by flash of lightning. Do you believe (& I really sh[oul]d like to hear) that God *designedly* killed this man? Many or most persons do believe this; I can't & don't. – If you believe so, do you believe that when a swallow snaps up a gnat that God designed that that particular swallow sh[oul]d snap up that particular gnat at that particular instant? I believe that the man & the gnat are in same predicament. – If the death of neither man or gnat are designed, I see no good reason to believe that their *first* birth or production sh[oul]d be

necessarily designed. Yet, as I said before, I cannot persuade myself that electricity acts, that the tree grows, that man aspires to loftiest conceptions all from blind, brute force.[59]

Here again is the question of designed or chance fate, of Zeus who deals either in planned death by lightning or in random bolts. If such deaths are a matter of "blind, brute" necessity, Darwin speculates, why should individual or species births have a less fortuitous origin?

Darwin had posed the same question to Gray earlier that year in May:

> I own that I cannot see, as plainly as others do, & as I sh[oul]d wish to do, evidence of design & beneficence on all sides of us. There seems to me too much misery in the world. I cannot persuade myself that a beneficent & omnipotent God would have designedly created the *Ichneumonidæ* with the express intention of their feeding within the living bodies of caterpillars, or that a cat should play with mice. Not believing this, I see no necessity in the belief that the eye was expressly designed. On the other hand I cannot anyhow be contented to view this wonderful universe & especially the nature of man, & to conclude that everything is the result of brute force. I am inclined to look at everything as resulting from designed laws, with the details, whether good or bad, left to the working out of what we may call chance. Not that this notion *at all* satisfies me. I feel most deeply that the whole subject is too profound for the human intellect. A dog might as well speculate on the mind of Newton. – Let each man hope & believe what he can. –

> Certainly I agree with you that my views are not at all necessarily atheistical. The lightning kills a man, whether a good one or bad one, owing to the excessively complex action of natural laws, – a child (who may turn out an idiot) is born by action of even more complex laws, – and I can see no reason, why a man, or other animal, may not have been aboriginally produced by other laws; & that all these laws may have been expressly designed by an omniscient Creator, who foresaw every future event & consequence. But the more I think the more bewildered I become; as indeed I have probably shown by this letter.[60]

Lightning kills good and bad men indiscriminately, and birth doles out varying fates to children, as a result of "even more complex" causality – laws that, if regular, could be traced back to a planning Creator. But do such laws, ascribable to divinity, govern all aspects of evolution? Darwin sees that Necessity, the nonrandom work of natural selection, appears to act on the aimless nods of Zeus – on a motley crew of differences that are a matter of luck. And even if we grant all-encompassing laws, do their effects – the desirability, the justice of their outcomes – point to foresight? Darwin is exceedingly aware of differential fates; he marks a disparity between the "details" of a given destiny ("whether good or bad") and its seeming deservedness (whether it befell "a good one or bad one"). He therefore comes to chance, and not to a loving God, as the author of the *Ichneumonidæ*, of one creature's predation on another, of the death of the man who is good, of the deleterious birth defect that pains the child who is innocent.

This view, as we saw in Chapter 1, became increasingly unpopular. Bertrand Russell felt obliged to counter a wave of anti-Darwinian philosophizing, epitomized by Bergson and Whitehead. Russell writes that "[m]ind, or some aspect of it – thought or will or sentience – has been regarded as the pattern after which the universe is to be conceived, for no better reason, at bottom, than that such a universe would not seem strange, and would give us the cosy feeling that every place is like home."[61] As the novelists of his lifetime do, Russell sees in the impersonal, nonanthropocentric, nonteleological natural world the reemergence of the Greek divinities of tragedy. Russell reads in both ancient drama and the modern biological sciences "the empire of chance," the "wanton tyranny that rules ... outward life," and "the trampling march of unconscious power."[62] Because tragedy pits overwhelming force against resistant but breakable human bodies, Russell repeatedly calls it the literary genre that best fits a universe void of thought or will or sentience. He characterizes a modern tragic fate as follows: "Brief and powerless is Man's life; on him and all his race the slow, sure doom falls pitiless and dark. Blind to good and evil, reckless of destruction, omnipotent matter rolls on its relentless way."[63] Woolf shares this perspective.

Bernard Williams captures the radicalism of such resurgent, twentieth-century Greekness in *Shame and Necessity* (1993):

> Plato, Aristotle, Kant, Hegel are all on the same side, all believing in one way or another that the universe or history or the structure of human reason can, when properly understood, yield a pattern that makes sense of human life and human aspirations.... [Yet] we are in an ethical condition that lies not only beyond Christianity, but beyond its Kantian and its Hegelian legacies.... In important ways, we are, in our ethical situation, more like human beings in antiquity than any Western people have been in the meantime. More particularly, we are like those who, from the fifth century and earlier, have left us traces of a consciousness that had not yet been touched by Plato's and Aristotle's attempts to make our ethical relations to the world fully intelligible.[64]

Woolf's neo-Greek iconoclasm, her aversion to rationalizing loss, departs from this Western tradition; Woolf conspicuously deviates from Plato and Aristotle, Christian thought, and Kant and Hegel. Woolf's work also stands in opposition to late nineteenth-century and early twentieth-century anthropological and philosophical endeavors to safeguard character and to present suffering as comprehensible. Woolf's tragic outlook runs counter to anthropologists Jane Ellen Harrison's and Gilbert Murray's sanguine visions of nature – elaborated in Harrison's 1912 *Themis* – and to Friedrich Nietzsche's fixation, first, on tragedy as the consolation of character and, second, on tragedy as the triumph of character.

Before turning to Woolf's representation of incommensurate human and nonhuman time scales, and of characters who, reading no anthropocentric narrative in the natural world, envision no salvific narratives for themselves, let us consider the very different interpretations of nature and tragedy that obtain in the decades prior to Woolf's writing. Late nineteenth-century anthropology turned toward a study of wildness and mutability in ancient Greek thought, away from the sedate and sanitized Hellenism that prized permanent and idealized forms. Picturing violent and ecstatic flux at the heart of the ancient rites of Dionysus, Nietzsche's philosophy and Harrison's anthropology nonetheless rendered the natural world of ritual, in all its volatility, as life-affirming. Nietzsche and Harrison believed that Greek tragedy originated in the cultic worship of Dionysus. To varying degrees, however, Harrison, Murray, and Nietzsche held that tragedy parted ways from ritual. Nietzsche ultimately sought to extract a fortifying philosophy from tragedy – *amor fati*, he called it – a philosophy that Woolf did not share. Woolf sounded a different note: the "it is enough!" that celebrates fleeting moments of affirmation, those that sustain us in otherwise perilous and redoubtable circumstances.

Jane Ellen Harrison's Ritual

Jane Ellen Harrison established and steered the anthropological society later known as the Cambridge Ritualists. Treating Greek religion and society in concert, Harrison combined and advanced the developing fields of anthropology, sociology, and psychology; she was both philologist and archeologist, and brought together fellow classicists Gilbert Murray and Francis Cornford. Woolf read, admired, corresponded with and published Harrison, and paid tribute to her in *A Room of One's Own*. In *Virginia Woolf, Jane Ellen Harrison, and the Spirit of Modernist Classicism*, Jean Mills describes Harrison's work as follows:

> The introduction of the theory of a pre-classical culture based on women that is communal and collective in nature is among her greatest contributions as a Ritualist, along with her articulation of Dionysus as a

Year-Spirit or *eniautos daimon* rather than as a drunken, pot-bellied Bacchus. She also portrayed and outlined the goddess Themis as representative of *polis*, as the integument or fabric of society, itself, especially when characterized by a sense of community.... Each of these new ideas was considered radical and controversial as her work shifted the focus in the Classics away from philology and the myths of a pantheon of named and individuated gods to the communal, women-guided ritual practices of ancient Greek culture.[65]

In Harrison's view, precisely the Greek tragedians' recourse to legendary epic heroes and Olympian gods constituted the denial of this earlier, ritual culture that celebrated communal and matrifocal rites. To comprehend such rites, Harrison argued, we must imagine not "the individual human soul" but "that thing at once more primitive and perhaps therefore more complex – the group-soul."[66] From this collectivity "[t]he god is projected, not by the thinking or the feeling of one man, but by such part of his thinking and feeling as he has in common with other men, such emotions and ideas as are represented by his customs and enshrined in his language."[67] This shared tissue of emotion and habit is the Themis of ritual culture; Dionysus is its half mortal and half divinized "projection of group-unity."[68] Dionysus is not fully anthropomorphic, is not a celestial king perched on high, but an earthly *daimon*, a spirit of fertility, who perishes and returns annually. He represents the religious hope of a totemistic community bound to the earth and its life cycles: "Dionysos is a daimon, he is *the* daimon, of death and resurrection, of reincarnation, of the *renouveau* of the spring, and that *renouveau*, that reincarnation, was of man as well as nature."[69]

Harrison locates the origins of tragedy in these rites of springtime regeneration: "The Dithyramb, from which the drama arose, was also a *dromenon* [ritual enactment] of the New Birth."[70] It is specifically in the *mythos*, the narrative structure of such ritual, that Harrison claims to locate the evolutionary link between Dionysiac ritual and Greek tragedy. *Mythos* proper, Harrison says, originates with the Bacchic rites. *Mythos* is the story line, the set of utterances, that accompanies the physical movements of the *dromenon*. Harrison contends that the life story of Dionysus, repetitive and ever-same, bequeaths the idea of narrative form to tragedies' later plots, which concern a far more varied cast of characters:

> The *mythos*, the plot which is the life-history of an Eniautos-daimon, whether performed in winter, spring, summer or autumn, is thus doomed by its monotony to sterility. What is wanted is material cast in less rigid mould.... [I]n a word – *the forms of Attic drama are the forms of the*

*life-history of an Eniautos-daimon; the content is the infinite variety of free and
individualized heroic saga – in the largest sense of the word "Homer."*[71]

This shift from Dionysus and his doubles to a profusion of Ionian heroes
and Olympian divinities signifies, to Harrison, a decided cultural transformation. Citing her agreement with Nietzsche, Harrison writes that
"Apollo is of man's life, separate from the rest of nature, a purely human
accomplishment; Dionysos is of man's life as one with nature, a communion not a segregation."[72] Harrison often speaks appreciatively of
Nietzsche's distinction between Dionysiac and Olympian religions:

> We touch here on the very heart and secret of the difference between the
> Olympian and the mystery-god, between Apollo and Zeus on the one hand
> and Dionysos on the other: a difference, the real significance of which was
> long ago, with the instinct of genius, divined by Nietzsche. The Olympian
> has clear form, he is the *"principium individuationis"* incarnate; he can be
> thought, hence his calm, his *sophrosyne*. The mystery-god is the life of the
> whole of things, he can only be felt – as soon as he is thought and
> individualized he passes, as Diosysos had to pass, into the thin, rare ether
> of the Olympian. The Olympians are of conscious thinking, divided,
> distinct, departmental; the mystery-god is the impulse of life through all
> things, perennial, indivisible.[73]

For Harrison, such merging with the movement of the seasons, a sense of
belonging to cyclical time, is essential to Bacchic religion, whereas the
denial of time's passing is the Olympian stance: "all life and that which is
life and reality – Change and Movement – the Olympian renounces.
Instead he chooses Deathlessness and Immutability – a seeming Immortality which is really the denial of life, for life is change."[74]

Harrison sees in the Olympians the projection of a new Themis, a "form
of society with which we are ourselves most familiar, the patriarchal
family," which accompanies profoundly altered views of nature and divinity.[75] Whereas Bacchic nature was all-inclusive and uncontrollable, and
ritual sought both to propitiate and to harness its powers, the supernatural
and changeless Olympians begin to suggest, in Harrison's view, that
natural events are the expression of divine will, even of divine morality:

> Man's first dream of a god began, as we saw, in his reaction towards life-
> forces not understood. Here again we begin with the recognition of, or
> rather the emotion towards, a truth. There *is* a mystery in life, life itself
> which we do not understand, and we may, if we choose, call that mystery by
> the name of god, but at the other end of the chain of evolution there is
> another thing, a late human product which we call goodness. By a desperate
> effort of imagination we try to link the two; we deny evolution and say that

the elementary push of life is from the beginning "good," that God through all his chequered career is immutably moral, and we land ourselves in a quagmire of determinism and teleology. Or, if we are Greeks, we invent a Zeus, who is Father and Councillor and yet remains an automatic, explosive Thunderstorm.[76]

Harrison is adamant that the brute power of the elements – the automatic and insentient, explosive, chance thunderstorm – should not be viewed as the divine communiqué of any Father. She opposes the view that nature is shot through with "determinism and teleology." Harrison writes that to set Themis, Social Order, as the progenitor of Dike, Natural Order, is to deny the order in which evolution itself occurs and to miscast natural menaces and bounties as so many signs of a priori design. Harrison does not, then, see the gods of Greek tragedy as the incarnation of mutable fortune, but as the incipient representation of a theistic creationism. Tragedy, in Harrison's view, takes the skeletal form of the life of Dionysus, but sets this infrastructure within a wholly different context – one of individuation and patriarchy, in which male violence rains down from the anthropomorphized sky and dominates the earth. Harrison much prefers the Dike and Themis of ritual, wherein, in her estimation, nature is not the reflection of God-given edicts and values but the terrestrial engine of all life, vital force and *durée*, that which human communities attempt to honor and to rejoin.

Gilbert Murray's Tragedy

In *Themis*, Harrison also includes Gilbert Murray's "Excursus on the Ritual Forms Preserved in Greek Tragedy." In agreement with Harrison, Murray seeks to further demonstrate the kinship between the rites of Dionysus and Greek tragic drama. While Harrison, however, emphasizes the discontinuity between ritual and tragic worldviews, Murray pursues with care the idea that the formal staples of ritual survive into and structure the Greek plays – and continue to dictate the plays' meaning, one of ritual rebirth. Murray's excursus evidences the anthropological impulse to discover foundational archetypes preserved in later cultural artifacts – the remnants of a past that is never entirely gone.

Acknowledging that tragedy's "content has strayed far from Dionysus," Murray proceeds to show the ways in which the "forms of tragedy retain clear traces of the original drama of the Death and Rebirth of the Year Spirit."[77] Murray first enumerates the six components of the Dionysiac ritual itself:

1. An *Agon* or Contest, the Year against its enemy, Light against Darkness, Summer against Winter.
2. A *Pathos* of the Year-Daimon, generally a ritual or sacrificial death, in which Adonis or Attis is slain by the tabu animal, the Pharmakos stoned, Osiris, Dionysus, Pentheus, Orpheus, Hippolytus torn to pieces....
3. A *Messenger*. For this Pathos seems seldom or never to be actually performed under the eyes of the audience. (The reason of this is not hard to suggest.) It is announced by a messenger. "The news comes" that Pan the Great, Thammuz, Adonis, Osiris is dead, and the dead body is often brought in on a bier. This leads to
4. A *Threnos* or Lamentation. Specially characteristic, however, is a clash of contrary emotions, the death of the old being also the triumph of the new....
5   and 6. An *Anagnorisis* – discovery or recognition – of the slain and mutilated Daimon, followed by his Resurrection or Apotheosis or, in some sense, his Epiphany in glory. This I shall call by the general name *Theophany*. It naturally goes with a *Peripeteia* or extreme change of feeling from grief to joy.[78]

Of signal importance is that death and dismemberment occur in the service of – are necessary to – resurrection and rebirth. The *anagnorisis*, the recognition of the loss of the god himself, gives way to the assurance of his restoration. The course of reversal, of *peripeteia*, is from grief to joy, and the purpose of ritual is theophany, celebration of the endless life of Dionysus.

Murray argues that both tragedies and satyr plays are the progeny of Dionysiac rites and that they are best understood together. Murray suggests that with the demarcation between tragedy and satyr play at the City Dionysia, "the cutting-off of the Satyr-play left the tragic trilogy without its proper close."[79] The satyr play, Murray contends, held the dénouement of the Bacchic rites: "the Satyr-play, coming at the end of the tetralogy, represented the joyous arrival of the Reliving Dionysus and his rout of attendant daimones at the end of the Sacer Ludus."[80] Seeing the problem of tragedy as the problem of retaining this conclusion, ritual theophany, Murray writes:

> What was [tragedy] to do? Should it end with a threnos and trust for its theophany to the distinct and irrelevant Satyr-play which happened to follow? Or should it ignore the Satyr-play and make a theophany of its own? Both types of tragedy occur, but gradually the second tends to predominate. Secondly, what is to happen to the Anagnorisis and Peripeteia? Their proper place is, as it were, transitional from the Threnos of tragedy to the Theophany of the Satyr-play; if anything, they go rather with the Satyrs.[81]

Here is another decidedly affirmative reading of tragedy, in which its *threnos*, its lamentation, must never be separate from its theophany, its soothing assurance of the eternal life of Dionysus.

Less concerned than Harrison with collectivity versus individualism, matriarchy versus patriarchy, Murray signally reimbues the Greek plays with the epiphanic comfort he claims for earlier ritual. Yet closer to the Greek tragedians themselves, Plato and Aristotle, on the contrary, reject what they take to be a very different religiosity at the heart of tragic drama. While Murray fits the gods of tragedy into contemporary anthropology's vision of regenerative ritual and redemptive Dionysus, Plato and Aristotle view these same gods as manifestations of chance and labor to discard them in favor of rationality. And in Woolf we find a tragic *threnos* for the mortal individual still subject to chance – which is not commuted into redemptive epiphany.

Friedrich Nietzsche's Love of Fate

Nietzsche writes prior to Harrison and to Murray – and is theorist and philosopher rather than anthropologist – but adopts the widest swath of views concerning ritual, tragedy, and nature. Nietzsche's first account of Greek drama appears in *The Birth of Tragedy* in 1872. He, too, suggests that the Greek tragic chorus was originally comprised of satyrs who represented Dionysus in the springtime ritual of the Dithyramb. This band of satyrs, he argues, roused both tragedy's audience and dramatic characters to desire Dionysiac self-dissolution – reimmersion in the totality of undifferentiated life. The satyrs of the Greek tragic chorus, says Nietzsche, fleetingly rekindle the infectious ecstasies of the Dionysiac mysteries. As Joshua Dienstag writes, these satyrs begin "severed from the eternal flux and individuated."[82] They then achieve liberating intoxication and are "torn to pieces and reunited with the whole."[83]

Yet the culture of tragedy is not the culture of ritual. Nietzsche would agree with Harrison that Dionysus has ceased to provide succor. Nietzsche concludes that when the satyrs' ecstatic trance ceases, returning them to individual self-consciousness, life-negating sorrow awaits them. They find themselves exiled from the totality of nature. At a remove from communal, ritualistic practices, they experience Dionysiac temporality as menacing – it now represents an eternity no longer theirs. Nietzsche theorizes that it is in response to this loss of temporal expansiveness that tragedy develops its compensatory "Apolline" *mythos*. Bernard Reginster describes Nietzsche's view as follows:

> The lesson of this tragedy ... is that "wisdom, and particularly Dionysian wisdom, is an unnatural abomination" (ibid.), which must be "transfigured" by Apollonian illusion, a transfiguration that involves, as in the case of Oedipus himself, a kind of voluntary blindness.... Tragic wisdom, at that early stage, thus prescribes eschewing the Dionysian depths and remaining at the Apollonian surface with its beautiful appearances – being, in other words, "superficial – *out of profundity*" (GS, Preface 4).[84]

Here Oedipus' blindness is the figure for the curative concealments of art. Oedipus, in Reginster's reading, protects himself from beholding further horrors. Now that boundless Dionysiac collectivity cannot be experienced, it is Apolline dreamscape, elaborate fantasy, that resolves the problem of suffering by commuting the agonies of individuation into beautiful form.

Thus Nietzsche establishes fictional *mythos* as the new purveyor of consolation, because nature has become the site of "terrors."[85] And it is out of this account of the origin and function of ancient tragedy that Nietzsche develops his "literary" approach to life as a whole in *The Gay Science* (1882): "*What one should learn from artists. – What means do we have for making things beautiful, attractive, and desirable when they are not?*"[86] Nietzsche suggests that we each become – given his early theory of tragedy – the tragic "poets of our lives," writers of our own transformative *mythos*.[87] Nietzsche commits to literary self-fashioning, to narrative's powerful justificatory arsenal; he suggests that life stories can construe any character's or man's prior sufferings as necessary to and inseparable from his future glory. *The Gay Science* signally reprises the lexicon of *The Birth of Tragedy*: "I want to learn more and more how to see what is necessary in things as what is beautiful in them – thus I will be one of those who make things beautiful. *Amor fati*: let that be my love from now on!"[88] Martha Nussbaum reads Nietzsche in this way, evidencing his 1886 draft for a revised preface to *The Birth of Tragedy* in which he calls on "Art as the *redemption of the sufferer* – as the way to states in which suffering is willed, transfigured, deified, where suffering is a form of great delight."[89] Nussbaum remarks that in this fragment Nietzsche is well aware that *The Birth* "portrays the world of nature as 'false, cruel, contradictory, seductive, without meaning.'"[90] Nietzsche's own philosophy then reflects the very panacea he attributes to tragic drama: to fashion, as Nussbaum puts it, "a meaning where nature herself does not supply one."[91] Alexander Nehamas also contends that Nietzsche's theory of identity dovetails with this view of art.[92] We have no a priori essence in Nietzsche; instead, every iota of our experience is essential to our character. To wish to revoke any one detail of our past is to wish to cancel our identity in its entirety. But to affirm any one detail of our experience is to embrace our life in its entirety. Our happiness is necessarily the product of *all* that has befallen us and should be narrated to emphasize the interdependence of joys and griefs. Reginster explains that, for Nehamas, Nietzsche's "affirmation does not require that I abandon the standards by which I find them [my sufferings] detestable and horrible. It only demands that I manage to 'redeem' them, for example by creating a context in which they precisely cease to be detestable and horrible."[93]

Yet Nietzsche himself comes to doubt that these artistic ministrations can sufficiently hide from view the pains of individual self-awareness. Nietzsche questions whether the anguish that tragic characters and audiences experience in relation to nature and their individual finitude can be eclipsed by the creation of heroic plots and Olympian gods, by the creation of recuperative story lines. As Dienstag writes of Nietzsche's second, far less cheerful view of Greek tragedy:

> The ravages of time could not be cured or compensated through tragedy, only understood.... [T]ragedy simply serves to lay bare for us the horrible situation of human existence that the pre-Socratic philosophers describe, a situation from which our minds would otherwise flee: "The hero of tragedy does not prove himself ... in a struggle against fate, just as little does he suffer what he deserves. Rather, blind and with covered head, he falls to his ruin: and his desolate but noble burden with which he remains standing in the presence of this well-known world of terrors presses itself like a thorn in our soul" (*KGW* 3:2:38).[94]

This is Nietzsche's strikingly revised reading of the tragic hero. Oedipus now falls to his ruin blindly, unknowingly, and undeservedly, and his literal blindness does not symbolize his protection from outside terrors. It instead marks the very fact that he has known them – has registered their horror by gouging out his eyes. Oedipus has not been able to elude this nightmare world, in Nietzsche's new reading, and must endure the continuous, unmitigated wrenching of his soul – which in turn wrenches ours.

Nietzsche comes to recharacterize the Olympian divinities as well. He no longer associates them with a beautiful fantasy of anthropomorphic perfection. Nietzsche now associates the Olympians with the crushing "realm of *chance*," with the blind striking down of character.[95] In *Daybreak* (1881), Nietzsche writes of such chance and the gods:

> [E]verything happens senselessly, things come to pass without anyone's being able to say why or wherefore. – We stand in fear of this mighty realm of the great cosmic stupidity, for in most cases we experience it only when it falls like a slate from the roof on to that other world of purposes and

intentions and strikes some treasured purpose of ours dead.... The Greeks called this realm of the incalculable and of sublime eternal narrow-mindedness Moira, and set it around their gods as the horizon beyond which they could neither see nor exert influence.[96]

Destiny is no longer heroic and beautiful, but the irrevocable bad luck that frustrates "some treasured purpose." Resurrected Dionysus, whose worshippers were to be, like him, reunited with the unending continuousness of life, has become not even the glorious Olympian of tragic theophany but the puppet of the "cosmic stupidity," of incalculable *tuchē*. Ian Hacking describes Nietzsche's views of tragedy and chance as follows: "Gilles Deleuze has a succinct summary of one of Nietzsche's thoughts here. The dice of creation 'thrown once are the affirmation of *chance*, the combination which they form on falling is the affirmation of *necessity* ... What Nietzsche calls *necessity* (destiny) is thus never the abolition but rather the combination of chance itself.'"[97] This is a view that Woolf held and dramatized also: she dared to picture necessity as no more than irreversible chance.

In *Daybreak*, Nietzsche proceeds to characterize Christianity as the fullest realization of the impulse to reclaim design from chance – to make it design, at least, that human beings can "neither see nor ... influence." In Nietzsche's view, Christianity insists "that that almighty 'realm of stupidity' was not as stupid as it looked, that it was *we*, rather, who were stupid in failing to see that behind it there stood our dear God who, though his ways were dark, strange and crooked, would in the end 'bring all to glory.'"[98] Unreason, Nietzsche says, became the proof of superior and supreme reason:

> This new fable of a loving god who had hitherto been mistaken for a race of giants or for Moira and who himself span out purposes and nets more refined even than those produced by our own understanding – so that they *had* to seem incomprehensible, indeed unreasonable to it – this fable represented so bold an inversion and so daring a paradox that the ancient world, grown over-refined, could not resist it, no matter how mad and *contradictory* the thing might sound.[99]

Nietzsche therefore leaves behind his own theory of tragic art (and of art per se) as Apolline cover-up – for it too much resembles the rationalization of chance that he ascribes to Christianity – and undertakes a revaluation of the Dionysiac itself. Now articulating the meaning of tragedy for a third time, Nietzsche comes to posit that individual human psyches *do* relish the ceaseless, the perilous, the unpredictable flux and flow of existence. It is not the gods of chance who must be transformed into the God of wisdom

and love, but terrestrial chance itself that must be loved. The Dionysiac
nature that proved so life-affirming in early Greek ritual, as Nietzsche,
Harrison, and Murray envisioned it, had become the terrifying existential
substrate of tragic art – the terrifying raison d'être of all art in Nietzsche's
view – but he now dismisses the resultant wisdom that whispers that only
"as an aesthetic phenomenon" is existence "*bearable* for us" and labors for
"a Dionysian affirmation of the world as it is."[100] He will not hide or
counteract the world's "well-known terrors" – he will deny their power to
terrify. He will abolish the desire to abolish them.

According to Reginster, Nietzsche goes about this by determining that
prevalent Western values – a hatred of time, change, and suffering, the
prizing of compassion, the hedonistic definition of happiness as the
elimination of pain – are what keep people in misery and are therefore
life-negating.[101] These values, that is, cannot be realized in life; afterlives
have been discredited; and unfulfilled desire for them leads us to loathe the
world as it is. So Nietzsche recharacterizes human psychology itself and the
values that spring from it. He assigns to human beings a second-order
desire for obstacles to the fulfillment of our first-order desires; accidents
that frustrate our hopes nourish a stimulated character, strong, active,
replete with desire.[102] Nietzsche elects to valorize Dionysiac becoming
over Apolline being and develops his ethics of power, of the inherent
gratification that attaches to striving and strife. Nietzsche reaches a new,
Dionysiac understanding of *amor fati*: we can love the very process of
overcoming impediments to our most cherished objectives, of being
thrown into the rough waters of life. We can love this suffering in its
own right. Nietzsche's new tragic hero is doomed only because he is
eventually, laudably, attracted to a fatal portion of suffering. Nietzsche,
Reginster argues, adopts a new and more radical theory of art; he considers
a relish for creativity to be the proof of recalibrated values, because
creativity itself craves its struggles, and is tragic because it meets with
inevitable failure as its daring escalates.[103] In Nietzsche's final apology
for tragedy, therefore, suffering does not even provoke lamentation because
our biology hungers for it. Suffering becomes a badge of honor, a sign of
character fulfilled.

If Schopenhauer encouraged the quieting of the will, the cessation of
desire, in order to diminish life's pains, Nietzsche wishes to resist this
quietism and to rescue desire. Yet in order to do so, he must will suffering
itself. In this way, the herald of modernism, who curses Socratic rational-
ism, scientific optimism, and Christian sin – who wishes to refute
Schopenhauer's argument for resignation and to ensure the world's

endorsement once and for all – cannot live with suffering as we know it. Nietzsche first reads Greek tragedy as the epitome of mitigation, consoling us for worldly ills via transformative art. When he then ceases to believe that ancient drama proffered such palliatives – and does not want to peddle "metaphysical solace" himself – he revalues the very Dionysiac nature whose terrors he had exposed.[104] Nietzsche revalues our vulnerability to loss so entirely that mitigation ceases to be necessary.

Not *"Amor fati"* but "It is enough!"

Woolf's *To the Lighthouse* and *The Waves* dispense with these transfigurations of pain. Woolf instead interprets tragedy as the expression of unassuaged suffering. Woolf signals this emphasis in her treatment of Sophocles' *Electra* in "On Not Knowing Greek." Woolf's Electra is "blunted and debased by the horror of her position" and announces it relentlessly.[105] Woolf draws our attention to Electra's "loud, almost vulgar, clamour to the world at large."[106] Woolf's Electra does not model Dionysiac ritual's release from the pains of individuation or Apolline myth's aestheticization of them. Nor does Electra welcome and savor adversity, as late Nietzsche counsels. What Woolf lauds is Electra's untempered lamentation: the "bare" "cries of Electra in her anguish," which express "something suffering in her, outraged" and irresolvable.[107] Woolf's own fiction, then, represents forces that blunt and debase the vulnerable and lead them to cry out.

Woolf confronts her characters with inhuman timelessness, a stability that is not theirs, in conjunction with the innumerable threats that inhere in time. While Plato objects to tragedy because it depicts discomfited men who do not "accept the fall of the dice," Woolf's tragedy accentuates capricious dice-throwing time – Hardy's "dicing Time" – that wounds and grieves mortals.[108] Woolf presents harrowing and aleatory time severed from Christian providential narrative and from Aristotelian plot in which heroes fall for intelligible reasons native to themselves. Woolf instead shares Bertrand Russell's conception of time as a succession of discrete instants, possessed of objective, abstract continuity and independent of human existence, onto which subjective experience may be mapped.[109] Such nonteleological time could, as Banfield says, "be summarized as 'Greek,' understood as non-Heraclitian."[110] It is this impersonal time that "according to Russell, Bergson 'condemns' – as 'static, Platonic, mathematical, logical, intellectual.'"[111] Insofar as Woolf does, then, evoke Dionysiac time in her fiction – time that feels unbroken and immersive – it proves a repository of dicey and unpredictable eventualities, which harden into necessity. It is not a restorative and sustaining totality.

In the midst of his final, famed monologue in *The Waves*, Woolf's protagonist Bernard comes face to face with the atemporal fixity of logic. Bernard repeatedly evokes a willow tree that has arrested his interest since childhood:

> I was saying there was a willow tree. Its shower of falling branches, its creased and crooked bark had the effect of what remains outside our illusions yet cannot stay them, is changed by them for the moment, yet shows through stable, still, and with a sternness that our lives lack. Hence the comment it makes; the standard it supplies, and the reason why, as we flow and change, it seems to measure.[112]

What exactly does Bernard see in this tree? It seems to "comment" on his life, he says, as it stands unmoved – both stationary and unfeeling. He contrasts its suggestion of permanence with his mobile impressions. The willow appears to emphasize human movement because it does not participate in it, lies "outside" human points of view. We cannot possess its stillness and it cannot "stay" our passing existence. Indeed, our own "illusions" may claim the tree "for the moment," subsume it within our realm of temporal and affective experience, and fleetingly "change" it. Yet it reasserts its otherness, its intimation of changelessness. Its alterity "shows through." We cannot humanize it.

Bernard's willow seems to supply its own measuring standard for immobility and longevity. Even more than the tree's lifespan, Bernard seems to register the timeless "universals" that subtend it – the knowable, immutable constants of mathematics that Banfield has demonstrated to be essential to both Russell's and Woolf's conceptions of reality.[113] Russell distinguishes universals, in the timeless sphere of "being," from sense data and physical objects in the time-bound realm of "existence":

> We shall find it convenient only to speak of things *existing* when they are in time, that is to say, when we can point to some time *at* which they exist (not excluding the possibility of their existing at all times). Thus thoughts and feelings, minds and physical objects *exist*. But universals do not exist in the sense; we shall say that they *subsist* or *have being*, where "being" is opposed to "existence" as being timeless. The world of universals, therefore, may also be described as the world of being. The world of being is unchangeable, rigid, exact, delightful to the mathematician, the logician, the builder of metaphysical systems, and all who love perfection more than life. The world of existence is fleeting, vague, without sharp boundaries, without any clear plan or arrangement, but it contains all thoughts and

feelings, all the data of sense, and all physical objects, everything that can do either good or harm, everything that makes any difference to the value of life and the world.[114]

Universals, that is, exist in a domain apart from trees and people. These universals are themselves "stable, still, with a sternness our lives lack." They are independent of consciousness. In Russell's analysis of them in *The Problems of Philosophy* (1912), they consist not only in the abiding propositions of mathematics but also in abstract or generalized qualities (e.g., smoothness, loudness) and in all forms of spatial, temporal, and comparative relation: "the relation 'north of,' which is a universal," "the relation which I call 'being to the left of,'" "the relation of before and after in time," "the universal *resemblance* or *similarity*."[115] They do not indicate a subjective manner of organizing appearances. It is not the case that Reality (noumena, the Thing in Itself, the Absolute) remains beyond our ken, as philosophical idealists contended. These universals are knowable and undergird a physical world that we can know.

Russell does, however, mark the difference between our "sense data" and "physical objects" themselves. We possess immediate "knowledge by acquaintance" of sense data but do not possess direct knowledge of the objects that occasion such sensation: "the sense-data are to be regarded as resulting from an interaction between the physical object and ourselves."[116] Nonetheless, Russell maintains that we can know our physical surroundings in an alternate manner. He reminds us that "we also have acquaintance with what we shall call *universals*, that is to say, general ideas, such as *whiteness, diversity, brotherhood*, and so on."[117] It is our acquaintance with both sense data ("existence") and universals ("being") that allows us "knowledge by description" – indirect but reliable – of the outside world as it is apart from sensation. Via knowledge by description, we can understand natural history, astronomy, geology, physics, and physical objects. We can also come to understand more remote and complex universals. We can credibly infer how the world is or was, distinct from a subjective vantage point. This is what Kant deemed impossible. For Russell, however, there exist both a sensible willow and a universal willow, and because of our acquaintance with both we can arrive at description of the physical willow as it is whether we behold it or not. Bernard, then, both senses the willow and intuits the logical – conceptually still – aspects of the tree.

As Banfield shows, Russell in 1910 returned from the immutability of logic to the mutable sensible environment and our knowledge of it: "the completion of the logicist project [Russell's and Whitehead's *Principia*

Mathematica] turned the philosopher to the physical world."[118] Russell's new researches led him to postulate "sensibilia," sense data that no one need see.[119] Sensibilia further prove a world independent of us. Russell recommends that we imagine sensibilia as unperceived sense data that are in theory perceptible, existing in unoccupied or not yet occupied perspectives.[120] These points of view, he claims, exist regardless of anyone's inhabiting them. Added together, they attest to a real outside world. They, too, possess spatial and temporal coordinates and can be adumbrated by description. The world does not, then, require a viewing subject or Berkeley's omniscient God to ensure its existence. Banfield contends that these logical relations, underpinning sense perception, constitute in Russell and Woolf not F. H. Bradley's idealist Absolute, a hallowed Reality, but an invisible, ghostly frame, spectral yet hard as "granite" – Woolf's elected noun.[121] A latticework of "still" universals underlies the transient "rainbow" impressions of first-person experience and of all possible experience.[122] Impressionable Bernard flows and changes while the willow represents a version of unchanging eternity. "The tree alone resisted our eternal flux," he observes, "the populous undifferentiated chaos of life which surged behind the outlines of my friends and the willow tree."[123] The willow seems to Bernard nearly as indestructible as the logical relations that subtend it. Such constants minimize human being and reveal its contrasting fluidity.

Woolf's tragic time, however, also takes a second form – as the endlessly mutable "eternal flux," the teeming, chameleon time of evolution and its innumerable chances. In this second instance of extrahuman scale, it is not perennial stillness but perennial motion that dwarfs and consumes human actors. It is the "very trees . . . [as] symbols of the vast external world which recks so little of the happiness, of the marriages or deaths of individuals."[124] Rather than trees as seemingly immobile markers of an invariable world of being, we see them as participants in ceaseless mutability, over a vast expanse of time. Now blind evolutionary process, in all its variability, stands as humanity's uncaring opposite:

> [T]he stars did their usual work upon the mind, froze to cinders the whole of our short human history and reduced the human body to an ape-like, furry form, crouching amid the brushwood of a barbarous clod of mud. This stage was soon succeeded by another, in which there was nothing in the universe save stars and the light of stars; as she looked up the pupils of her eyes [Katharine's in *Night and Day*] so dilated with starlight that the whole of her seemed dissolved in silver and spilt over the ledges of the stars for ever and ever indefinitely through space.[125]

Here we have not the rigid intransigence of logic but devouring Heracli-tean nature – populous, undifferentiated, chaotic, surging – as the context in which necessity bursts forth. It is the eyeless purveyor of irrevocable fortune, as well as the encircling reminder that the individual human hourglass runs down while all else that is natural appears to cycle and change "for ever and ever and indefinitely." This second species of tragic time, showing human life to be the insecure product of the promiscuous flux of all life, is the very antithesis of the productively protean, Bergsonian flux that Harrison praises in her preface to *Themis*. Dionysiac time, for Bergson and Harrison, fortifies humanity, whereas for Woolf it "reduce[s] the human body."

Woolf's Rhoda in *The Waves* hungers for Bergsonian temporality to cradle and include her. But she denies that it does so: "'If I could believe,' said Rhoda, 'that I should grow old in pursuit and change, I should be rid of my fear: nothing persists.... I cannot make one moment merge in the next. To me they are all violent, all separate.... I have no end in view. I do not know how to run minute to minute and hour to hour, solving them by some natural force until they make the whole and indivisible mass that you call life.'"[126] For Rhoda, time appears a senseless train of disjointed beats: "Meaning has gone. The clock ticks."[127] Bernard, on the contrary, can conceive of an indivisible mass of moments, ever-changing and unified. For him, however, such a time stream is not intrinsically meaningful either; its "end" is not safety or homecoming. It does not produce the sense of interconnection that Rhoda craves. In Bernard's experience, such time only reinforces the postulate that "nothing persists." This Dionysiac temporality, so life-affirming to Harrison and Bergson, is not so to Bernard:

> With dispassionate despair, with entire disillusionment I surveyed the dust dance; my life, my friends' lives, and those fabulous presences, men with brooms, women writing, the willow tree by the river – clouds and phantoms made of dust too, of dust that changed, as clouds lose and gain and take gold or red and lose their summits and billow this way and that, mutable, vain.[128]

How much *more* ephemeral must Bernard feel when even the willow proves a short-lived creature in the history of the natural world? It, too, participates in this dust dance – is a passing phantom, on a level with the clouds, billowing without fixity ("mutable") and devoid of preassigned purpose in a teleological narrative ("vain"). Bernard's despair is that of Nietzsche's Greek chorus who awaken, disillusioned, to their finitude, to their tenuous billowing amid the persistent changefulness of nature.

Bernard therefore confronts his willow under multiple aspects: first, there is its seeming immortality, like that of an abstract mathematical form, and then there is its living, mortal presence. And it is to this vulnerable biological existence that Bernard's thoughts ultimately turn – to the willow's fluidity rather than to its fixity. Once the willow, even, seems to him subject to erasure, his perspective is so far expanded, his imagination so far outside its usual bounds, that his own life appears to measure nothing at all. In such "I-less" moments, Bernard owns a world bereft of conscious design, and his usual designing powers do not rush in to transform the scene in front of him. His senses, his customary spurs to creation, cease to inspire him; his characteristic phrase-making grinds to a halt. He experiences his keenest bouts of self-dissolution when he registers no hint of authorship in this universe of impersonal and staggering change. In these rare moods, Bernard perceives the days, the waves, the clouds, the trees themselves, to cycle endlessly, and it is this recognition of perennial movement which reduces his existence, and his stories, to a felt impossibility.

Confronted with deep time, Bernard announces the vanity of taking "notes in the margin of [the] mind for some final statement" on life:[129]

> How tired I am of stories, how tired I am of phrases that come down beautifully with all their feet on the ground! Also, how I distrust neat designs of life that are drawn upon half sheets of note-paper. I begin to long for some little language such as lovers use, broken words, inarticulate words, like the shuffling of feet on the pavement. I begin to seek some design more in accordance with those moments of humiliation and triumph that come now and then undeniably. Lying in a ditch on a stormy day, when it has been raining, then enormous clouds come marching over the sky, tattered clouds, wisps of cloud. What delights me then is the confusion, the height, the indifference and the fury. Great clouds always changing, and movement; something sulphurous and sinister, bowled up, helter-skelter; towering, trailing, broken off, lost, and I forgotten, minute, in a ditch. Of story, of design I do not see a trace then.[130]

This vision of size and indifference, of "great clouds always changing, and movement" initially pleases him; at first, the sky's unruly grandeur, its vast scope and confusion, "delight" him as he lies supine in his declivity in the earth. Yet he senses, too, "something sulphurous and sinister" in this pageantry of nature. It appears to him both "helter-skelter" and "towering," immense without "a trace" "of story, of design" to inform its passage across the sky. Its careless fury and magnitude diminish his own existence, endanger it. Bernard cannot escape the intimation of something "bowled up" and foreboding in the "march of day across the sky."[131] He feels his "I" "forgotten, minute."

In this way, Woolf naturalizes human beings and places them in peril, without dissolving her characters, ritualistically, into collective, undying "group-unity." Woolf writes repeatedly in *The Waves* that "[t]he being grows rings, like a tree. Like a tree, leaves fall."[132] The days pass and the mind ages: "Tuesday follows Monday; then comes Wednesday. The mind grows rings."[133] The mind is part and parcel of the natural world, racking up years, in no way exempt from the dust dance. The mind grows symbolic rings, too, aiming to rein in the confusion, the fury, with scripted form, forging designs: "So the being grows rings; identity becomes robust. What was fiery and furtive like a fling of grain cast into the air and blown hither and thither by wild gusts of life from every quarter is now method-ical and orderly and flung with a purpose – so it seems."[134] Signally, Bernard comes to question these seemingly stable arrangements, these pat coming-of-age narratives. He expresses his skepticism of them: "[t]he true order of things – this is our perpetual illusion."[135] His corrective is the "world seen without a self," "without illusions."[136] Prostrate in a ditch with the sky "towering" over him, Bernard embraces a reduced aesthetic fit for his reduced position: "a howl; a cry" will better capture his relation to the world.[137] With an anti-anthropocentric perspective comes an altered artistic credo: "When the storm crosses the marsh and sweeps over me where I lie in the ditch unregarded I need no words. Nothing neat. Nothing that comes down with all its feet on the floor. None of those resonances and lovely echoes that break and chime from nerve to nerve in our breasts making wild music, false phrases."[138] His will be a messy and "unfinished" account of himself and his fellows.[139] It will remain true only to "the welter; to the torture" of insecure human life, to the "rushing stream of broken dreams, nursery rhymes, street cries, half-finished sen-tences and sights – elm trees, willow trees, gardeners sweeping, women writing."[140] But an unfinished life is not a meaningless one. For all that Bernard regrets that he has "been sedulous to take note of shadows," to pay tribute to what "merely changes" – and for all that he is finished with immodest "phantom phrases" that trumpet transcendent truths – he does solemnize moments with his scraps of language and this practice affixes him to others and to the world.[141]

It is not the bellicose, imperialist sagas of king and country, those which Percival epitomizes – Percival around whom Bernard and his companions initially rally – that in the end sustain him. Bernard comes to resist such rhetoric, its false promise of all-encompassing order. Bernard in his final soliloquy parts ways from the certainties that Percival had represented. Moments of closeness and bodily satisfaction are what Bernard comes to value in lieu of Percival's grand (but hollow and pernicious) symbolic resonances. In his youth, that is, Bernard had felt in proximity to Percival that "we . . . stride not into chaos, but into a world that our own force can subjugate and make part of the illumined and everlasting road."[142] In his maturity, Bernard forgoes this notion of an "illumined and everlasting road" that legitimizes subjugation. He pursues instead "some design more in accordance with those moments of humiliation and triumph that come now and then undeniably" – moments of humiliation that guard against triumphalism, and moments of triumph that ward off self-abnegation, total silence. Embracing such moments, Bernard seeks safe harbor between narrative and nothingness.

Woolf spurns the notion of tragedy as propagandistic *mythos* that would sanctify and champion Percival's heroic commitments and death in their name. Tragedy instead consists in Bernard's mortal vulnerability to Dionysiac nature, wherein a roll of the dice of mutability can mean "'death among the apple trees' for ever."[143] Bernard finds that no narrative armor, no mythic greaves, can protect him. Fleeting intersubjective intimacy is now what offers him passing security – what he commemorates in words and seeks among friends. It is their small shared *telos*, their tragic sociality, perennially threatened with dissolution:

> "Now once more," said Louis, "as we are about to part, having paid our bill, the circle in our blood, broken so often, so sharply, for we are so different, closes in a ring. Something is made. Yes, as we rise and fidget, a little nervously, we pray, holding in our hands this common feeling, 'Do not move, do not let the swing-door cut to pieces the thing that we have made, that globes itself here, among these lights, these peelings, this litter of bread crumbs and people passing. Do not move, do not go. Hold it for ever.'"[144]

Theirs is "this common feeling," "the thing that we have made"; it supports them, "that immersion – how sweet, how deep!" as Bernard later recalls it.[145] Such intimacy hovers above "'these roaring waters,' said Neville, 'upon which we build our crazy platforms.'"[146] They hold such security like an object, and wish to hold it perpetually. Yet it is more prone to disintegration than even the crumbs and peelings: "'But soon, too soon,' said Bernard, 'this egotistic exultation fails. Too soon the moment of ravenous identity is over.'"[147] All share this sense of imperilment: "'For one moment only,' said Louis. 'Before the chain breaks, before disorder returns, see us fixed, see us displayed, see us held in a vice. But now the circle breaks. Now the current flows. Now we rush faster than before."[148] Theirs is the rounded moment in all its doubleness, materializing and dissipating: "Let us hold it for one moment," begs Jinny and yet, as Rhoda attests, "The circle is destroyed. We are thrown asunder."[149]

Bernard later recounts, too, that they "drew apart," "were consumed in the darkness of the trees."[150] Bernard remembers that painfully "Neville, Jinny, Susan and I as a wave breaks, burst asunder."[151] He experiences such separation, even at the time, as a kind of submersion in an unwelcome river, as a kind of drowning. He never forgets this annihilation of a closeness that afforded him his sense of identity:

> I could not collect myself; I could not distinguish myself; I could not help letting fall the things that had made me a minute ago eager, amused, jealous, vigilant and hosts of other things into the water. I could not recover myself from that endless throwing away, dissipation, flooding forth without our willing it and rushing soundlessly away out there under the arches of the bridge, round some clump of trees or an island, out where sea-birds sit on stakes, over the roughened water to become waves in the sea – I could not recover myself from that dissipation. So we parted.[152]

Like Neville, who needs "the limbs of one person" because "nature is too vegetable, too vapid," "[s]he has only sublimities and vastitudes and water and leaves," Bernard can only combat this disintegration of himself, this onslaught of time – these incessant waves whose sound he interprets as "the pounding of death" – with revival among people:[153]

> Thus I visited each of my friends in turn, trying with fumbling fingers to prise open their locked caskets. I went from one to the other holding my sorrow – no, not my sorrow but the incomprehensible nature of this our life for their inspection. Some people go to priests; others to poetry; I to my friends, I to my own heart, I to seek among phrases and fragments something unbroken – I to whom there is not beauty enough in moon or tree; to whom the touch of one person with another is all, yet who cannot grasp even that, who am so imperfect, so weak, so unspeakably lonely.[154]

For Bernard, as for Neville, "the touch of one person to another is all." Such connection proves nearly impossible to obtain, uncertain and precarious. It survives "unbroken" only in rare moments of relieved isolation. "Moon or tree," even in their beauty, are not "enough" to sustain him. Indeed the "darkness of the trees" and "that endless throwing away, dissipation, flooding forth without our willing it" communicate the "incomprehensible nature of this our life."

Woolf is not, then, the pure subjectivist, consumed by the mind in all its solipsism, that many have claimed her to be.[155] She is committed to

representing the extent to which time exceeds a merely human measure –
to placing human perspectives in perspective. She brings to the fore, as
Bernard describes it, "that unfeeling universe that sleeps when we are at
our quickest and burns red when we lie asleep."[156] It is not the case, as she
writes in To the Lighthouse's "Time Passes," that "beauty outside mirrored
beauty within."[157] The external world is not the internal world writ large:
"the mirror was broken."[158] Woolf's characters, as a result, aim to create
their own modest brand of stability, aim to make certain moments in time
stand out and endure in their minds. They seek to emulate the solidity of
the "granite" of logical form, all the while knowing that their lived
moments cannot possess such solidity. Finitude becomes a condition that
besets their loves, rather than the source and raison d'être of their loves.
Bernard makes "the contribution of maturity to childhood's intuitions"
and recognizes "what is unescapable in our lot; death; the knowledge of
limitations."[159] He feels that "I, too, am dim to my friends and unknown;
a phantom, sometimes seen, often not," in danger of disappearance: "Our
flame, the will-o'-the-wisp that dances in a few eyes is soon to be blown
out and all will fade."[160] And yet he persists in feeling "the need for
opposition" in "the presence of an enemy" – and he battles to "have
dispatched the enemy for a moment."[161]

Mrs. Ramsay, too, feels threatened by the deep time of nature and takes
what action she can to shore up countervailing safety. She hears the waves
"like a ghostly roll of drums remorselessly beat the measure of life" and
intimate that her allotment is "ephemeral as a rainbow."[162] She feels "an
impulse of terror," and to stave off its recurrence that evening, she
cultivates "this peace, this rest, this eternity," as "a wedge-shaped core of
darkness."[163] Even in this pared-down privacy, she resists self-dissolution.
She does not relish vacant impersonality but her own resilience and
freedom. Mrs. Ramsay voyages as the wedge: "There were all the places
she had not seen; the Indian plains; she felt herself pushing aside the thick
leather curtain of a church in Rome. This core of darkness could go
anywhere, for no one saw it. They could not stop it, she thought, exulting."[164] It becomes her avatar, a ghostly vessel traversing foreign lands.
What appeals to her is not nothingness, sheer absence, in place of her
quotidian responsibilities; instead, she moves through the world unhin-
dered, a mobile explorer. When Mrs. Ramsay's gaze then turns outward,
toward the sea, she attaches her still exulting subjectivity to an object, to
the lighthouse beam. In her imagination, her wedge, having traversed
space unseen and unchecked, becomes the eternal light stroke, infused
with its temporal expansiveness, its regular beat as steady as the waves'

own.[165] In this way, Mrs. Ramsay succeeds in feeling herself more than "a little strip of time."[166] She locates in the light not a kindred spirit, not a universe that shares in her sensations, but her own keen emotion; watching the light, she plumbs and illumines her own personality. She recognizes that the character she ascribes to the beam is her own. She knows that it is "odd" how one "leant to inanimate things"; she knows her "tenderness" for the light is "irrational," and still she allows the beam to express her, know her, be her.[167]

So soothed does she feel, that "suddenly she added, We are in the hands of the Lord."[168] Then her peace is rent, the candor of her experience sullied – "[t]he insincerity slipping in among the truths roused her, annoyed her."[169] She turns again to the beam to extirpate this falsehood: "she had been trapped into saying something she did not mean. She looked up over her knitting and met the third stroke and it seemed to her like her own eyes meeting her own eyes, searching as she alone could search into her mind and her heart, purifying out of existence that lie, any lie."[170] She corrects her error: "How could any Lord have made this world? she asked. With her mind she had always seized the fact that there is no reason, order, justice: but suffering, death, the poor. There was no treachery too base for the world to commit; she knew that. No happiness lasted; she knew that."[171] Mrs. Ramsay registers, too, that the beam itself is heartless, impersonal, "the steady light, the pitiless, the remorseless."[172] Yet "for all that," she remains "hypnotised" by the stroke and she feels "as if it were stroking with its silver fingers some sealed vessel in her brain whose bursting would flood her with delight."[173] The beam's caress catalyzes her remembrance of past happiness: "she had known happiness, exquisite happiness, intense happiness."[174] Her rush of present ecstasy constitutes a fresh moment of being that draws from her a cry of affirmation: "it is enough!"[175]

Having assigned her personality to an object and assumed its longevity in imagination, Mrs. Ramsay proceeds to cultivate this same feeling of permanence, of joy in a treacherous world, among people, among subjects. Woolf lifts the party from a frivolous – recreational, trivial – pastime (Wyndham Lewis, with misogynistic disparagement, calls Woolf herself a "party-lighthouse") to a feat of decided existential significance.[176] Mrs. Ramsay responds to nonhuman nature, its implacable rhythm, its promise of tragedy, with another stilled moment of being, a product of shared feeling, and yet (as she conceives it) akin to an elm in its fixity. While Mr. Ramsay inclines to behave "as if to be caught happy in a world of misery was for an honest man the most despicable of crimes," Mrs. Ramsay recognizes that happiness itself is the mark of labor, of rare and "great reconciliation scenes" with "this thing that she called life" and found "terrible, hostile, and quick to pounce on you if you gave it a chance."[177] Such happiness is not a sign of complacency or mendacity, as Mr. Ramsay might have it. Mrs. Ramsay's "effort of merging and flowing and creating" requires its own brand of "sternness" and heroism.[178] Mr. Ramsay's truth ("it would not be fine," "There is no God"), which the waves have whispered to her as well, spurs her to rebellious creation.[179] Mrs. Ramsay is determined to "secrete" at her dinner party what Woolf refers to in her diary as the "envelope" of "party consciousness."[180] Mrs. Ramsay purposefully reproduces her earlier shock of joy:

> Now all the candles were lit up, and the faces on both sides of the table were brought nearer by the candlelight, and composed, as they had not been in the twilight, into a party round a table, for the night was now shut off by panes of glass, which, far from giving any accurate view of the outside world, rippled it so strangely that here, inside the room, seemed to be order and dry land; there, outside, a reflection in which things wavered and vanished, waterily.
>
> Some change at once went through them all, as if this had really happened, and they were all conscious of making a party together in a hollow, on an island; had their common cause against that fluidity out there.[181]

For the moment, all refuse the reminders of "outside" time; endlessly waving nature is defied but not denied. In this candlelit room, the windows have become mirrors; "that fluidity out there," really, is a reflection of persons within. So they have "common cause," too, against their own vanishing, rippling natures, which flow and change in much more short-lived a manner than the hidden landscape beyond the glass. "Out there," as they persist in calling it, remains blurred and impressionistic; in here proves a "composed" tableau. Mrs. Ramsay glances once again at "the window with its ripple of reflected lights," sees it relegate the external world to obscurity and mirror the human scene within, and proclaims that something shines out "in the face of the flowing, the fleeting, the spectral," and stays its movement temporarily.[182] "Conscious of making a party together in a hollow," they stave off human wavering for the moment; no wonder when the party disperses, "they wavered about."[183]

Bernard experiences an equivalent "summoning together" at dinner, in defiance of human transience, in defiance of "the huge blackness of what is outside us, of what we are not":

And, half-way through dinner, we felt enlarge itself round us the huge blackness of what is outside us, of what we are not. The wind, the rush of wheels became the roar of time, and we rushed – where? And who were we? We were extinguished . . . and the blackness roared. . . . For me this lasts but one second. It is ended by my own pugnacity. I strike the table with a spoon. If I could measure things with compasses I would, but since my only measure is a phrase, I make phrases – I forget what, on this occasion.[184]

"The wind, the rush of wheels, became the roar of time," the hand of annihilation, Mrs. Ramsay's waves. Bernard fights it too, not with the instruments of mathematics, not with the compass – although he would prefer the compass's exactitude. But his measure, as he says, is the phrase. He must build a safe enclosure out of words ("assemble a few words and forge round us a hammered ring of beaten steel," "a steel ring of clear poetry").[185] For the compass suggests a timeless circle, which Bernard can only approximate with his clumsier tool:

Against the gateway, against some cedar tree I saw blaze bright, Neville, Jinny, Rhoda, Louis, Susan and myself, our life, our identity. . . . [A]gainst the brick, against the branches, we six, out of how many million millions, for one moment out of what measureless abundance of past time and time to come, burnt there triumphant. The moment was all; the moment was enough.[186]

Here the cedar is an emblem of the ceaseless continuance of nature, against which these six stand out for a moment only. The expansive time of wind and water, of creeping airs in "Time Passes" ("there was time at their disposal"), is allied with the timelessness of the circles the compass draws: Bernard, like Mrs. Ramsay, aspires to both and cannot have either.[187]

But "[t]he moment was all; the moment was enough." In one sense, these two clauses bound together by a semicolon are equivalent – the moment is everything, and this "all" suffices. "It is enough" is high praise in Woolf's fiction, the pinnacle of affirmation. Yet Bernard's "all" is not All with a capital A, is momentary and not eternal; it bespeaks no all-inclusive confederacy with the sum total of existence. It is not bound up with Greek ritual's promise of collective rebirth. Nor does Bernard's "all" implicate him in a mythic destiny that rationalizes, even valorizes, the necessity of the moment's dissolution. "It was enough" captures the poignancy, the smallness of this "all" upon which Bernard's entire affirmation of life must rest. Woolf envisions moments that burn triumphant before an inevitable defeat. At once the moment is the zenith of self-realization and intersubjective intimacy, and yet it is the most precarious container of value, gone when time passes. The moment's flame of happiness bears within it the promise of grief. These short-lived bursts of feeling, ballasts in the tide of life, contest *amor fati*. In contradistinction to a Nietzschean love of fate, Woolf stages moments snatched from the maw of becoming and elegizes their loss.

Woolf's Tragic Chances

Greek tragedy's preoccupation with cosmic unconcern and the insecurity of human time is Woolf's also. The inevitability of the past and the uncertainty of the future resurface prominently in *To the Lighthouse*'s "Time Passes." This is Woolf's extraordinary evocation of the unfathomable "cosmic stupidity" that Nietzsche describes. Here Woolf dramatizes both inhuman permanence and Darwinian natural history. She confronts the ill luck and undeserved suffering that attend survival and reproduction. Ominously, the section commences:

> "Well, we must wait for the future to show," said Mr. Bankes, coming in from the terrace.
>
> "It's almost too dark to see," said Andrew, coming up from the beach.[188]

We have left a deterministic universe, idealist or materialist, in which all is "too dark to see" because of human ignorance only. We have left a "necessitarian" universe, as Peirce calls it, in which all is in principle predictable, knowable in advance.[189] Characters "must wait for the future to show" for the new reason that both Peirce and Darwin recognize: time, like the evolutionary process, involves chance. This is Euripides' universe, too, in which characters are buffeted about by aleatory, not rationally foreordained, forms of necessity: "the swings and swerves of mortal fate," time in which "change rolls upon change" unpredictably, for "[t]he life of man is a wandering thing, pounded from all sides."[190] Not only do these inevitable poundings seem fortuitous from the human perspective, but they may be swerving, changing, wandering things in and of themselves, outside the regularities of nature.

"Time Passes" characterizes the universe as massive, material volatility "pierced by no light of reason":

> Listening (had there been any one to listen) from the upper rooms of the empty house only gigantic chaos streaked with lightning could have been heard tumbling and tossing, as the winds and waves disported themselves like the amorphous bulks of leviathans whose brows are pierced by no light of reason, and mounted one on top of another, and lunged and plunged in the darkness or the daylight (for night and day, month and year ran

shapelessly together) in idiot games, until it seemed as if the universe were battling and tumbling, in brute confusion and wanton lust aimlessly by itself.[191]

Amid this "gigantic chaos," the universe plays its "idiot games," games of chance, "aimlessly." The changeless constants of physics reside outside this realm of "brute confusion." Banfield reminds us of Russell's distinction between these spheres as follows: "Universals have being, but things in time exist: the word 'exist' is taken to mean "'being at some part of the time-series.'" Herein lies the difference between the atemporal permanence of universals and the permanent, nondeictic, temporal relations of empirical facts."[192] There is the stability of Russell's logical universals in the timeless realm of "being"; in the mobile realm of "existence," nature's evolution occurs. Once past, nature's time is "permanent, nondeictic." Such beats of past time, in their immobility, have all the mausoleum-like stillness of those occurrences locked in place when Zeus nods "yes" to goddess Necessity. Every motion of every mote in the dust dance is fixed within a sequence of earlier and later occurrences – irrevocable. But future coordinates are not yet set.

It is the irreversible emergence of such unforeseeable chances that inhabits the well-known brackets of "Time Passes." The first and paradigmatic lightning bolt of misfortune runs as follows, in a bracketed aside: "[Mr. Ramsay, stumbling along a passage one dark morning, stretched his arms out, but Mrs. Ramsay having died rather suddenly the night before, his arms, though stretched out, remained empty.]"[193] Here is the image of seeking and not finding – companionship and comfort – that dominates "Time Passes." For Mr. Ramsay, the master predictor of the morrow's weather in a deterministic cosmos, it was too dark to see this event. Mr. Ramsay's quintessentially demanding embrace meets with nothing. Open arms are made empty arms. Death comes "rather suddenly," threaded, in this section, into no compensatory narrative. Not even a causal explanation is given, as the central consciousness of the novel is withdrawn; the encircling context, one of idiot games and brute confusion, implies that no explanation of any sufficiency can be given. Fate is in no way tempered or mitigated – not because the section is told from the impersonal, nonnarrative perspective of nature, but because precisely this perspective nullifies the possibility that contingent, sudden, unforeseen luck can possess justification.

When the *renouveau* of spring then comes and it seems "impossible to resist the strange intimation which every gull, flower, tree, man and woman, and the white earth itself seemed to declare (but if questioned at once to withdraw) that good triumphs, happiness prevails, order rules," the next bracketed catastrophe occurs: "[Prue Ramsay died that summer in some illness connected with childbirth, which was indeed a tragedy, people said, everything, they said, had promised so well.]"[194] This flimsy report, bandied about by a gossipy "people," speaking casually of tragedy and its *peripeteia* – everything "had promised so well" – contains all the cold contingency of time's passing. Prue dies in "some" illness; if people do not know or remember which, it seems equally the case that a complete etiology will go no further toward sufficient explanation. Springtime birth, here, has nothing of renewal in it. Generation is not regenerative. If reproduction, a new life, is to be a solace, what of Mrs. Ramsay's dashed hopes that Prue "her own daughter must be happier than other people's daughters"?[195] Woolf demolishes ritual faith in redemptive springtime. And in the following bracketed episode, on the world-historical stage, "[A shell exploded. Twenty or thirty young men were blown up in France, among them Andrew Ramsay, whose death, mercifully, was instantaneous.]"[196] This chance mercy attends the idiot games of war, wherein the general odds of survival are once again unjustifiable. To what, we are asked to imagine, must the poetry of Augustus Carmichael attest, composed in this period of inexplicable death, sans resurrection – his book also having come out in the brackets of "Time Passes"?

This section confronts readers with sweeping destruction, natural and historical. It focuses primarily on the natural, within which human convulsions are set. Woolf also emphasizes the inhuman staying power of qualities that characterize the scene: "So loveliness reigned and stillness, and together made the shape of loveliness itself, a form from which life had parted."[197] In the Ramsays' vacated summer house, Woolf locates abiding form, that of Russell's universals, of Platonic "loveliness itself." It is distinct from the mobile particulars of "life." Cohabiting concepts, "loveliness and stillness clasped hands in the bedroom" and outlast "even the prying of the wind, and the soft nose of the clammy sea airs, rubbing, snuffling, iterating, and reiterating their questions."[198] These loquacious airs interrogate their surroundings: "'Will you fade? Will you perish?'"[199] Posing the question to abstractions, it "scarcely needed that they [loveliness and stillness] should answer: we remain."[200] They stand outside the ledger of time. Within time are breezes and change. Woolf evokes both in this climactic passage:

> In spring the garden urns, casually filled with wind-blown plants, were gay as ever. Violets came and daffodils. But the stillness and the brightness of

the day were as strange as the chaos and tumult of night, with the trees standing there, and the flowers standing there, looking before them, looking up, yet beholding nothing, eyeless, and so terrible.[201]

Unwavering "stillness and brightness" are as disconcerting as the "chaos and tumult" of time's passing. Eerily, Woolf depicts plants as if they possess human bodies, as if they stand and look. At the same time, she seeks to wean us from this anthropomorphizing tendency. She juxtaposes personification with its retraction. She accentuates the trees' and flowers' absence of human perspective. They are "eyeless." Here is the expectation of resemblance thwarted. These flowers are deficient in eyes and should – says human narcissism – have eyes. But Woolf revokes their sight and rescinds their subjectivity. It is the same with Hardy's "eyeless countenance of the mist." Hardy conjures a face that is not really there. Woolf and Hardy invoke human characteristics (we hear the homonyms "eye" and "I") only to withdraw them. It is anthropomorphizing undone, alterity laid bare, that is "so terrible." Woolf choreographs this confrontation with a desacralized, nonanthropocentric world. No divine "I am" oversees creation.[202] Life carries on undeterred: "Let the wind blow; let the poppy seed itself and the carnation mate with the cabbage."[203] Let there be (imagined) a self-sufficient world independent of divine or human oversight. Nancy Worman writes that this tableau of unconcerned urns and flowers "captures the shock of loss in a world that lives on, in a resonantly Aeschylean mode that also nods to Keats' 'Ode on a Grecian Urn,' with its invocation of stillness ... and inhuman things enduring while generations pass away."[204]

Language that joins inhumanity and loss is, for Woolf, the language of tragedy. In "On Not Knowing Greek," Woolf writes that Aeschylean phrases themselves "rise up and stalk eyeless and majestic through the scene."[205] Woolf suggests that Aeschylean lines stand and move, personifying poetry as she does flowers. But like the flowers risen on their stalks, these lines are eyeless; they evince inhumanity. Both nonhuman surroundings and Greek verses testify to "visionless" realities, beyond the "I's" purview and control.[206] The language of Aeschylean tragedy, Woolf posits, is reverberant in its "richness of metaphor," as it circles around people in pain and in danger.[207] "Take this from the *Agamemnon*," Woolf writes: "ὀμμάτων δ' ἐν ἀχηνίαις / ἔρρει πᾶσ' Ἀφροδίτα."[208] "In the eyes' blank gaze / all Aphrodite is lost," Worman translates.[209] Here the Argive Chorus conjures a bereft Menelaus, following Helen's departure. Worman translates the passage in full:

> In the longing for her gone across the sea,
> a phantom will seem to rule the halls;
> and the grace of statues is hateful to the husband;
> in the eyes' blank gaze
> all Aphrodite is lost.
> Mournful dream-visions come
> seeming to bear vain delight;
> for in vain when someone thinks he sees
> the sight, slipping through his hands, is gone,
> at once it wings away
> along pathways of sleep.[210]

Woolf herself translated the *Agamemnon* in 1922. She largely followed A. W. Verrall's 1904 prose text. Her version is this:

> He shall pine for her that is far beyond sea, till he seem, but a phantom lord of the house. Grace of beautiful the husband hateth: with the want of the eyes all the passion is gone. Dream-forms stay with him a while, convincing semblances, & offer delight in vain; for lo, when vainly he thinks to grasp the phantom, the vision escapes through the arms & is gone that instant on wings that follow the passing of sleep.[211]

In his notes, Verrall comments on the specific line that Woolf includes in "On Not Knowing Greek." Verrall connects "the want of the eyes" to the mention of "colossuses" (statues) above it. He speculates that this word "colossuses" might serve to reinforce Aeschylus' focus on the "eyeless":

> ὀμμάτων ἐν ἀχηνίαις *in the want of the eyes*. The question is raised whether the "eyes" are those of the husband, or of the lost wife, or of the blankly-gazing statues, a question which cannot and must not be answered. The eyes of the husband seek, but no longer find, the eyes that were wont to answer, and, for lack of this response, love is for him no more. It is the advantage of the language here that it is ambiguous between "absence of eyes" and "hunger of eyes." – Prof. Bury (*Class. Rev.* II 182) points out that to a Greek ear κολοσσός (κόλος, ὄσσε) would suggest *eyeless*, and supposes the exceptional word to be chosen for this reason. This, for Aeschylus, is quite possible and would even be characteristic.[212]

Woolf's chosen line is resoundingly ambiguous. Bound up in its "blast of meaning," as Woolf calls it, is the intimation that eyeless conditions (uncaring, ruinous) issue in loss (less for the eyes to feast on) and that such deprivation itself is deadening.[213] In Anne Carson's 2009 translation, it is Helen's eyes that are no longer present: "Without her eyes / all Aphrodite is gone."[214] In 1947, Richmond Lattimore gives us: "in the emptiness of eyes / all passion has faded."[215] If these are the statues' vacant eyes, it is such haunting simulacra that cannot requite love. Copies of Helen are at a remove from her, as Plato would say. Even if her likenesses immortalize her in the vein of Keats's urn, still they attest to her absence. For Robert Fagles, "the eyes starve."[216] Someone wanting, wanting someone, famishes Menelaus. He can discern no loveliness in the world around him; or he has contracted the statues' insensibility. Like Oedipus, who blinds himself in his grief, seeking to sever connection to the world – "convulsed with anguish, the eyes out on stalks," says Beckett – Menelaus, too, may become senseless, "beholding nothing."[217] In *Mrs. Dalloway*, war veteran Septimus is terrified of this condition: "the panic was on him – that he could not feel," "the appalling fear came over him – he could not feel."[218]

"Time Passes" also takes up the Aeschylean imagery of dreaming in vain and waking empty-handed. Mr. Ramsay, too, embraces bodiless air. In the natural world, "[t]hat dream, of sharing, completing, of finding in solitude on the beach an answer" has no corresponding reality.[219] "Time Passes" represents this desire for a legible Book of Nature – the natural world as holy writ, the premise of William Paley's natural theology – but retracts its possibility. "The mystic, the visionary" futilely searches the natural world for "tokens of divine bounty"; these clues do not reliably materialize.[220] When beach roamers endeavor to "ask of the sea and sky what message they reported or what vision they affirmed," they uncover only signs of manmade crimes: "This intrusion [of an ashen-colored warship] into a scene calculated to stir the most sublime reflections and lead to the most comfortable conclusions stayed their pacing."[221] War intrudes upon the landscape, and in both Woolf and Aeschylus, it shadows private loss. Just as the Chorus follows their evocation of Menelaus' pains with their account of "woes surpassing" these, Woolf broadens her purview to include nameless men and sinking ships.[222] The Chorus registers collective loss in war, all Greece returned as "urn & ashes," in Woolf's translation. Woolf, too, suggests mass casualties.[223] Worman writes of Woolf that "this is what she claims for and wants from tragedy – namely a means of staring down the terrible losses and emotional devastations of war."[224] But Woolf also places the urns of the Aeschylean war dead in the garden, where all life emerges and expires. Woolf reaches for this outermost narrative frame – that of time's passing on nonhuman terms – to signal that evolution itself is lethal and insentient. Emblematic, for Woolf, of this unsupervised unspooling of the hours are the bodiless elements (airs, waters) and eyeless vegetation (trees, flowers) that do not, so to speak, look out for us. They leave us cognizant of the unscripted and insensate processes that give rise to life and annul it. What prodigious vitality, then, must attach to Woolf's moments of camaraderie and love, braces against such multifarious and encircling hazard.

Lily affirms these resurgent and treasured moments. Lily stands before her easel, with gratitude recalling Mrs. Ramsay's uniting "herself and Charles Tansley and the breaking wave; Mrs. Ramsay bringing them together; Mrs. Ramsay saying, 'Life stand still here.'"[225] But these moments belong to no transcendent, recuperative whole. In producing her painting, Lily is not the worshipper who "participates, briefly, in an eternal life force," as Martha Carpentier reads her in Harrisonian fashion.[226] Nor has Mrs. Ramsay herself achieved ritual fusion with the breaking wave. It is instead one wave, one slice of Dionysiac time, that she has commanded for once to stand still. Mrs. Ramsay has made this moment, as Lily attests, matter and endure in memory. It does not dissipate, forgotten, into the irretrievable past. It is this resistance to time's remorseless measure, to its erasure of human meanings, that constitutes Mrs. Ramsay's triumph over "her old antagonist, life."[227] Lily recognizes the Dionysiac menace that Mrs. Ramsay in this way tames, and realizes that her own practice is the same:

> Mrs. Ramsay making of the moment something permanent (as in another sphere Lily herself tried to make of the moment something permanent) – this was of the nature of a revelation. In the midst of chaos there was shape; this eternal passing and flowing (she looked at the clouds going and the leaves shaking) was struck into stability. Life stand still here, Mrs. Ramsay said. "Mrs. Ramsay! Mrs. Ramsay!" she repeated. She owed it all to her.[228]

Like the Greek tragedies' papyrus rolls, left to disintegrate by indifferent Roman scholars, Lily's painting may molder in the attic. But it is still her act of resistance, her stand against instability and loss. And precisely its uncertain future is another of Woolf's unsparing evocations of chance and fragility.

Lily registers the extreme insecurity of the tragic universe. She would like to demand of it an explanation. Poignantly, her vision of the only acceptable reply is the resurrection of Mrs. Ramsay. As usual, the answer does not come:

> Was there no safety? No learning by heart of the ways of the world? No guide, no shelter, but all was miracle, and leaping from the pinnacle of a tower into the air? Could it be, even for elderly people, that this was life? – startling, unexpected, unknown? For one moment she felt that if they [she and Carmichael] both got up, here, now on the lawn, and demanded an explanation, why was it so short, why was it so inexplicable, said it with violence, as two fully equipped human beings from whom nothing should

be hid might speak, then, beauty would roll itself up; the space would fill; those empty flourishes would form into shape; if they shouted loud enough Mrs. Ramsay would return. "Mrs. Ramsay!" she said aloud, "Mrs. Ramsay!" The tears ran down her face.[229]

Woolf represents "implacable," "immitigable" destiny in her writing. Lily weeps for a form she cannot revive – Mrs. Ramsay's. In lieu of the consolatory, Woolf pens the irremediable. In lieu of the returned god of ritual, she depicts the perishable persons of tragedy.

Woolf parts ways from that singular contradiction in terms, counter-tragic tragedy, which is hostile to the notion that undeserved or uncompensated loss can befall characters. Like Hardy, hers is not the Aristotelian view that heroes' own inadvertent missteps inaugurate their doom. Nor does she adopt a Christian construal of the genre in which characters are the culpable agents of their own misfortune, punished for their immoral passions, their sufferings the route to salvation. Woolf also refuses the anthropological assessments of tragedy, as we have seen, that treat the death of the individual as a ritual enactment of communal renewal and theophany. Woolf leaves behind, too, Nietzsche's philosophical renderings of tragedy as justificatory narrative or "heroic" psychology. In each of these discarded models, it is the fearsome chanciness of mortal luck that is to be exorcized at all costs – just as the chance at the heart of Darwinian evolutionary theory, as many critics said, had to be denied.

Woolf follows Aeschylus, Sophocles, Euripides, Hardy – a *literary*, not a philosophical or anthropological, heritage – when she sees in tragedy the overthrow, not the apotheosis, of character. Woolf's interpretations of tragedy and natural history do not yield theodicy – or attest to the ritual or biological consolations of terrestrial life. In her tragic novels, Woolf nonetheless celebrates an ethos of opposition to reasonless fatality, without justice on its side – Bernard's "[a]gainst you I will fling myself, unvanquished and unyielding, O Death!"[230] Yet she deflates whatever presumption to triumphalism resides in Bernard's final, rebellious outcry. Woolf closes her novel with the impersonal, italicized reminder of human impermanence in relation to the waves, of the external world that will check Bernard's defiance: "*The waves broke on the shore.*"[231] Like Hardy, Woolf backs human nature in an unequal contest.

CHAPTER 4

Camus's Modernist Forms and the Ethics of Tragedy

Camus's Idea of Tragedy

In Camus's estimation, modern history now breaks human bodies as Greek destiny did. It claims the same incontestable right to do so. Camus makes this point in 1955, delivering a lecture in Athens, "On the Future of Tragedy." The subject of Camus's talk is whether the current age may foster the revival of the Greek genre, and Camus's answer is a provisional yes. Camus suggests that Greek tragic characters, in challenging divine and social orders, overreached in their defiance and met with a disproportionate response: with merciless repression. The gods or the state did not rein in hubristic heroes; they overstepped in turn, mirroring characters' extremism. So Greek tragic characters learned the merits of moderation and the evils of inordinate force. Camus argues that modern European nations, however, have foresworn all measure; their ethos is one of unbridled individualism and of power that knows no bounds. Having dethroned the pagan and monotheistic gods, they are the new sources of terror.

Camus speculates that literary tragedy may recur today because Europe has behaved as if no limits apply to it, initiating new and indomitable orders of violence. Tracing the etiology of a genocidal modern Europe, Camus points to his countrymen's eighteenth-century mania for domination, which, he insists, instituted and incubated "monstrous" forms of "human reign":

> The world that the eighteenth-century individual thought he could conquer and transform by reason and science has in fact taken shape, but it's a monstrous one. Rational and excessive at one and the same time, it is the world of history. But at this degree of *hubris*, history has put on the mask of destiny.... In a curious paradox, humanity has refashioned a hostile destiny with the very weapons it used to reject fatality. After having deified human reign, man turns once more against this new god.[1]

Deified human reign now takes the form of fascism, which invokes "reason and science" in its defense. Communism, too, Camus determines, risks totalitarianism if it concludes that its ends justify all means. Capitalist, colonialist liberal democracy is no better. "[T]he Europe we know," Camus writes in 1948, "is the daughter of excess.... In our madness, we push back the eternal limits, and at once dark Furies swoop down upon us to destroy."[2] Camus numbers himself among this "we," both caught and complicit in a rapacious and malignant excess that has issued in the twentieth century's "most monstrous wars."[3]

Camus repeatedly describes himself as the inheritor of an apocalyptic imperialism that has terrorized the entire world: "We have preferred the power that apes greatness – Alexander first of all, and then the Roman conquerors, whom our school history books, in an incomparable vulgarity of soul, teach us to admire. We have conquered in our turn, have set aside the bounds, mastered heaven and earth."[4] Modern European states are the product of "this degree of hubris." They represent a manmade, "refashioned," "hostile destiny." Frantz Fanon speaks of Western politics in similar terms in *The Wretched of the Earth* (1961): "Europe now lives at such a mad, reckless pace that she has shaken off all guidance and all reason, and she is running headlong into the abyss."[5] Tragedy, Camus theorizes, is the genre best suited to expose Europe's murderous and unsustainable ideologies.

In *Albert Camus' Critique of Modernity*, Ronald Srigley makes the complementary case that Camus finds in Greek tragedy a much-needed antidote to the various messianisms of Christianity, Nazism, Stalinism, and capitalist liberal democracy. As Matthew Sharpe puts it: "Srigley's book rightly highlights how [Camus] ask[s] us, in some way, to reanimate the tragic vision of the Greeks as a counterpoint to all political theologies, medieval or modern."[6] Camus registers the same "dialectic of enlightenment" that Horkheimer and Adorno do; "in a curious paradox," Camus observes, Europe's so-called emancipation from the superstitions of church or king results in the very tyranny – the drive to tyrannize, to breach natural and moral limits – that revolutionary Europe had claimed to oppose. For this reason, in Camus's view, tragedy must be modernity's narrative paradigm: because it showcases these evergreen abuses of power. Here Camus departs from Horkheimer and Adorno, for whom ancient Greek religion and literature were already celebrations of the desire to command and to dominate. For Camus, rather, it is Greek tragedy that laments people's subjection to injurious forces. Contrary to Horkheimer and Adorno, Camus does not see the gods of tragedy as early manifestations of the will to power. For Camus, then, tragedy is not an early instance of "enlightened" claims to banish fear and unreason. Tragedy is instead enlightenment's opposite and corrective – the genre that reveals the lie of lethal belief systems that masquerade as salvation.

For Camus, tragedy shows all people in thrall to a nature that no one enslaves. In Camus's work, Western pretensions to control the environment – to occupy land, to commercialize and militarize it – prove sterile and deadening. Camus's tragedy concomitantly presents human masters not to be trusted. It demands that tragic characters remain vigilant, alive to insalubrious political shackles: not compliant, not complacent. Camus derives this ethics of tragedy from his reading of the Greek plays and proceeds to invent contemporary tragic heroes and heroines in *The Plague* (1947), "The Adulterous Wife" (1957), and his unfinished novel *The First Man*. These modern-day tragic characters recognize a restricted compass for action and agency, but determine to act nonetheless. Such figures cleave to lyrical, time-dilating moments that serve as temporary reprieves from unjust persecutions. These moments constitute "revolt," Camus's term for resistance to powers that we cannot vanquish entirely. Camus contrasts revolt (or rebellion) with practices of revolution. Revolutions, in Camus's view, purport to end suffering completely. Overzealous, cocksure revolutions evince the triumphalism that returns us to tragedy. The salvific aspirations of revolution, in Camus's assessment, devolve into nihilism; contemporary programs for total social redemption come to license all species of cruelty in pursuit of their promised outcomes.

In analyzing and composing tragedy, then, Camus illustrates the work of revolt: tragic heroes and heroines answer life-negating circumstances with life-affirming moments. These moments are amnesties from fate. In possession of such moments, tragic characters seek to delimit further incursions of undeserved suffering into mortal life – wherever change and amelioration are possible – condemning persons and institutions in league with indefensible destruction. They refuse to concede one inch more to tyrannous ill luck, undue pain, and wanting justice. Laying the foundation for this ethics, Camus speaks with humility in his 1955 lecture on tragedy, admitting the perennial difficulty of defining the Greek genre. But he volunteers his own conception of tragedy's development. Rather conventionally, he suggests that tragedy proper has appeared only twice before – in fifth-century Athens and in England, Spain, and France beginning in the Renaissance. In Camus's estimation (echoing Nietzsche's in *The Birth of Tragedy*), these efflorescences of the genre mark a world in pronounced transition from a theological to a human-centered belief system. One passes from pre-Socratic to Socratic thought via tragedy; one passes from the thought of the Middle Ages to that of the Enlightenment via tragedy.[7] Rehearsing a well-known appraisal of fifth-century BCE drama, Camus declares that we move from the quasi-religious and ritualistic tragedy of Aeschylus to the paradigmatic tragedy of Sophocles to the psychological tragedy of Euripides.[8] Greek tragedy, Camus concludes, thrives in the middle space, as do sixteenth- and seventeenth-century tragedy:

> On two occasions, twenty centuries apart, we find a struggle between a world that is still interpreted in a sacred context and men who are already committed to their individuality, that is to say, armed with the power to question.... And each time the final triumph of individual reason, in the fourth century in Greece and in the eighteenth century in Europe, causes the literature of tragedy to dry up for centuries.[9]

For this reason, Camus determines that the revolutionary and romantic German drama of the nineteenth century is not tragedy at all – the reasoning individual is invariably right, actively makes history, and over-comes all opposition to his aims.[10] If there is loss involved in his triumph, it is well compensated.

Camus defines ancient tragedy in the opposite manner: characters' inaugural mistake is to believe that they can wholly remake, or even survive, their world. Tragedy is predicated on their delusive faith in the perfectibility or enduring security of their circumstances. Camus seems to accept the German Idealist premise that two positions collide: "Antigone is right but Creon is not wrong. Similarly, Prometheus is both just and unjust, and Zeus who pitilessly oppresses him also has right on his side."[11] Camus grants that Greek tragic characters nourish valid aims and so do their foes. But the problem, for Camus, is that these opposed commitments come to exist in explosive – not moderate and productive – tension. It is the irredeemable scourge of excess, rather than the Hegelian promise of reconciliation between two interdependent necessities, that Camus understands to be central to tragic conflict. Two forces that would be legitimate within measure, self-determination and the enforcement of limits, give themselves over to extremity:

> The ideal tragedy ... is first and foremost tension, since it is the conflict, in a frenzied immobility, between two powers, each of which wears the double mask of good and evil.... Tragedy occurs when man, through pride (or even through stupidity as in the case of Ajax) enters into conflict with the divine order, personified by a god or incarnated in society.[12]

Singly or collectively, Greek tragic characters overestimate their agency, their righteousness and the protections it confers. Camus contends that Greek tragedy "stems from" this disproportionate confidence and its disproportionate correction.[13] Camus's concern is that each side – "man and his desire for power" and "the order that strikes him down" – attempts to dictate terms exclusively.[14] Moderation is nowhere in sight.

In Camus's sense of modern tragedy, however, we begin with voracious and excessive ruling orders that believe themselves invincible. In contrast to Camus's Greek tragic antagonists, these modern mainstays of power do not lash out at hubristic opposition. Instead, tragic characters start at their mercy and shudder at their lethal extremism. Tragedy may reemerge in France in the twentieth century, Camus reiterates, because Western "individualism is visibly changing today," forgoing its own pursuit of omnipotence: "beneath the pressures of history, little by little the individual is recognizing his limits ... [he] proclaims his revolt, knowing this revolt has limits, demands liberty though he is subject to necessity."[15] Tragic individuals denounce claims to limitless power (over history, over nature), acknowledge that the "triumph of individual reason" has only produced new forms of tyranny, and commit to shared revolt: moments free from domination. They recognize that they cannot match modern politics' excessive force, nor would they want to. They learn moral limits (to their action) and practical limits (to their contestation of injustice). Opposing immoderate violence, they become diagnosticians of the systemic conditions that oppress them and others.

For Camus, then, modern tragic heroes commence where ancient tragic heroes ended: with a searing indictment of malign power. They know that neither religious nor secular ideologies have liberated them from harm:

> In both religious and atheistic [counter-tragic] drama, the problem has in fact already been solved. In the ideal tragedy, just the opposite, it has not been solved.... There is no Oedipus without the destiny summed up by the oracle. But the destiny would not have all its fatality if Oedipus did not refuse it.[16]

Camus's Greek examples crystallize his interpretation of the genre. Antigone is undaunted by Creon's law, nor does Ajax submit to the Greek army's. Prometheus flies in the face of Zeus and Oedipus flouts Apollo. Sisyphus, Camus's own tragic exemplar, refuses to stay in the underworld. Yet their claims to autonomy are checked utterly: Antigone may twice bury Polynices but she is discovered and entombed alive. Prometheus may bring fire to humanity but he is left to the vultures.

Ajax bears arms against Odysseus and Agamemnon but is made to slaughter the Greek herds instead. Oedipus leaves his adoptive family in Corinth only to reunite horribly with his blood relations. Sisyphus, too, manages to "put Death in chains," to steal unauthorized and glorious years "facing the curve of the gulf, the sparkling sea, and the smiles of earth," but finds that "[h]is scorn of the gods, hatred of death, and passion for life" have "won him that unspeakable penalty," "in the wild and limited universe of man."[17]

This, however, is only the first movement of Camus's Greek tragedy. Next comes characters' all-important action (revolt) within the confines of fate. Think of Sisyphus, bound to his rock, casting it off in moments only. In such action Camus sees grounds for characters' endorsement not of undue suffering per se but of lives inseparable from it. Theirs is not Nietzschean *amor fati*: a masochistic love of pain. Instead, Camus's tragic characters continue to take the utmost stand against deleterious external power, now knowing that their revolt is bounded (in two senses: in a positive vein, they recognize that they mustn't resemble such power, and in a negative vein, they recognize that they cannot dismantle oppression entirely or make full restitution for its injuries). Tragic characters prove rebellious in a more clear-eyed manner. Camus therefore insists in both "The Myth of Sisyphus" and "On the Future of Tragedy" that Oedipus, sightless and diminished, can pronounce that "all is well."[18] In each piece, Camus cites this phrase from Sophocles and calls it the miraculous "ancient wisdom" of tragedy.[19] Camus explains:

> Oedipus at the outset obeys fate without knowing it. But from the moment he knows, his tragedy begins. Yet at the same moment, blind and desperate, he realizes that the only bond linking him to the world is the cool hand of a girl. Then a tremendous remark rings out: "Despite so many ordeals, my advanced age and the nobility of my soul make me conclude that all is well."... [This remark] drives out of this world a god who had come into it with dissatisfaction and a preference for futile sufferings. It makes of fate a human matter.[20]

In the face of his "futile sufferings," Oedipus' "only bond" to life comes from the touch of his daughter's hand. Oedipus does not bow to Apollo's law approvingly, but reduced and in pain, he attests to an attachment that is enough. Oedipus practices Bernard's small, rescaled loves – the recalibration of affirmation, the redefinition of heroism on display in Woolf's *The Waves*. Reading *Oedipus at Colonus* as the epitome of curtailed freedom and countervailing perseverance, Camus locates in Sophocles the model for his own ethical and aesthetic commitment to tragedy.

Composing his own tragic myth in prose, Camus writes that Sisyphus "too concludes that all is well" and that we "must imagine Sisyphus happy."[21] Sisyphus is akin to Mrs. Ramsay: face to face with her mortality, her "little strip of time," Mrs. Ramsay is nonetheless willfully and fleetingly happy.[22] Sisyphus, likewise, relishes "a breathing-space which returns as surely as his suffering," when he travels down the mountain, momentarily liberated.[23] What engrosses Camus, then, are characters' actions once they are conscious of an inexorable condition: "from the moment [Oedipus] knows, his tragedy begins," but he proceeds to register a new basis for modest and defiant affirmation. This stance, Camus intimates, stands between the two extremes of Greek tragic outcome: the ostensibly full contentment restored to pardoned Prometheus and the intolerable lucidity of shame-faced Ajax, who finds nothing left to affirm and takes his own life. Instead, Camus's Oedipus and Sisyphus both elect to cling to their small but Herculean means of going on. It is the same for Camus's Rieux and Tarrou in *The Plague*. Both resist their foe indefatigably, but when it nonetheless checks their defiance, they not only continue to fight it from their positions of circumscribed agency but rely for sustenance on a resuscitating moment of being, the tiny feat that they can accomplish: swimming in tandem in the sea.

Camus expressly positions tragedy between "the two poles of extreme nihilism and limitless hope."[24] Tragic heroes and heroines attain awareness of an "unintelligible and limited universe" wherein "[a] horde of irrationals has sprung up and surrounds [them]."[25] But they also reach the conclusion that while such fate "can be painful . . . it is still worse not to recognize that it exists."[26] It is worse, Camus argues, to harbor unrealizable hopes, destined for disappointment, or to deny tragic constraint in the opposite manner, by hewing to nihilism, claiming concern for nothing and no one.[27] Camus's own fiction, then, presents tragedy that corresponds to his conception of the Greek genre: as an anguishing encounter with brute power that engenders a rebellious, Sisyphean battle for happiness. In Camus's atheistic fiction, the problem of existence has not "in fact already been solved." It is still the case that "[e]ven by his greatest effort man can only propose to diminish arithmetically the sufferings of the world. But the injustice and the suffering of the world will remain and, no matter how limited they are, they will not cease to be an outrage."[28] In lieu of divine order, there are natural and social orders not made to human measure; human beings continue to confront shackles they wish to throw off and cannot.

In the face of the irremediable, Camus pictures characters who cherish hard-won intervals of respite. Wherever objectionable conditions permit of alteration, these moments are also templates for change, and characters labor to reduce senseless suffering. Camus himself describes modern fiction as the expression of just such a conflict between crushing realities and revolts against them:

> The greater an artist's revolt against the world's reality, the greater can be the weight of reality to balance that revolt. But the weight can never stifle the artist's solitary exigency. The loftiest work will always be, as in the Greek tragedians, Melville, Tolstoy, or Molière, the work that maintains an equilibrium between reality and man's rejection of that reality, each forcing the other upward in a ceaseless overflowing, characteristic of life itself at its most joyous and heart-rending extremes.[29]

In his 1955 lecture, too, Camus describes all tragedy as "theater in which the creature and creation are pitted one against the other."[30] It is, therefore, the atheist Rieux who "believed himself to be on the right road – in fighting against creation as he found it."[31] In ancient and modern tragedy, Camus contends, the paining, inordinate "weight of reality" cannot be denied. It cannot be lifted in its entirety. Nor can our resultant "rejection of that reality" be stifled. Our responsibility to contest it cannot be abdicated.

The Moment in Camus and Woolf

Camus suggests that it is now the task of the novelist to resolve "the problem of a language for modern tragedy."[32] His own solution – bringing small, sustaining moments when "all is well" into his rendition of "heart-rending" "reality" – is on display in his account of Sisyphus and in his reading of Oedipus. As we saw in the previous chapter, this was Woolf's strategy also.

In recurring to tragedy, Camus works to challenge historical eschatologies that would replace chance with inevitable progress. Camus holds that Marx and Engels associated Darwinian evolutionism with such determinism. Camus, however, weds chance to evolution, eschewing the notion that natural laws underlie contemporary social formations or transformations. He likewise rejects the notion that an amoral, nonteleological natural world authorizes Western "reason and science" in their crusade to dominate the earth; as he says in his lecture on tragedy, such determinations "to conquer and transform," to vanquish perceived "fatality" in this manner, have only "refashioned a hostile destiny."[33] Unwittingly, Camus discerns the etiology of climate catastrophe: specific human conduct ratchets up the lethality of the natural world. Culpable human actors decimate landscapes where those least responsible for this escalation of harm reside. In his own thought, Camus critiques what he takes to be a twentieth-century campaign to expunge tragedy and chance from the natural and historical records:

> Marx wrote to Engels that the Darwinian theory constituted the very foundation of their method. For Marxism to remain infallible, it has therefore been necessary to deny all biological discoveries made since Darwin. As it happens that all discoveries since the unexpected mutations established by De Vries have consisted in introducing, contrary to the doctrines of determinism, the idea of chance into biology, it has been necessary to entrust Lyssenko with the task of disciplining chromosomes and of demonstrating once again the truth of the most elementary determinism.... As far as that is concerned, the twentieth century has also witnessed the denial of the principle of indeterminism in science, of limited relativity, of the quantum theory, and, finally, of every general tendency of contemporary science.[34]

Camus comments in *The Rebel* (1951), his nonfiction treatise on revolt, that "[a]lready, as we can see, the great problem of modern times arises: the discovery that to rescue man from destiny is to deliver him to chance. That is why the contemporary mind is trying so desperately hard to restore destiny to man – a historical destiny this time."[35] Matthew Sharpe remarks that "epistemically a realist, Camus talks (in contrast to Kant) of a nature independent of us: 'inhuman' or 'not made to our scale.'"[36] Camus is familiar, too, with the science of his friend Jacques Monod, the Nobel prize–winning molecular biologist who endeavored to demonstrate the inaccuracy of evolutionary theory yoked to utopianism, anthropocentrism, and theism.[37]

In his scientific treatise *Chance* and *Necessity* (1970), Monod made the final lines of "The Myth of Sisyphus" his epigraph; Monod, too, suggests that we must labor for happiness in a world not designed for our flourishing. Uniting Darwinism and genetics, Monod argues that not only does evolution proceed without humankind as its goal, but the origin of life cannot be traced to either mechanistic determinism or vital forces. Life itself has arisen by chance. The invariance with which hereditary material is then transmitted constitutes the necessity of his title. Mutations are the chance occurrences that make for evolution: "chance *alone* is at the source of every innovation, of all creation in the biosphere. Pure chance, absolutely free but blind, at the very root of the stupendous edifice of evolution.... There is no scientific concept, in any of the sciences, more destructive of anthropocentrism than this one."[38] Monod, like Camus, decries modern recourse to directive and redemptive teleologies, biological or historical. In Monod's words, "[w]hat is very plain, however, is that the ideas having the highest invading potential are those that *explain* man by assigning him his place in an immanent destiny, in whose bosom his anxiety dissolves."[39] In this light, Monod understands the "track which nineteenth-century scientism saw leading infallibly upward to an empyrean noon hour for mankind."[40] Like Camus, Monod aims to debunk "religiosity, scientific progressism, . . . [and] the materialist and dialectal religion of history."[41]

Monod, however, conceives of a more victorious response to the chanciness of mortal life than Camus does. Monod's conclusion to *Chance and Necessity* envisions a reigning "kingdom of ideas, of knowledge, and of creation" that abolishes the very sense of exile within the "universe's unfeeling immensity" that Monod had expounded.[42] While Camus, then, does concur that natural history promises no perfected future, he does not advance Monod's faith in human ingenuity (knowledge, creation) that will armor us against all menace. For Camus, we are not craftsmen of impregnable citadels or transcendent kingdoms of ideas.[43] Our moments of security are more provisional and tenuous. Far more modestly, Camus captures the ways in which natural vistas variously solace, grieve, and overwhelm us. He writes of a communal impulse to shore up natural beauty to counter the pain of losing it. He writes of the shared compulsion to seek shelter from harsh and annihilating climates. Camus, that is, takes a Woolfian message of human limitation and solidarity – not domination – from his vision of nature.

Camus describes his own moments of being, documented in his notebooks and essays, in much the same terms that Woolf's novels conceive of them. Like Mrs. Ramsay, young Camus feels his passion for existence, his keenest happiness, kindled by a beam of light which he encounters in solitude. Mrs. Ramsay, as we saw in the previous chapter, projects her own "exulting" personality onto the lighthouse beam in an interval of privacy.[44] Camus, at age twenty-two, recounts just such an ecstatic experience in his literary notebooks:

> Who am I and what can I do – except enter into the movement of the branches and the light, be this ray of sunlight in which my cigarette smolders away, this soft and gentle passion breathing in the air? If I try to reach myself, it is at the heart of this light that I am to be found. And if I try to taste and understand this delicate flavor that contains the secret of the world, it is again myself that I find at the heart of the universe. Myself, that is to say this intense emotion which frees me from my surroundings. Soon,

my attention will be filled again with other things and with the world of men. But let me cut out this moment from the cloth of time as other men leave a flower in the pages of a book.[45]

In prose almost fit for *To the Lighthouse*, Camus recognizes in the light not a sentient companion, not a universe that joins in his sensations – not the universe's resemblance to him – but his own concentrated pleasure, as Mrs. Ramsay does. Camus, too, treats such a moment as a solid object, binding him to life, to be treasured and stowed away. Echoing Mrs. Ramsay, who "looked up ... and met the third stroke and it seemed to her like her own eyes meeting her own eyes," he concludes: "Today is a resting place, and my heart goes out to meet itself."[46]

Like Mrs. Ramsay, too, Camus manifests a double persona – both "solitaire et solidaire," as his daughter characterizes him.[47] He is committed to these solitary moments of satiety, of sudden delight within a world of inhuman alterity, and committed, also, to promoting and sharing such moments with others, for community heightens their power. Just as Mrs. Ramsay recreates her earlier feeling of affirmation at her dinner, Camus himself develops a scene of solitary nighttime swimming first drafted for his unpublished novel *A Happy Death* (composed between 1936 and 1938) into a scene of shared nighttime swimming in *The Plague*. Séverine Gaspari traces Camus's transformation of the first, more loosely sketched scene into the exquisitely choreographed second. Gaspari shows us that in the first version of this episode the sea possesses a warmth, a body, a character all its own.[48] Contact with its nonhuman physicality brings Patrice Mersault more fully to life; he experiences the sea as quasi-maternal, birthing, cradling him, throwing his vitality into sharper relief.[49] In *The Plague*, however, it is Dr. Rieux who recognizes the sea's warmth and registers the moonlight and the scratchiness of the rocks on the shore; but the moonlight, rocks, and water, rather than entities forming a dyad with him alone, the solitary swimmer, prove the backdrop against which he attunes his perception to his dear friend Tarrou.[50] Now Rieux is in harmony with this human companion. They stroke through the waters in sequence, Gaspari notes, speed in concert through a patch of cold – display a human intimacy at odds with their evocative and stirring, but unconscious and unconcerned environs.[51] In *A Happy Death*, the same glacial patch of sea quickens the lone Mersault's sensibility and leaves him shivering, exhilarated, happy on shore, his vitality surging in response to the sea, as Mrs. Ramsay's and Camus's own emotions had surged before their beams of light. Yet it is Camus's mature novel that envisions feelings of personal vitality and of human intimacy intertwined.[52] Responsiveness to the natural environment now begets a shared quickening of feeling, of rejuvenation and affection in response to nature but also, concomitantly, in opposition to its endless waves that signal the tininess of human lives and bodies. Rieux's and Tarrou's ephemeral, arresting moment of being – the plague on pause, held fleetingly at bay – nourishes both men in their return to battle. This moment acts as that for which they fight. Rieux, then, sees the end of the plague only after it has killed his companion. Rieux includes this moment in the sea in his record of the catastrophe – as Lily's painting commemorates past moments with Mrs. Ramsay – making it clear that despite the plague's cessation, this is a tragic account of solidarity and loss.

Camus himself comes to feel, as Mrs. Ramsay and Bernard do, that exquisite moments can and must be shared. For Camus these moments are emblems of common human value, and he devotes *The Rebel* to describing the community of feeling they inspire. Like Lily, Camus comes more and more explicitly to ground his art and philosophy in such moving and foundational scenes: "a man's work is nothing but this slow trek to redis-cover, through the detours of art, these two or three great and simple images in whose presence his heart first opened."[53] Camus writes these words two years before his death, in his 1958 preface to a reissued volume of *The Wrong Side and the Right Side*, a collection of his earliest essays composed in 1936 and 1937. He reflects in this preface on his childhood and on the convictions and sources of inspiration it inspired:

> "There is no love of life without despair of life," I wrote, rather pompously, in these pages. I didn't know at the time how right I was; I had not yet been through years of real despair. They came, and managed to destroy every-thing in me except an uncontrolled appetite for life. I still suffer from this both fruitful and destructive passion that bursts through even the gloomiest pages of *The Wrong Side and the Right Side*. It's been said we really *live* for only a few hours of our life. This is true in one sense, false in another. For the hungry ardor one can sense in these essays has never left me.... My [childhood] revolts were brilliant with sunshine. They were almost always, I think I can say this without hypocrisy, revolts for everyone, so that every life might be lifted into that light.[54]

For Camus, these rare moments – "we really *live* for only a few hours of our life" – never leave him, sustain him, and implant in him his "hungry ardor" for existence. When he finds his youthful, sun-soaked revolts checked by "years of real despair," his ethics is only further solidified: "that every life might be lifted into that light," shackled as little as immovable circumstance and respect for others permit. It is Camus's own receptivity to such moments, which he also sketches in the essays *Nuptials* (1938) and *Summer* (1954), that allows him, as it does Mrs. Ramsay and Bernard, to say of life, for all its barbs and anguishes: "[t]he moment was all; the moment was enough," "It is enough!"[55] Ruthless fate continues to check the human refusal of death, but it is this refusal that seems justified – provided that it does not pass, precisely, into excess and totalitarian ambitions. The rebel learns moderation, not because he, Camus's modern-day tragic hero, bows willingly to fate – he fights the plague, he cannot accept it – but because faced with such measureless destruction, he vows never to author plague himself, to manufacture another's doom. He learns moderation not because he is reconciled to destiny, but because he is loath to compound it. He is committed to its antithesis, to an ethics of preservation.

Camus versus Sartre

Camus distances himself from Sartrean existentialism because it is *too* empowering: it avows that whatever "facticity" (necessity, fate) one faces, one is free to transform it in light of a future project. Simone de Beauvoir's *Ethics of Ambiguity* (1947) reiterates this contention that people are not products of brute, aleatory circumstance, but are a generative lack of being, a negativity. According to Beauvoir, such negativity is the source of genuine identity and existence: we must practice the refusal of being, stepping back from facticity and regarding it at a distance. This movement of consciousness, which allows us to judge and interpret the past and to elect the future, is what Beauvoir, like Sartre, calls "transcendence." Our willed endeavors represent a "triumph of freedom over facticity."[56] Yet Beauvoir adds to Sartre's theory that we can, in fact, be limited in our ability to act, restricted by oppressive forces and blamelessly so; facticity can indeed quash freedom, and such constraint, Beauvoir contends, demands opposition from those still empowered to contest it. Cognizance of any freedom, Beauvoir argues, should require from us a commitment to freedom for all. Knowing that we must choose our projects, she concludes, we should feel a considerable burden, a sense of risk and even anguish: "it is because there are real dangers, real failures and real earthly damnation that words like victory, wisdom, or joy have meaning. Nothing is decided in advance, and it is because man has something to lose and because he can lose that he can also win."[57] Evil, for Beauvoir, is a real prospect: it consists in avoiding transcendence, choice, where it is possible. Camus would agree. Still, for Camus the sphere of action to which Sartre and Beauvoir commit is too vast ("nothing is decided in advance"). Camus's attraction to literary tragedy accentuates his divergent starting place for ethics: significantly circumscribed freedom and irreparable damages that we cannot transform. If we do not feel ourselves masters of fortune, we will be, in Camus's view, more strategic in the projects we elect. We will be less liable to fateful hubris.

In this vein, Camus militates against the excesses that he diagnoses in twentieth-century politics, including Sartre's: the presumption that a program of murder in the name of a given end can be justified. Set against the notion that ends justify means, Camus's fiction also rejects the idea of "*l'esquive*" (sidestepping, dodging), the notion that all suffering can be overcome either in a Christian afterlife or in a historical future. It is belief in such a *telos*, Camus reiterates, that makes for atrocity. As Joshua Dienstag writes of Camus's outlook:

> Eluding [*l'esquive*] is that mental maneuver that allows human beings to exist in linear time without being deflated by it, but without fully facing its challenge either, thus "the typical act of eluding . . . is hope. Hope of another life one must 'deserve' or trickery of those who live not for life itself but for some great idea that will transcend it, refine it, give it a meaning, and betray it" (*MS* 8). In this criticism, Camus means to sweep together both the transcendent hope of Christianity and the hope of historical optimists that, to him, is typified by Marxism. Both ultimately "betray" human life because they do not accept it in the time-bound, absurd state that is, in fact, its single unalterable condition.[58]

Camus equally rejects the notion that without such *esquive* our confrontation with "unalterable" checks on our transformative powers must issue in the cessation of action or in suicide. As Arnaud Corbic writes in *Camus et l'homme sans Dieu* (2007), Camus is fiercely opposed to "tout ce qui nie l'homme, le mutile et tend à l'écraser, voilà le fil conducteur de son œuvre. La lucidité tragique n'interdit pas l'exigence d'humanité" (all that denies man, mutilates him and tends to crush him, that is the central theme of his oeuvre. Tragic lucidity does not preclude the demand for humanity).[59]

Yet the central indictment of Camus, brought against him during his lifetime and grown more robust afterward, is that tragic lucidity did preclude his demand for humanity. First in the infamous exchange among Francis Jeanson, Sartre, and Camus in Sartre's journal *Les temps modernes*, and then in postcolonial criticism of Camus in relation to Algeria, Camus is charged with turning his back on the sufferings of his contemporaries.

In 1952, Sartre tasks staff writer Jeanson with reviewing Camus's 1951 *The Rebel*. On the one hand, Jeanson admirably synthesizes a number of Camus's central tenets. Jeanson is certainly correct that "[a]près s'être efforcé, dans *Le Myth de Sisyphe*, de prouver l'existence de l'Absurde, [Camus établit] que la conscience de l'Absurde conduit non pas au suicide mais à la révolte" (after endeavoring in *The Myth of Sisyphus* to prove the existence of the Absurd, [Camus establishes] that awareness of the Absurd leads not to suicide but to revolt).[60] Jeanson also adroitly summarizes Camus's distinction between revolt and revolution: "toute révolution finisse par renier le mouvement initial de révolte, au profit d'une préten-tion totalitaire" (every revolution finishes by renouncing its initial move-ment of revolt in favor of a totalitarian pretention).[61] On these grounds Camus refuses some Marxist views of history. Jeanson equally refuses to ascribe any value to Camus's alternative program of revolt. For Jeanson, "Sisyphe savait déjà qu'il ne faut point se laisser prendre au piège de l'action: il faut agir, bien sûr, mais simplement pour agir et sans en attendre aucun résultat, sans nourrir l'illusion de donner un sens à ce qui n'en saurait avoir" (Sisyphus knew already that one must not let oneself fall into the trap of action: one must act, of course, but simply for the sake of action and without expecting any result, without nourishing the illusion of giving meaning to what can never have one).[62] Here Jeanson misreads Camus's account of Sisyphus; Jeanson makes resigned cognizance of absurdity, rather than tragic ethics, Sisyphus's endpoint. As we have seen, Sisyphus represents action that *is* productive – as productive as possible. It is essential that Sisyphus is happy in his journey down the mountain, that he has made his labor matter in fighting for that reprieve. Sisyphus is constrained, but motivated; he is now in a position to discriminate between action that counteracts and action that compounds the misery of his burden. He is far from a hopeless drudge. He is far from the ethical nihilist who values nothing. He is far from the political nihilist who condones the torture of others. Contra Jeanson, the philosophical message of Sisyphus is that life invariably acquires meaning for persecuted beings; this meaning is one of solidarity.

In this way Jeanson misconstrues Camus's rebel, his tragic hero. Jeanson contends that such a Sisyphus is locked in a battle with a personified divinity, with a Creator who is supremely unjust. Jeanson argues that such a hero, nursing a perennial grudge – a sense that he has been metaphys-ically wronged – cares nothing for terrestrial ills because they pale in comparison to this original cruelty. But we have seen that in Camus's evocations of modern tragedy the Greek gods cede their place to a godless nature and a post-Enlightenment history. The ravages of both incite the contemporary tragic hero's commitment to minimizing injustice where possible. Jeanson, however, ignores Camus's objection to men who resemble gods or insentient elements, who devastate others with impunity. Jeanson dismisses revolt's resultant call for moderation. As Camus responds to Jeanson, if the only marker of political engagement, the only proof against moral apathy, is unequivocal endorsement of Stalinism, then the rebel indeed consigns himself to failure – but is progress only possible via this mode of revolution? As Jeanson notes, Camus recoils from a totalitarian ethos lurking within revolutionary fervor, a desire for control which never leaves the human body intact and unmolested. This "principled," revolutionary disregard for human bodies is an instance of what Camus labels "*démesure*," his shorthand for an inhumane historical measure that brooks no restraint.

Camus pens an excoriating reply to editor-in-chief Sartre, accusing Jeanson of willful misunderstanding. Sartre then enters the fray, claiming that he can no longer spare Camus's delicate sensibility. Sartre's conclusion, the same as Jeanson's, is that Camus concerns himself with transhistorical human predicaments, with a fearsome existential fate, in order to duck participation in contemporary politics. Sartre's words, like Jeanson's, are especially cutting because they turn a keen analysis of Camus's works against Camus. Sartre addresses Camus directly:

> Être heureux, c'était faire son métier d'homme; vous nous découvriez "le devoir d'être heureux." Et ce devoir se confondait avec l'affirmation que l'homme est le seul être du monde qui ait un sens "parce qu'il est le seul à exiger d'en avoir." L'expérience du bonheur, semblable au *Supplice* de Bataille mais plus complexe et plus riche, vous dressait en face d'un Dieu absent comme un reproche mais aussi comme un défi: "L'homme doit affirmer la justice pour lutter contre l'injustice éternelle, créer du bonheur pour protester contre l'univers du malheur." L'univers du malheur n'est pas *social* ou du moins pas d'abord: c'est la Nature indifférente et vide où l'homme est étranger et condamné à mourir; en un mot c'est "le silence éternel de la Divinité.".... Mais puisque, d'après vos propres termes, l'injustice est *éternelle* – c'est-à-dire puisque l'absence de Dieu est une constante à travers les changements de l'histoire – la relation immédiate et toujours recommencée de l'homme qui exige d'*avoir* un sens (c'est-à-dire qu'on le lui donne) à ce Dieu qui garde éternellement le silence, est elle-même transcendante à l'Histoire.... On ne peut aller plus loin; aucun progrès ne peut trouver place dans cette tragédie instantanée.[63]

> To be happy, that was to do the job of being a man. You revealed to us "the duty to be happy." And this duty was mingled with the affirmation that

man is the sole being in the world who has a meaning "because he is the sole being who insists on having one." Similar to Bataille's *Le supplice* but richer and more complex, you erected the experience of happiness in the face of an absent God as a reproach, but also as a challenge: "Man must affirm justice to struggle against eternal injustice, create happiness to protest against the universe of unhappiness." The universe of unhappiness is not *social*, or at least not at first: it is the indifferent and empty Nature where man is a stranger and condemned to die. In a word it is "the eternal silence of the Divinity.".... But since, according to your own terms, injustice is *eternal* – that is, since the absence of God is a constant across the changes of history – the immediate and continually reaffirmed relation of man who insists on *having* a meaning (which is to say, who demands that one be given to him) to this God who maintains eternal silence, is itself transcendent to History.... One can go no further: there is no place for progress in this instantaneous tragedy.[64]

Echoing Jeanson, Sartre signally mischaracterizes Camus as one who still believes in and personifies God, as one who is not an atheist but an antitheist – conceiving of a God who has turned his back on the world. But by "the silence of the Divinity," Camus again refers to its inexistence, not to its recalcitrance. The latter interpretation is appealing to Sartre, perhaps, because it can establish a view of Camusian revolt as a merely recriminatory and apolitical dispute with the heavens. But what Sartre calls Camus's posture of "eternal" contestation, "transcendent to History," is a stance that bears directly on history: a baseline, lived repulsion to death, instinctive and shared, that makes for specific political and economic critique. As John Foley writes, "at no point does Camus assume that the immediate cause of political injustice is anything other than political."[65]

Camus, however, does challenge a Hegelian notion of world history and certain Marxist, materialist narratives of history. In his view, both wager that pain and death are unavoidable and generative: stepping-stones to saving social transformation.[66] Camus objects to a teleological justification of pain. Camus's sense that a greater or future good does not render innocent deaths acceptable echoes Darwin's conclusion that animals' pain, in the course of evolution, is not justifiable. Darwin saw that natural selection adapted species to their environments over time; at the species level creatures fared ever better. But this was because of innumerable individual losses. Camus likewise sees senseless and irredeemable – tragic – suffering in the course of history. While Kant, as Patrick Hayden writes, is already keen to "bemoan an attitude that eschews historical teleology as 'truly the stone of Sisyphus,'" Camus is committed to developing an ethics consistent with Sisyphean struggle.[67]

Camus's foundational belief in the existence of meaningless suffering does not translate into political reaction, as Sartre and Jeanson allege. Camus endorsed anti-imperialist and anticapitalist politics – transformative collective action, in line with anarcho-syndicalism – that took care, the best it could, to dismantle exploitative economic relations peacefully.[68] Jeanson and Sartre saw in this Camus's refusal to back real antibourgeois and anticolonial change, which necessitated violence; but Camus argued that modes of emancipation should balk at innocent sacrifice.[69] As Hayden writes of Camus: "If revolutionary practice builds coalitions and solidarity between diverse people, then revolt counters its totalizing and repressive tendencies."[70] Camus's idea was that the principles of revolt would keep revolutionary action humane. Camus did not insist, either, on nonviolence at every juncture.[71] Camus's point, as Hayden writes, was that "[v]iolence … can only be understood as a contingent weapon of defence, not as a normalized instrument of liberation."[72] While Sartre, then, witheringly insisted that Camus was drawn to revolt because it "wrenches him from his daily 'agitation' and from 'historicity,'" Camus cautioned that it was the political rationalization of murder that wrenched human beings from the reality of broken bodies.[73] Camus sought to counter this desensitization.

Janine: A Moment of Being

Sartre's contention is that to set human history within natural history – the latter accorded a tragic cast – is to passively lament a world hopelessly flawed in its constitution. For Camus, however, precisely this condition demands the revolts of Rieux and of Janine, Camus's first female protagonist. In "The Adulterous Wife," the opening story of *Exile and the Kingdom* (1957), Janine grieves the precarity of mortal life. She is fascinated by images of fixity and imagines a land where "no one would ever age any more or die."[74] Janine is moved by these unrealizable fantasies not to renounce a world in which time cannot be stilled but to accept and endorse the nearest substitute: moments of satiety within time. Janine's very desire for the sky's immensity and longevity comes to revive her, to rekindle her waning fires – to reawaken her pleasure in existing.

A moment of being melts the cold around her, the icy solitude of her marriage, and the insistent, frozen air of the North African desert. Janine and her husband Marcel have left behind their comfortable quarters in the city to travel across this chill and imposing landscape because Marcel's business is not what it was; at the tail end of colonial rule, French commerce is on the decline. Marcel insists that Janine accompany him as he peddles his wares on foot, in order to provide for her, he says, a suitcase full of goods planted between his legs.[75] It is Janine's perspective we follow. During their bus ride, she remarks that "[t]he sand now struck the windows in packets as if hurled by invisible hands."[76] Janine experiences the natural environment as a hostile and anonymous attacker and feels herself too large among the bus's Arab travelers. Only the one other Frenchmen on board takes notice of her, but not with desire; to her, then, he seems to resemble the sandy, impassive hardness of her surroundings.

On disembarking in a remote locale, Janine finds that an Arab man who will not move aside for her husband also reminds her of the intractable desert rigidity that she has attributed to the Frenchman. Janine reflects, too, in free indirect style, that "[p]robably [Marcel] didn't love her" and that he does not satisfy her.[77] Yet Marcel, she reflects, needed her:

> she did know that Marcel needed her and that she needed that need, that she lived on it night and day, at night especially – every night, when he didn't want to be alone, or to age or die, with that set expression he assumed which she occasionally recognized on other men's faces, the only common expression of those madmen hiding under an appearance of wisdom until the madness seizes them and hurls them desperately toward a woman's body to bury in it, without desire, everything terrifying that solitude and night reveals to them.[78]

Janine recognizes Marcel's loveless terror, his own desperation to escape time and death. In response to some inner prompting of her own, however, she insists that they visit an abandoned military fort, now, it seems to her, just a scenic lookout. A certain experience, previously wanting in her life, befalls her there. The sky's light itself "relaxed and softened"; it passes from hard crystal to seeming liquid.[79] By chance, she thinks, she glimpses what she takes to be a small, free band of travelers who manage to make an ever-shifting home within this "limitless" and inhospitable terrain – and this idea of hers helps to dissolve a calcified knot inside her. Janine imagines these "nomads" to have been there "[s]ince the beginning of time," "free lords of a strange kingdom."[80] She claims to know, too, that this enduring realm, to which these outsiders are bound, has "been eternally promised her" as well – and has always been the target of her desire – but that she can only take hold of it in this singular, initiatory moment.[81] Rapt, she beholds a silent and "suddenly motionless sky." She imagines a permanent stop to the "world's course," to both its temporal and spatial movement. As Mrs. Ramsay would say: "Life stand still here."[82]

Yet even Janine's perception of time's cessation and movement's suspension is filled with mobile vitality. The "motionless" sky beats with "waves of steady light."[83] While life for her, externally, is paused, internally "someone" – barely known, foreign and yet most intimate – is actively weeping with unprecedented, awestruck feeling.[84] This hiatus from her married life, from its colonial and commercial imperatives – from its oppressive emotional and economic transactions – catalyzes a furious need in her, "to be liberated," later that night:

> she too was afraid of death. "If I could overcome that fear, I'd be happy...." Immediately, a nameless anguish seized her. She drew back from Marcel. No, she was overcoming nothing, she was not happy, she was going to die, in truth, without having been liberated. Her heart pained her; she was stifling under a huge weight that she suddenly discovered she had been dragging around for twenty years. Now she was struggling under it with all her strength. She wanted to be liberated even if Marcel, even if the others, never were! Fully awake, she sat up in bed and listened to a call that seemed very close.... It came from the south, where desert and night mingled now under the again unchanging sky, where life stopped, where no one would ever age or die any more. Then the waters of the wind dried up and she was not even sure of having heard anything except a mute call that she could, after all, silence or notice. But never again would she know its meaning unless she responded to it at once. At once – yes, that much was certain at least![85]

Recoiling from Marcel, Janine sees herself as a "dragging" Sisyphus. She imagines this imploring and emancipatory wind to traverse the "again unchanging sky" of earlier that day, "where life stopped." Again, she feels "called" to reprise and pursue an experience akin to Mrs. Ramsay's "still space": a momentary sensation of reprieve from time and death that will sustain her in the face of them.[86]

Janine makes her way back to the fort, through freezing darkness: "The cold, no longer having to struggle against the sun, had invaded the night; the icy air burned her lungs."[87] She arrives shaken, benumbed, and emotionally famished. But ascending to the fort's parapet, Janine projects herself upon the "sparkling icicles" of the stars and moves with them across the sky toward the horizon:

> Breathing deeply, she forgot the cold, the dead weight of others, the craziness or stuffiness of life, the long anguish of living and dying. After so many years of mad, aimless fleeing from fear, she had come to a stop at last. At the same time, she seemed to recover her roots and the sap again rose in her body, which had ceased trembling.... Then, with unbearable gentleness, the water of night began to fill Janine, drowned the cold, rose gradually from the hidden core of her being and overflowed in wave after wave, rising up even to her mouth full of moans.[88]

Having drawn back from the "dead weight" of Marcel, she moans with pleasure. She associates herself with the stars instead, which "little by little identified her with the core of her being, where cold and desire" vie for ascendency.[89] Like Mrs. Ramsay and Camus, before their own light sources, Janine comes closest to herself as she revels in the landscape. She adopts its expansiveness and feels heady warmth steal over her. In their stillness, her stars nonetheless travel – make their "stationary progress" – and watching them, her desire begins to overcome the cold.[90] Janine opens herself more and more to the night; her persistent thoughts of death recede from consciousness. She momentarily forgets "the long anguish of living and dying" – "she forgot," that is, in the grips of a heated attachment to the "cold earth."[91] Her resurgent vitality makes for such amnesia, an alternative to the "mad, aimless fleeing from fear" that has only left her sapless and petrified. It is this fearless, intuitive relish for being that henceforward "roots" her to life. She banishes the "stifling," weighty need of her husband, the pressure of his ventures. As it does for Mrs. Ramsay, something quickens inside her: "the sap again rose." As Mrs. Ramsay's wedge-shaped core of darkness brimmed with happiness when "waves of pure lemon ... curved and swelled and broke upon the beach and the ecstasy burst in her eyes and waves of pure delight raced over the floor of her mind," so the "water of night began to fill Janine, drowned the cold, rose gradually from the hidden core of her being and overflowed in wave after wave."[92]

Hiroki Toura, in *La quête et les expressions du bonheur dans l'œuvre d'Albert Camus* (2004), traces Camus's own defining rapport with natural settings – the seaside of Tipasa and the desert of Djémila, for instance.[93] The connotations of these settings vary for Camus, as Matthew Sharpe notes: "the desert is at once a place of annihilation, as well as of higher epiphanies; so too the water" can be life-affirming or "drown and corrode"; "[i]n short, here again, we see the complexity of Camus' thought: which does not simply pit nature (positive) versus history (negative), but preserves a two-sided sense of nature herself."[94] Seaside scenes do not always reassure us, as Camus says, that "everything is on a human scale."[95] But it is the sun-warmed seascape of Tipasa that does lead Camus to open his heart to the world and to sense fully his love for others as he thinks of their shared responsiveness to such beauty.[96] The desert frightens Camus, but not Janine, with nonhuman otherness.[97] The dry, mineral intransigence of sun-scorched Oran or Djémila brings Camus face to face with human impermanence.[98] In the desert, as Toura shows, Camus records the menacing face of nature, which threatens to rob him of personhood.[99]

To be in accord with this hard, windswept place is to imagine himself a stone, divested of sensibility. Toura recounts: "C'est dans ces ruines que Camus croit pouvoir trouver 'le mot exact qui dirait, entre l'horreur et le silence, la certitude consciente d'une mort sans espoir'" (It is among these ruins that Camus believes that he can find 'the right word between horror and silence to express the conscious certainty of a death without hope').[100] Janine, however, comes alive in this forbidding place. For her, it dismisses from view the greater aridity of French colonial rule. She comes, in defiance of this history, to epitomize warmth and desire.

Camus composes "The Adulterous Wife" alongside some of his most fervent political commentaries on Algeria – his appeals to end its "fratricidal" bloodshed, to establish a civilian truce, and to envision an equitable multiculturalism on its soil.[101] But for postcolonial critics, Janine's epiphanic love affair with this "natural" setting seems a particularly blatant instance of Camus's erasure of colonial history from his fiction. These "nomads" who wander the desert far from any river are not timeless fixtures of the landscape; they are refugees who have been methodically robbed of their arable farmland. As Sartre makes clear in "Colonialism Is a System": "the French State gives Arab land to the colonists in order to create for them a purchasing power which allows French industrialists to sell them their products; the colonists sell the fruits of this stolen land in the markers of France."[102] French Algerian countryside is first and foremost land taken and stolen. "In short," says Sartre, "it has taken just a century to dispossess them of two-thirds of their land."[103] This land cannot be reparceled and reallocated equitably, Sartre argues, so long as the colonial machine, self-propagating and rapacious, persists. Sartre would find in Janine a pernicious ahistoricity and a culpable disregard for the very history of the fort in which she finds herself thawing and liberated. Janine, on such readings, romanticizes injustice (the military post, the displaced people). She enjoys a moment of respite, denying the evidence of state violence all around her. Conor Cruise O'Brien and Edward Said persuasively read such forgetfulness of historical circumstance as Camus's apology for colonial occupation, as the licensing of permanent amnesia.

These are damning critiques, to be sure, reducing Camus to a particularly clever apologist for capitalist and colonialist exploitation and for right-wing ideology: pushing colonial violence from view out of moral turpitude or out of nostalgic, obdurate love for the land of his mother and childhood.[104] Yet these indictments seem to miss the mark not simply because of the anticolonialist Camus of *Combat* or "Misery in Kabylia" but because of Camus the fiction writer. "The Adulterous Wife" might suggest that it is because Janine can recover her taste for existence that she is poised to reimagine her marriage, and even Algeria's future, on the basis of a universal human claim to such free and untrammeled moments. If desert vistas can awaken her appetite for life and quicken her despair at its impermanence, then this rapport with the land, far from eclipsing the significance of history, implies that all have equal stake in it. It is the aversion to bloodshed that this position entails, which Sartre finds moralistic and politically enervating, that leads Camus to his promotion of pacific solutions to war in Algeria.

For Sartre, colonialism makes explicit the vacuity of French human rights discourse: "since all human beings have the same rights," Sartre says in 1956, "the Algerian will be made a subhuman."[105] Camus, in a more muted manner, makes this point in 1945. French "colonizers," he writes, offer "only a caricature" of democracy to Algerians.[106] Camus cites Ferhat Abbas's 1943 manifesto, which asserts that universal equality under colonialism has proven itself *"an unattainable reality."*[107] Camus is not blind to French atrocities. He is not inclined to overlook them as he focuses on a more abstract and collective human fate. Instead, he finds that a shared human response to this fate – one of loathing and defiance – serves as the fiercest indictment of historical dehumanization and murder. Sartre asks for a "safeguard ... to stop nations or the whole of humanity from falling into inhumanity."[108] This may be Camus's answer: with a lyricism the opposite of his spare, "American" style in *The Stranger*, Camus celebrates Janine's break from Marcel and all that he signifies.[109]

Discussing his upcoming publication of *Albert Camus the Algerian* in a 2007 interview, David Carroll also argues, against postcolonial critics, for the continuing value of Camus's perspective:

> [Camus] condemned the use of torture and summary executions by the French army and the politics of the extreme right, which supported at any costs the continuation of French rule in Algeria.... In spite of harsh criticisms of his position from both the political left and right, Camus stubbornly continued to believe in the possibility of creating a democratic, multi-cultural society in a postcolonial Algeria in which all populations would have equal rights.... During the cold war Camus attacked Stalinist forms of Marxism and wrote polemical critiques of both the concept and reality of revolution in general. But at the same time he remained critical of what could be called imperialist forms of democracy, as well as what he feared was an emerging Islamic empire rooted in political and religious fanaticism.... By extension, he attacked all justifications for the assassination of political opponents, indiscriminate bombings of cities and villages, the torture and execution of suspects, and the use of both terrorist and

counterterrorist tactics against civilians. Camus placed justice before politics, the protection of the lives of individual civilians before the achievement
of political goals, no matter how just those goals were claimed to be or in
fact actually were. This explains why during the Algerian War he repeatedly
denounced the criminal nature of both the French army's counterterrorist
strategy and the FLN's use of terrorism against civilians.... [By an "age of
terror," Camus meant] an age in which politics is treated as religion, and
religion, the belief in an absolute Truth, considered the unquestionable
basis for politics.[110]

Detached from fanatical politics, Janine's desire for a momentary reprieve
from mortal fear, and from loveless marital and socioeconomic relations –
even her delusive figuration of "free" "nomads," an unsubujugated collective, at home everywhere, nationless, indestructible – might signify her
taste for anticolonial revolt. She might turn against death and its collabo-
rators: political orders that license it in service of their ends.

While for Sartre the foreign presence bleeding Algeria dry must leave in
order to cease and desist, for Camus, Janine's physical and affective
awakening might bear within it a promise of peace and reconstruction in
Algeria. "The Adulterous Wife" hints that history could be made afresh, on
the basis of a liberating and rehumanizing moment of bodily ecstasy, one
that stands apart from colonialism – like a haven, a steadfast source of
renewal – but inevitably bears upon it, by throwing into relief colonialism's
forced exiles and unconscionable ravages. Speaking of the lessons of Greek
tragedy in "Helen's Exile," Camus writes in this vein:

> it is indecent to proclaim today that we are the sons of Greece. Or, if we are,
> we are sons turned renegade. Putting history on the throne of God, we are
> marching toward theocracy.... History explains neither the natural uni-
> verse that came before it, nor beauty which stands above it. Consequently it
> has chosen to ignore them.... It is by acknowledging our ignorance,
> refusing to be fanatics, recognizing the world's limits and man's, through
> the faces of those we love, in short, by means of beauty – this is how we may
> rejoin the Greeks.[111]

Camus incorporates this natural universe and this beauty into his fiction,
not to deny history but to gain a vantage point – like Janine's from the
fort – from which to refashion it. Janine's military outlook (literal and
metaphorical) is transformed because she is transformed. She leaves Marcel
and his baggage (literal and metaphorical) behind. Janine militates against
the deformation and forgetting of the human body.

In keeping with this somatically rooted vision of value, Dienstag argues
that Camus's commitment to moments of being does not require "a kind

of radical romanticism that tells us to abandon all thought of the past and future to experience as deeply and intensely as we can whatever is in front of us."[112] Dienstag does not see Camus as a purveyor of such temporality that requires "withdrawing entirely from a historical perspective and narrowing our vision to the immediate, the instant. Living the moment is the attempt to reverse, or cancel, the fall into time."[113] Camus and his characters do not live the moment in this permanently escapist fashion. Their attachment to the momentary is not such a romantic endeavor to abolish historical time. It is the basis for contesting – not eluding – history.

Jacques and Jessica: Tragic Affirmation

Camus's unfinished opus, *The First Man*, was to be his most sweeping novel, passing from the colonization of Algeria to the French Resistance, and from a beloved mother to an impassioned love affair. He imagined it as his *War and Peace*.[114] Camus's notes for all that was to come (perhaps only one of three sections is provisionally drafted) shimmer and tantalize. The final pages of his manuscript just begin to introduce the novel's hero to its heroine:

> [Jacques Cormery] had loved her for her beauty and for the openhearted and despairing passion for life that was hers, and that made her deny, deny that time could pass, though she knew it was passing at that very moment.... [I]ntelligent and outstanding in so many ways, perhaps just because she was truly intelligent and outstanding, she rejected the world as it was.... Then, her blood on fire, she wanted to flee, flee to a country where no one would grow old or die, where beauty was imperishable, where life would always be wild and radiant, and that did not exist; she wept in his arms when she returned, and he loved her desperately.[115]

She "den[ies]" that time could pass," longs for a land of imperishable beauty where "no one would grow old or die," and weeps for this unrealizable place. She is very much akin to Janine, and Jacques, too, who is perennially "rebelling against the deadly order of the world."[116]

Critic Agnès Spiquel, analyzing Camus's recently unveiled notes for the novel – those published only in 2008 – identifies this unnamed rebel as "Jessica," a *femme révoltée* whom Camus began to sketch for *The First Man* as early as 1954, in his journals and elsewhere. Spiquel reminds us that Camus was already taken with Shakespeare's Jessica in *The Merchant of Venice*, celebrating her fiery, dauntless love in a 1939 essay on Pisa and Florence, "The Desert," in *Nuptials*. As Spiquel describes Jessica in "Qu'aurait été l'histoire d'amour dans la suite du *Premier Homme*?" (2010):

Jessica, c'est la femme à qui l'amour donne toutes les audaces; c'est l'anti-Juliette, l'amante heureuse qui court vers son bonheur et chante avec celui qu'elle aime le bonheur d'aimer. Dès 1939, tout est donné de Jessica: merveilleuse, elle est surtout l'occasion merveilleuse de l'amour. Dès 1945, Camus sait qu'elle sera l'héroïne du roman d'amour qu'il écrira un jour; il note dans ses *Carnets*: "Roman d'amour: Jessica."[117]

Jessica is the woman to whom love gives every audacity; she is the anti-Juliet, the happy lover who runs toward her happiness and sings the happiness of loving with the one she loves. Since 1939, everything is known about Jessica: marvelous, she is above all the marvelous occasion of love. Since 1945, Camus knows that she will be the heroine of the love story he will write one day; he notes in his *Carnets*: "love story: Jessica."

Spiquel contends that "Camus constitue Jessica comme une héroïne camusienne, très proche du narrateur de *L'Envers et l'Endroit*, pour qui 'il n'y a pas d'amour de vivre sans désespoir de vivre'" (Camus represents Jessica as a Camusian heroine, very close to the narrator of *The Wrong Side and the Right Side*, for whom "there is no love of life without despair of life").[118] Jessica indeed appears well matched to Jacques, who is repeatedly described in terms of his "famished ardor, that mad passion for living which had always been part of him and even today was still unchanged."[119] Spiquel cites Camus's envisioning of Jessica found in a section of his sketches for *The First Man* entitled "The Pyre" ("Le Bûcher"), the name itself commingling life's vital heat and irreversible losses:

> On pouvait croire qu'elle était l'insoumission elle-même et il est vrai que cet être couronné de flammes brûlait comme la révolte elle-même. Mais elle était surtout l'acceptation. "J'accepterais de mourir aujourd'hui (à 30 ans) car j'ai eu assez de joie. Et s'il me fallait revivre, je voudrais la même vie, malgré ses malheurs extremes."[120]

> One could believe that she was rebelliousness itself and it is true that this being crowned with flames burned like revolt itself. But she was above all acceptance. "I would accept dying today (at age 30) because I have had enough joy. And if I had to live again, I would want the same life, despite its extreme misfortunes."

Rather than nourishing a wish to flee the world, moments of happiness sustain Jessica, allow her even to pass Nietzsche's test of eternal recurrence.

In contrast to Jessica, Spiquel introduces Marie, whom Camus also outlines in his plans for the novel. Marie, decidedly, does not believe in the promise of a salvific future, yet she is drowning, as Camus describes her, in an anguishing present. She is borne downward by her knowledge of death and pain, with no countervailing joys to keep her afloat.

She experiences happiness, Camus writes, only as the precursor to loss, betrayal, and suffering. Camus evokes her in his notes:

> L'un des secrets de M. est qu'elle n'a jamais pu accepter, ni supporter, ou simplement oublier la maladie ni la mort.... La vie pour elle n'est que le temps, qui lui-même est maladie et mort. Elle n'accepte pas le temps. Elle s'arc-boute dans un combat d'avance perdu. Quand elle cède, la voilà au fil de l'eau, avec un visage de noyée. Elle n'est pas de ce monde parce qu'elle le refuse de tout son être, sinon dans les *instants* de gloire ou de beauté.[121]

> One of M.'s secrets is that she has never been able to accept, nor bear, or simply forget sickness or death.... Life for her is nothing but time, which itself is sickness and death. She does not accept time. She braces herself in a battle already lost. When she yields, there she is drifting with the current, with the face of a drowned woman. She is not of this world, because she refuses it with all her being, except in *moments* of glory or beauty.

Marie's despair comes of valuing what is insecure and terrestrial, and of wishing in turn to forgo it. She recognizes the inevitability of time's passing; she experiences temporal limitation as "a battle already lost." Her moments of glory and beauty act only as salt in the wound that is the world. Unlike Jessica, she cannot harness the power of these moments in a way that fortifies her, cannot make them life rafts in the Dionysiac flood of time. Jessica, like Janine, manages to stay afloat down the tragic river; Marie is going under, yielding to not being. She is "not of this world" because she eludes it – not via hope for celestial or earthly perfection to come, but via a life-negating hopelessness that causes her to abjure the here and now.

Jessica and Marie: both opposed to time, one because of passionate defiance, love for a life that she cannot bear to lose, the other because of unshakable despair at this same life and its losses. Camus's Janine begins as Marie – in thrall to loneliness, to the omnipresence of death – and ends as Jessica, exultant, weeping with the very love that accounts for death's fearsomeness. Janine ceases to drown in Marie's icy waters and is bathed in Jessica's fires. Janine is "adulterous" because she experiences this heated passion apart from Marcel. Camus celebrates this life-affirming adultery. Janine's revived body prefigures Jessica's, as Camus evokes the latter in his notes: "Son corps brûlait. Il brûlait littéralement par une sorte de foyer incandescent qui devait se trouver à l'intérieur" (Her body was burning. It was literally consumed by a sort of incandescent fire which had to be located inside her).[122] We may imagine that Janine has come to feel, too, what Camus sketches in relation to Jacques: "Illumination," the end of psychic drought.[123] Camus's notes seem to gloss Jacques's epiphany as follows: "même s'il devait revenir à cette sécheresse où il avait toujours vécu" (even if he had to return to this dryness where he had always lived), he had had the chance "une fois, une seule fois peut-être, mais une fois, d'accéder ..." (once, one single time perhaps, but once, to attain ...).[124] Camus's sentence ends in ellipses, but perhaps both Janine and Jacques attain what Sartre dismissed as happiness in a "universe of unhappiness." This attainment might secure their commitment not only to extraordinary moments ("one single time") and to their sources (landscapes and other people) but to the replenishment of a desiccated social world – one that produces famine and exile in the desert.

Janine and Jessica both realize Camus's 1950 imagining in his *Notebooks* of a novelistic character to come. From his notebook entry, Camus recopies the following line and places it at the head of "The Pyre": "As if at the first warmth of love the snows accumulated in her melted gradually to give way to the irresistible, gushing waters of joy."[125] At the close of her story, Janine also "weep[s] copiously, unable to restrain herself."[126] She does not weep in Marcel's arms, as Jessica weeps in Jacques's, but hers is the same love-induced, voluptuous testament to life.

The Absurd Meursault

Camus castigates nihilism because it denies such moments their value. Camus both theorizes and dramatizes two contemporary forms of nihilism. One is the realization of Nietzsche's predictions: transcendent belief systems have lost their credibility, and traditional bases for action are wanting. There is no reason to pursue – or not to pursue – given behaviors. Meursault in *The Stranger* (1942) exemplifies this rudderless orientation toward others. The second species of nihilism that Camus identifies, however, comes of belief systems themselves: political ideologies that rationalize their casualties in the name of a future *telos*. In a 1959 interview, Camus locates such nihilism in *The Fall* (1956): "My hero is indeed discouraged, and that is why, as a good modern nihilist, he exalts servitude. Have I chosen to exalt servitude?"[127] Matthew Sharpe describes Camus's critique of such vicious modes of thought as follows: "It is above all this revolutionary willingness 'to do whatever it takes,' given which the taking of human life becomes a matter of indifference that Camus will finally call 'nihilism.'"[128] Sharpe argues that Camus's analysis of this nihilism internal to politics appears in his works from 1942 onward:

> From this time, centrally, when Camus talks of "nihilism" and the need for European civilization to pass beyond it, he no longer means only the

collapse of all universally agreed metaphysical or theological bases of moral and political order. "Nihilism" for Camus, *pace* both the Nietzschean and theological usages, has an irreducibly ethical meaning, directed toward how we relate to really-existing Others.... It means the condition in which killing other human beings has lost all horror, as if they were so many marionettes, *homini sacrii* or administrative abstractions to be shunted between queues, columns and rail-yards and exterminated in the name of competing ideological doctrines.[129]

For Camus, these nihilistic ideologies have the aim and the effect of repressing tragedy: their proponents need not register or grieve the pain they cause. It is the danger of nihilism that motivates Camus to craft his morally disengaged protagonists – characters who have ceased all prosocial activity.

These case studies in nihilism work to purge audiences of deleterious ethics, of insensibility. They lead us to shrink from characters who forgo all ethical reasoning (Meursault) or who claim reasoned bases for dismissing harm to others (Clamence in *The Fall*). As Camus writes in *The Rebel*, to affirm nothing and to affirm everything prove twin moral failings:

> Each time that [rebellion] deifies the total rejection, the absolute negation, of what exists, it destroys. Each time that it blindly accepts what exists and gives voice to absolute assent, it destroys again. Hatred of the creator can turn to hatred of creation or to exclusive and defiant love of what exists. But in both cases it ends in murder and loses the right to be called rebellion. One can be nihilist in two ways, in both by having an intemperate recourse to absolutes.[130]

Camus prophylactically pens illustrations of such nihilism: narratives that warn against the abdication of caring in a war-torn, concentrationary environment.

Ronald Srigley makes the case that Camus also proffers two etiologies of this modern political nihilism in *The Rebel*. In one account, contemporary nihilistic politics begins with the modern rebel's outage at a merciless Judaic god. Christianity proposes Jesus as a solution. But what ensues are immanent secular messianisms – like Nazism, for example – that eschew the very constraints that a transcendent Christian God had placed on human endeavors to reach perfection.[131] On Camus's second model, however, which Srigley finds more iconoclastic and more consistent with Camus's oeuvre, both Christianity and its totalitarian successors refuse the restrained rebellion of Greek tragic characters.[132] Christianity, National Socialism, Stalinism, and capitalist liberal democracy are in the same way heedless of the devastations they wreak in the name of the futures they promise.[133] What I am contending, in line with this latter conception of Camus's thinking, is that Camus seeks to demonstrate the extent to which modern nihilisms try and fail to obscure the enduring reality of a Greek tragic world in which limits should not be violated.

Meursault in *The Stranger* is slotted into a plotline that destroys him, as tragic heroes are, but is largely indifferent to it. He little registers, bewails, and contests the nets that ensnare him. He is expressly a tragic hero *manqué*. Meursault seems to possess not even a repressed consciousness of moments of being. Up until the point at which he shoots another man, and even afterward, Meursault cannot fathom past or future losses, his own or others'. As Sartre finds in "An Explication of *The Stranger*" (1943), Meursault seems primarily to exist in "this succession of inert present moments"; for Sartre such immediacy demonstrates a kind of earthy candor, heroic rootedness, and existential realism.[134] Yet Meursault's is the timeless now of the absurd itself, unconscious and nonteleological, of the natural environment, of the sun-shattered landscape. He does not experience transformative moments because for all their rich, sensuous mooring in the present, such moments depend on a sense of past and future, of elapsing time; they are still spaces in the tide of life, safe havens, precious because their possessors feel their rarity and fragility, and wield them (remember and commemorate them) against linear time as tragic antagonist.

The famous conclusion to the novel's first section, its midway point and first of two apexes, is Meursault's much vexing commission of murder, his seemingly inexplicable, unnecessary, and unmotivated act, little comprehensible to Meursault himself. It is a decisive and irreversible occurrence that fails to make sense either as the culmination of prior plot points or as the culmination of a prior nexus of thought and feeling; it is an eerie moment of near nonbeing. For all the lyricism with which Camus depicts the scene – the passage has quite a breathtaking poetry – Meursault does not seem, here, to be the lyric subject, a lyric self constituted by a moment of quickened affect or self-knowledge:

> All I could feel were the cymbals of sunlight crashing on my forehead and, indistinctly, the dazzling spear flying up from the knife in front of me. The scorching blade slashed at my eyelashes and stabbed at my stinging eyes. That's when everything began to reel. The sea carried up a thick, fiery breath. It seemed to me as if the sky split open from one end to the other to rain down fire.[135]

Meursault's already circumscribed interiority is melting away entirely; he becomes a sensorium only, receptive to light and heat. Only at the section's close does he relay to us two lines of quasi-reflection, between which he recounts his further inexplicable action:

> I knew that I shattered the harmony of the day, the exceptional silence of a beach where I'd been happy. Then I fired four more times at the motionless body where the bullets lodged without leaving a trace. And it was like knocking four quick times at the door of unhappiness.[136]

It is this last line, with its ominous foreboding – its presentiment of future unhappiness – that seems so decidedly *out* of character. This simile seems too self-aware, too predictive, too conceptual for sun-and-sea Meursault. But blindly and without motive, he has sealed his fate, shooting four more times.

Even though he presages his passage into misfortune, even though he feels the loveliness of the day rent and spoiled, he does not feel motivated to fight for his own life during his trial. Even as he begins to speak aloud tirelessly in his cell, and to invoke and retrace past enjoyments in memory, resurrecting so many treasures – seeming to awaken, simultaneously, to voice and to personal history, to temporal consciousness – and even as he grows desperate to be spared the guillotine, his final epiphany appears a regressive disavowal of human time and human value. Meursault determines that "[n]othing, nothing mattered and I knew why" and that he had always been right to live as he did, in nearly unconscious and somnolent, preferably pleasurable, apathy, giving no thought to past or future.[137] Unless this is the disingenuous and anguished cry of a man who must persuade himself no longer to care about a world he has indeed come to love – because he must now lose it and that loss is unbearable – Meursault's final, "enlightened" return to the complacency with which he began reveals the extent to which his philosophical recognition of absurdity proves sterile and life-negating. It affords him only this rationale for self-satisfied indifference. Faced with the chaplain who insists upon God, Meursault denounces life as much as Camus, writing his university thesis on Saint Augustine and neo-Platonism, believes that Christianity does.

When Sartre in *Les temps modernes* accuses Camus of a self-absorbed embrace of ephemeral delights, akin to Meursault's, Sartre overlooks Meursault's frank and unnerving nihilism, the antithesis of Camus's tragic ethics. This was never Camus's conception of the consequences of contending with an absurd natural and cosmological history. It was only Meursault's. Camus resembles Meursault no more than Sartre resembles the fascist anti-Semite Lucien Fleurier, of his own *Childhood of a Leader*. Yet Alain Robbe-Grillet maintains in "Nature, Humanism, Tragedy"

(1958) that *The Stranger* does represent the querulous and apolitical tragedy of which Jeanson and Sartre accuse Camus. Robbe-Grillet writes that in the twentieth century "the novel is tragedy's chosen field" but that this mixed genre only resurrects anthropocentric humanism, showing characters hounded by a cruel God who expresses himself through wounding nature.[138] Robbe-Grillet finds in *The Stranger* a personified landscape persecuting Camus's hero and dooming him to death:

> The crucial scene of the novel affords the perfect image of a painful solidarity: the implacable sun is always "the same," its reflection on the blade of the knife the Arab is holding "strikes" the hero full in the face and "searches" his eyes, his hand tightens on the revolver, he tries to "shake off" the sun, he fires again, four times. "And it was – he says – as though I had knocked four times on the door of unhappiness."
>
> Absurdity, then, is really a form of tragic humanism. It is not an observation of the separation between man and things. It is a lover's quarrel, which leads to a crime of passion. The world is accused of complicity in a murder.[139]

Yet it is the impersonality, chanciness, and extrahuman endurance of nature that have become humanity's tragic antagonist in Camus's fiction; precisely because there is no tragedy from the rock's point of view, there is from Sisyphus's. Modernist tragedy is anti-anthropomorphic. The sun does precipitate Meursault's act, but it is not made to human measure. As Raymond Williams maintains, Camus's "sense of tragic absurdity" consists in the "recognition of incompatibilities: between the intensity of physical life and the certainty of death; between man's insistent reasoning and the non-rational world he inhabits."[140] Absurdity, for Camus, is what defies human beings' mythologizing, personifying tendencies; absurd nature has no love to withhold, nor any intention of ushering in fatal unhappiness. Absurdity is only tragic from a human point of view. Meursault is not, then, a tragic hero in Robbe-Grillet's sense – one for whom conflict still signifies underlying unity, the promise of reconciliation with a temperamental God, of "victory ... in being vanquished."[141] Nor is Meursault a tragic hero in Camus's sense, in which life's "incompatibilities" are recognized, painful, and insoluble.

Meursault does fail to comprehend "the separation between man and things" – not because he personifies nonhuman nature, but because he too much resembles it. He is more of a thermometer than a character: he is responsive principally to temperature, is controlled by climate. He burns, rages, and strikes as the sun does. In lieu of engaging in psychological realism – in lieu of depicting Meursault as mourning son, as French colonialist, or even as persecuted, universal Other – *The Stranger* proves nearly science fictional in its representation of this "man" possessed by the elements.[142] Whereas Robbe-Grillet blames a persistently humanist conspiracy between hero and nature for Meursault's act, Camus signals that it is Meursault's failure to retain his humanity before the sun's insistent inhumanity that occasions his killing. Meursault cares more for the scorching Algerian heat than for another's life or for his own. His sense of camaraderie lies with the "gentle indifference of the world" (la tendre indifférence du monde), "[f]inding it so much like myself – so like a brother, really"; indeed, he maintains that the sky's indifference vindicates him, justifies his denial of God as well as his conviction that "nothing mattered."[143] For all that he acknowledges past pleasures, Meursault ceases to fantasize a stay of execution at the novel's close. A mob can greet him at the guillotine with "cries of hate" – such is his final wish – and he will relish the crowd's antipathy, precisely because these cries will confirm his defection from the human and his allegiance to the nonhuman.[144] *The Stranger* is a cautionary tale, the portrait of a character with no sense of tragedy, who kills without compunction – as thoughtlessly as an absurd sun, and as the court that condemns him to death.

The Stranger, that is, is ethically productive precisely because it spurs readers to recoil from its first-person narrator. Blocked identification is the ethical modus operandi of the novel. Built around two climaxes, the novel is a double illustration of how not to be. Its first half ends with Meursault's sun-struck, lackadaisical murder of the unnamed Arab man on the beach. Its second denouement is Meursault's diatribe against the society that feels so hubristically confident in his execution. Camus painstakingly designs part one of the novel to establish the emotional and ethical barrenness of this imperturbable murderer. With no peep of resistance, Meursault falls into a plotline in which his neighbor Raymond abuses an Arab woman and threatens violence to her brother – and Meursault becomes Raymond's accomplice in misogyny and racism, and his instrument of death, shooting this man with Raymond's gun. Meursault's thralldom to his environment – natural and social – is mechanical and unquestioning. Then, in part two of the novel, Meursault continues blandly to reflect the world around him. He conveys to us that the legal system, the high seat of justice in French Algeria, does not in fact find him guilty for the right reason – because of his reflexive collaboration in the murderous heat of the day and in Raymond's murderous ideologies. Tellingly, the court instead transforms Meursault's crime from one of ethical lethargy into one of premeditated, self-aware, and monstrous intent. Meursault's absence of grief at Maman's funeral, his want of remorse on firing into a human body, are deployed by the prosecution not as evidence of Meursault's divorce from meaningful action but in order to miscast his character as the embodiment of all that is malevolent, organized, and inhumanely violent – a displaced figuration of the colonial state itself. The court makes Meursault in its image, labeling him its antithesis, and then scapegoats and excoriates him. Insofar as Meursault exposes the misinterpretations and moral hypocrisy of the court, and insofar as he refuses membership among them, we feel inclined to rally around and applaud him. At the same time, Meursault also reasserts his brotherhood with nothing and no one. He is still, indefatigably, the nihilist of part one, who cannot attach himself to any values, only to their absence. Our protagonist is not an "existential hero," an appraisal that commonly surfaces in the high school classroom. Meursault is a vehicle of exposé; he exposes a morally vacuous inner life and a totalitarian criminal justice system that likens its moral infallibility to God's.

For Meursault, then, a reckoning with the absurd does not launch a recognition of life's value and of its tragedy – a sense that life is no less valuable for its absurdity, but tragic because loving aspects of life makes for irremediable loss. It is this very awakening to a sense of precarious value that grounds both Camus's and Mrs. Ramsay's revolts, that constitutes their resistance to the absurd and galvanizes their commitment to happiness. Camus makes explicit his own rejection of nihilism and his sense that tragedy is coeval with a passion for life in his 1938 review of Sartre's *Nausea*:

> [I]t is the failing of a certain literature to believe that life is tragic because it is wretched. Life can be magnificent and overwhelming – that is its whole tragedy. Without beauty, love, or danger, it would be almost easy to live.... The realization that life is absurd cannot be an end, but only a beginning.[145]

Camus reiterates this stance in his interviews of 1945 and 1951: "But does nothing have a meaning? I have never believed that we could remain at this point.... Accepting the absurdity of everything around us is one step, a necessary experience: it should not become a dead end. It arouses a revolt that can become fruitful."[146] Camus shares Woolf's conception of the heightened, secular moment that "shines forth fleetingly," and finds life tragic because there *are* such moments of value to lose – whereas *Nausea*'s principal character, Antoine Roquentin, deems existence unrelentingly repugnant, anathema to the "perfect moments" he claims for art alone.[147] Unlike Proust's Marcel, for whom subjectivity is a site of full retrieval – all of Marcel's time is regained, none is lost – for Woolf and Camus, rare intervals, replete and unforgettable, must suffice for life's affirmation.[148] Camus records one such impression in his literary notebooks of 1936: "If a cloud covers up the sun and then lets it through again, the bright yellow of the vase of mimosa leaps out of the shade. The birth of this single flash of brightness is enough to fill me with a confused and whirling joy."[149] The endangerment of what he loves and finds beautiful then awakens his sense of tragedy: "If I still feel a grain of anxiety, it is at the thought of this unseizable moment slipping through my fingers like a ball of quicksilver.... A cloud passes and a moment grows pale. I die to myself."[150] To invoke Rei Terada's term, Camus does not "look away," as Nietzsche in *The Gay Science* recommends – "*looking away* shall be my only negation" – in response to the tick of the clock.[151] Camus faces anguishing ephemerality. He writes of "a delicate, transparent band of blue sky" whose "presence is a torture for the eyes and for the soul, because beauty is unbearable, drives us to despair, offering us for a minute the glimpse of an eternity that we should like to stretch out over the whole of time."[152] Like Hardy and Woolf, Camus does not avert his gaze as *The Birth of Tragedy* encourages, nor does he look and affirm continually, in all circumstances, delighting in transience, as mature Nietzsche counsels. These tragic writers look and feel Mrs. Ramsay's "impulse of terror," Camus's impulse to despair, then look again and feel Mrs. Ramsay's joy in the candlelit dinner party, Camus's in the sunlit sky and Mediterranean.[153] They brandish the one looking at the other, as Mrs. Ramsay "brandish[es] her sword at life," as the finest art for Camus "disputes reality, but does not hide from it."[154]

Two convictions, therefore, run throughout Camus's work: "the perpetual tension between beauty and pain" and "neither complete rejection nor complete acceptance of what is."[155] To feel the first – "ecstasy of joy punctuated by the sudden counterpunches" of sorrow – is to refrain from indifference, from nihilism, from absolute negation.[156] To feel the second is to refuse Nietzsche's indiscriminate affirmation of all aspects of life, for "[rebellion] says yes and no simultaneously. It is the rejection of one part of existence in the name of another part, which it exalts."[157] The rebel pits moments of happiness against absurdity, cruelty, and despair. For love of that beautiful patch of sky hemmed in by dark clouds, Camusian rebellion "protests, it demands, it insists that the outrage be brought to an end, and that what has up to now been built upon shifting sands should henceforth be founded on rock."[158] It yearns to say that "[o]f such moments ... the thing is made that endures," to command "Life stand still here."[159]

In Camus's view, art's task is necessarily double. It must inscribe life's tragedies and characters' heroic, Sisyphean resistance to them. Art must acknowledge a "real universe," independent of minds, indifferent to our wishes, as well as our responses to it: "The real universe which, by its radiance, calls forth bodies and statues receives from them at the same time a second light that determines the light from the sky."[160] Art must evoke the absurd Algerian sunlight, alien to all subjectivity, and the "second light" of the mind that refuses absurdity. "Bodies and statues" – creatures and their artifacts – in this way determine physical and sociocultural environments. It is this light of the mind that Mrs. Ramsay sheds at her dinner, forging and memorializing a moment solid "like a ruby."[161] Hers is the light that Meursault cannot shed upon the human being opposite him on the beach.

The "good modern nihilist" Clamence

Jean-Baptiste Clamence of *The Fall* (1956) represents the Camusian antihero desperate to elude tragedy's call to action. Beyond fate's curtailment of his freedom, Clamence fears that his own cowardice inhibits him – he wagers that he has failed to sustain revolt in the sphere of action permitted him. Confronted with irremediable disorder and suffering, Clamence does not meet them with moral courage, as do Camus's Oedipus and Sisyphus. Camus has invented, with serpentine subtlety, an egomaniacal yet self-loathing narrator who cannot bear his own ethical shortcomings. Because revolt's compromised but valiant action intimidates him, he is drawn to Christianity's rationalization of personal fault and to nihilistic politics' rationalizations of mass suffering. Here we see the birth of Christian modernity from the (unendurable) spirit of tragedy. Clamence's specific trouble is that he cannot exonerate himself for having made no move to intercede in a woman's suicide in Paris, and for having drunk a dying man's water in a prisoner-of-war camp. He abhors what he suspects to be his chronic weakness of character – what these fateful circumstances have revealed. He endeavors to undo his tragic lucidity and derides all freedom because of its restrictions, complications, and risks.

Clamence's titular fall is not into belief in original sinfulness. His is reversed, in Greek tragic fashion, into clear-eyed awareness of his bounded self-sovereignty. But this is why the notion of Christian fallenness, as well as the notion of state terror, appeal to him – to his mind, both universalize and account for his deficiencies. As Srigley has shown, both also promise apocalyptic solutions to human fallibility.[162] Clamence, then, promotes the idea that the depravity of the world is so pervasive that it is useless to counter it oneself. He lauds the notion of everyone's forced complicity in political violence because such widespread guilt requires a corrective beyond his means. It eliminates the need for rebellion. What good is the promotion of altruism, happiness, or love? Why exert yourself to diminish the sufferings of others? In the worldview Clamence endeavors to espouse, only redemption or successful revolutionary politics (triumphant remaking of the world) can address evils so vast and so entrenched. *The Fall* condemns this conclusion, however, and shows that even Clamence is not persuaded by it.

Self-exiled to Amsterdam, Clamence recites his former accomplishments and conquests, glories in them afresh, only to dazzle (he presumes) with his ensuing self-indictment: even as he had represented widows and orphans in the law courts, his goodness of heart had been feigned. He casts his recognition of this duplicity as a virtue that once again sets him above the brutishness of the stock variety of men. This wordsmith who so frankly owns his misconduct, his systematic degradation and humiliation of women, for instance, wishes to be understood as a saint of self-scrutiny. How admirable a feat, he suggests, is the diagnosis of one's own megalomania. At once Clamence convicts and stokes his narcissism. This strategy will serve him throughout his narrative; his narrative itself is a carefully executed strategy.

Having beguiled his listener with these preliminaries, Clamence discloses more of his past – for what has induced this access of insight? A laugh, he maintains, has initiated it. A hallucinated laugh that he has heard one night on the Pont des Arts in Paris; it seems to reach him from downriver, when no one is there. Clamence claims that he initially forgets the incident. Yet this moment, this "surprise," marks a definitive rupture in his complacency, his self-satisfaction, his assumption of easy dominance.[163] His image in the mirror, he relates, comes to seem to him "double," as if he wore a comedian's mask.[164] He no longer feels vastly powerful and complete. On occasion, the laughter even appears to ring out from inside him: "Once in a great while, I seemed to hear it within me.... I must admit that I ceased to walk along the Paris quays.... [I]ts benevolent, almost tender quality ... hurt me."[165] He begins to feel, too, that everyone is laughing at him:

> For a long time I had lived in the illusion of a general agreement, whereas, from all sides, judgments, arrows, mockeries rained upon me, inattentive and smiling. The day I was alerted I became lucid; I received all the wounds at the same time and lost my strength all at once. The whole universe then began to laugh at me.[166]

Lucidity proves his claim to faultless character, his vaunted strength, to be a sham. But this dawning awareness of his own reversal does not resemble that of Oedipus or Sisyphus, as Camus reads them. They are made to see their finite powers but continue to act nobly within a limited compass. Clamence grows increasingly averse to action.

At the novel's midpoint seems to come the climatic revelation of the incident that induced the laughter: Clamence believes that he has overheard a woman committing suicide on the Pont Royal. This episode occurs two or three years, he explains, prior to his hearing the laughter on the Pont des Arts. He passes the woman dressed in black on the bridge and begins walking eastward along the quay toward Saint Michel, cigarette in hand. He then hears what he interprets to be a body hitting the water, and hears a cry that, like the laughter, seems to come from downstream. He does not turn, see her, attempt to save her, or report the incident; he is paralyzed. We are left to wonder if he could have rescued her, with the space between them, with the current and the cold. Was he under moral obligation to take this chance? Perhaps it is first and foremost a situation that Clamence cannot control that appalls him. Following the laughter, however, he comes to laud slavery – because, he says, restricted agency means no moral responsibility. Without freedom, he imagines, the guilt that he feels would be less shameful and less lonesome: "on the bridges of Paris I, too, learned that I was afraid of freedom. So hurray for the master, whoever he may be, to take the place of heaven's law."[167] Clamence pretends that he would welcome the atrocities of history. If heaven's law has made guilt congenital, political tyranny can render altruism (he hopes) impossible.

In his final, most feverish avowals, Clamence then returns to a past seemingly prior even to the woman's plunge. Clamence tells us that he once found himself in a prisoner-of-war camp in Tunisia, during the Second World War. In France, "[t]he French army ... merely asked me to take part in the retreat"; he went south "tempted by the Resistance," and then crossed to North Africa with the vague idea of reaching England.[168] In desultory fashion, he became involved with a woman whose own clandestine activities, unbeknownst to him, issued in his arrest. Once in the camp, he encountered a fervent antifascist, a "Du Guesclin type," whom he claims, unprecedentedly, to have loved.[169] What transpires is that Clamence drinks the water of a dying man; he insists that had Du Guesclin, the courageous, principled warrior, still been alive, he (Clamence) would have resisted longer. It is in this uncontrollable camp environment that a sense of unshakable fault and powerlessness seems first to overtake him.

Having armored himself, then, against charges of hypocrisy – by numbering himself among the world's offenders – Clamence curses all humanity, in an attempt to entice his listener into agreement:

> I have no more friends; I have nothing but accomplices. To make up for this, their number has increased; they are the whole human race.[170]

> Moreover, we cannot assert the innocence of anyone, whereas we can state with certainty the guilt of all. Every man testifies to the crime of all the others – that is my faith and my hope.[171]

This is indeed the desperate hope and faith of a guilt-monger who insinuates that every human endeavor, individual or collective, is corrupt. He is the animation of Sartre's and Jeanson's unflattering portrait of Camus – the narcissistic judge who should, in their estimation, be ashamed of his arguments for eluding action.

Camus brings to life this self-absorbed, craven, and ineffectual moralizer. Rather than Camus's mea culpa, however, this exposé of Clamence seems a kind of bluff-calling: only such a man, now attached to no one and condemning all, could embrace despotism as Clamence does. Debarati Sanyal argues that, far from resembling Camus, Clamence embodies the ideology of state terror, and his language itself is totalitarian:

> The totalitarian state creates its subjects in its own image and legitimates its violence through the imposition of universal guilt.... The narrative's oscillating frames of reference (Paris, Amsterdam, Jerusalem, Auschwitz, Hiroshima, North Africa) underscore the pervasion of this violent representational logic to finally disclose its dormant presence in the everyday practices of even a liberal democracy.[172]

Clamence's very apology for totalitarian violence is what Camus, in *The Rebel*, denounces and ascribes to fascism and revolution both. As Srigley, too, argues, Clamence himself ascribes such totalizing control and indoctrination to bourgeois liberal democracies.[173]

Certainly, Sartre's goals and motivations bear no resemblance to Clamence's, but how telling, Camus's novel implies, if Sartre should find himself espousing a Soviet cause that sanctions the same brutality that this mad weaver of fictions claims to desire. Shoshana Felman reads Clamence in this vein, as emblematic of a refusal of witnessing and a condoning of history's horrors. Felman connects Camus's disagreement with Sartre over Stalinism to this novelistic indictment, in her view, of Sartre's silence and inaction in relation to Soviet labor camps:

> While Sartre thinks Camus has failed as witness since he has ceased to be the witness of a cure [as he was in *The Plague*], Camus thinks it is Sartre

who is failing as a witness, since he neglects to witness and to take into account the labor camps in Soviet Russia, and fails to recognize through them the non-cessation of the Plague. While Sartre sees Camus as a *man of the past* who fails to recognize the progress made by history and thus essentially *fails to march toward the future*, Camus sees Sartre as a man who, in the name not of the real future but of the prophetic gesture – and projection – of an ideology, fails to *recognize the present* and thus *denies*, specifically, *the implications of the past*.... Camus *puts side by side* the blindness and contradictions of historicism and the blindness and the contradictions of antihistoricism. "He who believes *nothing but history*" is walking toward terror," warns Camus [in his response to Jeanson in *Les temps modernes*]; but at the same time, "he who believes *nothing of history*" is authorizing terror."[174]

Felman reads Clamence, who calls himself "an enlightened advocate of slavery," as an embodiment of the failure to question and to contest history that Camus himself exposes in *The Rebel*.[175] But it is also the case that Clamence is not really taken in by totalitarian apologetics; it is not that he "believes nothing but history," convinced of its "enlightened" rationales for violence. Nor does he "believe nothing of history," denying its stakes and casualties. He knows that oppression is pervasive and indefensible; he has no faith in the benevolence of authoritarian philosophies. "Enlightened" in this sense, he knowingly applauds their criminality.

Setting Clamence's prisoner-of-war camp in North Africa, Camus also pointedly includes French colonialism in his novel's catalogue of atrocities. He draws together multiple histories of lethal imprisonment. From 1955 to 1961, during the Algerian war of independence, France forcibly relocated millions of Algerians to *camps de regroupement* (regroupment camps) in Algeria and France:

> [In 1957] the discretionary special powers were extended to the metropole and camps such as Larzac or Rivesaltes interned over 14,000 Algerians suspected of harbouring ties with the Front de Libération National (FLN). But in Algeria, a network of underground repression camps was already well in place, and as early as 1955, entire sectors of the rural population had been displaced into regroupment camps in an effort to isolate insurgents.[176]

Sanyal remarks, too, that "Camus was one of the first to articulate the ironic proximities between Nazi Germany and the post-war French republic; his writings on Algeria in the press of the day opened a dialogue between these two repressed histories of occupation and racialized violence."[177] Clamence, on the contrary, connects and purports to defend these genocidal regimes.

They are his alibi for moral torpor, yet even to him his words ring hollow. Even Clamence experiences his wanting ethical and political engagement – his vapid egotism, the "sclerosis" of his indifference, his pleas for tyranny – as a failure and as a malady.[178] Clamence "could not forgive" himself this disinterest in others' sufferings; the judgment came from "in me."[179] He craves escape: "No more emotions!"[180] But he cannot forget or overcome this "indifference that spoiled everything": "In short, we should like, at the same time, to cease being guilty and yet not to make the effort of cleansing ourselves."[181] He is coming undone at the novel's close: "I'm not weeping.... But when you don't like your own life, when you know that you must change lives, you don't have any choice, do you? What can one do to become another? Impossible."[182]

He hungers, then, for a fellow coward who also yearns for a second chance to save himself, by saving another:

> Then please tell me what happened to you one night on the quays of the Seine and how you managed never to risk your life. You yourself utter the words that for years have never ceased echoing through my nights and that I shall at last say through your mouth: "O young woman, throw yourself into the water again so that I may a second time have the chance of saving both of us!" A second time, eh, what a risky suggestion! Just suppose, *cher maître*, that we should be taken literally? We'd have to go through with it. Brr...! The water's so cold! But let's not worry! It's too late now. It will always be too late. Fortunately![183]

Clamence has condemned himself because he has "managed not to risk his life," on the quay or anywhere else. He should like his interlocutor to confess an equal incapacity for selflessness and self-sacrifice. He hopes to be arrested, executed, and proven to bear everyone's likeness: "I would be decapitated.... Above the gathered crowd, you would hold up my still warm head, so that they could recognize themselves in it and I could again dominate – an exemplar. All would be consummated."[184] Clamence's is the opposite of Meursault's closing wish for "consummation": Meursault maintains that "[f]or everything to be consummated, for me to feel less alone," he would require "cries of hate," exile from human company, communion with the indifferent sky.[185] On the contrary, Clamence begs for entry into a human community, and all that he can permit himself to envision is a confederacy of narcissists powerless to intercede on behalf of others – prohibited by some master from doing so. Clamence is anguished and broken in a way that Meursault is not; "indifference" for Clamence (his own) is neither tenable nor "gentle."[186]

If it is Meursault who, in Camus's most famous negative example, fails to rebel against absurdity and never becomes fully alive to tragedy, it is Clamence who, in Camus's most sophisticated negative example, is never reconciled to dangerous and rebellious action within tragic confines. Camus's fiction depicts, then, not only tragic heroes and heroines, those who contend with oppression, bent on making what strides they can toward compensatory happiness and justice, but characters whose ethically disastrous, tragedy-averse philosophies leave no happiness or justice in sight.

CHAPTER 5

Beckett
Against Nihilism

The Unnamable: "alleviations of flight from self"

The narrator of Beckett's *The Unnamable* (1953) vehemently refuses to weep for his undeserved, undisclosed pains. He does not want to suffer them. But unlike Camus's Meursault, he registers and indicts them unceasingly. When the ambient "voices" of normative culture demand that he embrace life, he recoils from this directive; still he fails to silence them.[1] Meursault's somnolent conscription into others' narratives of him – and his one eruption of rage, followed by his return to indifference – are not viable courses of action for the Unnamable. Nor can he applaud his tormentors, as Camus's Clamence seeks to do; Clamence tries and fails to be the tyrant's apologist. The Unnamable cannot sign on to Clamence's devil's advocacy. Instead, the Unnamable scorns purveyors of pain. He likewise condemns all attempts to rationalize or to minimize his and others' pains. In a concerted manner, he spurns both the worldviews of tragedy (in which you suffer for no good reason) and of counter-tragic theology (in which you suffer for a reason) and counter-tragic philosophy (in which you vanquish suffering). He denounces both unmerited torments and the philosophical and theological commitments that endeavor to justify them. Erik Tonning describes Beckett's refusal of both terrestrial and celestial narratives of deliverance as follows:

> Beckett, then, may be said to accept the basic terms of Schopenhauer's description of the phenomenal world as a prison-house of being, a cycle of perpetual torture; he simply intensifies the philosopher's pessimism by insisting that there is *no* possible salvation or "way out.". . . Beckett's vehement ethical resistance to the Christian "answer" of eschatological hope fundamentally colors his reading of both Eastern and Western mystical traditions, as well as his reading of Romantic transcendent yearning, or "Sehnsucht."[2]

Possessed of this conviction – that there is "*no* possible salvation" – Beckett composes one of the twentieth century's most trenchant exposés of the sheer impossibility of evading tragic knowledge. The Unnamable retreats from Christian, Romantic, and mystical modes of doing so; his denial of any and all sentient experience, his own strategy to nullify pain, proves impracticable as well. His ineliminable discontinuity with the "nothing" that he craves is proof of his still existent character – of character despite itself, bent on imagining its own extinction.[3]

Such an assessment of *The Unnamable* counters readings of Beckett that hold this narrator to be in search of mystical self-dissolution and word-lessness. Chris Ackerley outlines Marius Buning's foundational studies in this vein:

> [Buning] argued the value of considering Beckett's work in the dark light of "classic negative or apophatic mysticism." Beckett's insistence on dispos-session, self-annihilation, solitude, silence ("in short 'nothingness'"), he considered, intimated equally the mystical experience.[4]

Buning himself references "Helene L. Baldwin's *Samuel Beckett's Real Silence* (1981), which claims that 'the progressive stripping down of the self which takes place in many of Beckett's works is ... in fact the "negative way" of mysticism, whose object is to break through the bonds of time and place.'"[5] In these interpretations, repudiation of terrestrial "voice" is a marker of negative theology. Shira Wolosky's *Language Mysticism* elaborates three other "antiwordly" appraisals of Beckett: that he is a "failed Christian or a 'mystic manqué'"; that he is a gnostic opposed to the material world, in search of its antithesis; and that he is a "secular nihilist" who anticipates "void" instead of "fullness" in the "transcendent nothing."[6] Common to these analyses, Wolosky argues, is the conviction that Beckett subscribes to a "metaphysical hierarchy" "that assumes a realm beyond time, beyond space, beyond physical and multiple conditions, to be the realm of truth."[7] Beckett is presumed to espouse a "scale of values that asserts eternity over time and unity over multiplicity, and that excludes the body, externality, and tempo-rality as alien to true, unitary, eternal truth."[8] In these readings, Beckettian characters are said to be toiling to "escape from the prison of time and words into the timeless and changeless condition of Selfhood."[9] Words are the paradigmatic hindrance to this "way out": "In such a system, language stands for the life of the body, of space, of time, of division and individuation."[10] Because language delineates and participates in "difference from unity," the "defeat of language forms the central thesis in study after study of Beckett."[11] Beckettian "silence" comes to mean transcendence of earthly existence.

For other critics, this coveted "silence" refers to unmediated knowledge of the terrestrial world. Beckett and his characters are designated as those who long to relinquish words in order to apprehend their material surroundings more directly. In this regard, Ackerley remarks on "the importance to Beckett of Fritz Mauthner's critique of language."[12] Shane Weller details Mauthner's conviction that "all language is metaphorical and that we never manage to get beyond these metaphors to the extralinguistic reality to which they are supposed, albeit indirectly, to refer."[13] Mauthner is more radical than Wittgenstein, Weller maintains, because he denies that any verbal statement can represent any worldly fact: "Mauthner insists that language as such is irredeemably unreliable, and that no form of linguistic purification can overcome this intrinsic unreliability."[14] Neither symbolism nor Joyce's "apotheosis of the word" can surmount this mendacity.[15] Little wonder that such falsehood, on this theory, would provoke characters' resolution "to abolish the word to break through to the world."[16] As Ackerley writes, characters' disenchantment with words' anthropocentrism and anthropomorphism would precipitate "what Carla Locatelli has termed 'unwording,' the *via negativa* that begins because escape from language is felt as an imperative."[17]

The language skeptic, however, meets with failure: "Yet 'unwording' proves that escape is impossible."[18] This for Mauthner is the limitation that words impose. While Bertrand Russell maintained the opposite, that we can pass from embodied subjectivity to knowledge of the world independent of us, this scholarship holds that for Beckett and his characters language is an insuperable barrier to reality.[19] To expose the referential poverty of words, then, in an effort to move beyond them, only to remain caught in their snare, is the Sisyphean labor that Dirk Van Hulle and Shane Weller identify in *The Unnamable*:

> *The Unnamable* engages directly with Mauthner's conviction that *only through language* can language be undone.... Beckett arguably places his entire text under the sign of Mauthner's *Sprachkritik* not only thematically, but also stylistically. Unwording here becomes, for the first time, not only the *matter*, but also the very *manner* of the literary work. In this respect, *The Unnamable* both anticipates and makes possible – albeit after considerable difficulties – the unwording procedures that characterize Beckett's later prose works.[20]

Rather than prosecuting an impassioned battle with undue suffering, the Unnamable is presumed to engage in an epistemological "attempt to reach what is described in the novel as 'le vrai silence' [the true silence], which is to say that silence which *is* the real beyond the language veil."[21] Here "the real" is a physical world that lies beyond human sense perception and symbolic representation.

Against these arguments for the Unnamable's concerted pursuit of "the real," whether otherworldly or worldly, I contend that the Unnamable labors unavailingly to elude "the real," understood as exclusively bodily and verbal. His body is proof of real, nonlinguistic pains. His language is impotent to palliate them. He hungers to renounce his body and his words in order to neutralize the real suffering that they occasion. He finds this visceral desire frustrated. More than God or nonverbal truth, Beckett's fiction unceremoniously dismisses the prospect of painless ecstasy: "Watt's attempt to 'eff the ineffable' is disastrous; quests in the *Three Novels* and *Texts for Nothing* end in an impasse; and *How It Is* concludes that the impulse toward the light is finally 'all balls.'"[22] The more Beckett's narrator wages war on individuation, embodiment, and language, the more he aims to sever himself from all experience. Animosity toward words and sweeping doubt are his instruments of pain management. While he meets with little success, this shunning of thought and sensation is his goal. This chapter, then, reads *The Unnamable* as a warning against such attempted self-abnegation. This chapter proceeds to contend that Beckett rewrites *The Unnamable*'s self-effacing protagonist in his late novella *Company* (1979), revisiting the Unnamable's tactics but supplying an alternative to them. Now Beckett's lonesome narrator speaks of himself in the second and third person not to flee self-knowledge but to people an otherwise intolerable solitude. Beckett affords this character lyrical bursts of feeling and recollection that lead him toward *anagnorisis*: "That was I. That was I then."[23] Here we see that Beckett participates in modernism's modest and fleeting affirmations.

Beckett tells us in his early study of Proust that "[t]ragedy is not concerned with human justice."[24] Tragedy is not concerned, in Beckett's view, with a "miserable expiation of a codified breach of a local arrangement, organized by the knaves for the fools."[25] Tragedy is not concerned with legal jeopardy or moral fault. These juridical and psychological measures of culpability are not the substance of the genre. Instead, Beckett recurs to Athenian tragedy's religious model of guilt: it swallows you up and defines you, despite you, and to spite you. Beckett writes that the tragic hero commits "the original and eternal sin ... of having been born."[26] Beckett implies that it is the origin of species rather than a transgression of God's law that seals human fate. Like his characters, Beckett does not accept the Christian postulate of original sinfulness and a fallen world as causal or moral explanation for human suffering. Beckett's fiction instead evokes a mortal sentence conferred at birth, without rationale: a congenital tragedy. Beckett's trouble is the Nietzschean trouble of being individuated at all. But Beckett does not share Nietzsche's "joyous hope that the spell of individuation can be broken."[27]

While Aristotle meant reassuringly to eliminate senseless pain from tragedy, the Unnamable's wrathful, life-denouncing logorrhea is his reply to such pain. Jonathan Lear presents the Aristotelian turn away from sufferings of obscure provenance as follows:

> The world of tragic events must, Aristotle repeatedly insists, be rational. The subject of tragedy may be a good man, but he must make a mistake which rationalizes his fall. The mere fall of a good man from good fortune to bad fortune for no reason at all isn't tragic, it's disgusting.... It is significant that, for Aristotle, *Oedipus Rex* is the paradigm tragedy rather than, say, *Antigone*. For the point of tragedy, in Aristotle's eyes, is not to portray a world in which a person through no fault of his own may be subject to fundamentally irreconcilable and destructive demands.... [T]he world remains a rational, meaningful place in which a person can conduct himself with dignity. Even in tragedy, perhaps especially in tragedy, the fundamental goodness of man and world are reaffirmed.[28]

Beckett's character is no Aristotelian. Instead of a fall "for no reason at all" that "isn't tragic, it's disgusting," in Beckett's fiction the inexplicable fall – into humanity, into mortal pain – is the quintessence of tragedy. And rather than disallow disgust with it, Beckett suggests that such disgust is an appropriate response to suffering that is unwarranted. His novel also suggests, however, that to turn against the whole of existence because of repugnance to part of it is to go down the path of nihilism. It is Beckett's narrator in *The Unnamable*, epitomizing such total repulsion, who wishes to flee from consciousness of himself as a fragile human subject – and who might in turn spur readers to balk at his suicidal practices.

The Unnamable is a 52,000-word monologue without a story. Beckett's speaker, as if channeling the lesson of Woolf's brackets in *To the Lighthouse*, introduces a plight whose origins are impenetrable, and if known would not satisfy: "No matter how it happened," he says of his condition on page one of the novel.[29] All appears ill-explained and contradictory: "I seem to speak, it is not I, about me, it is not about me."[30] What narrator, we are compelled to ask, disowns his narrating "I," devalues his every assertion, and insists that his existence cannot be verified? His first-person interior monologue seems to him no guarantee of authentic self-expression. But how can he be wholly fraudulent, ventriloquized, or inhuman, as he variously surmises, and still articulate the murmuring opposition of some truer "I," demanding expression and subsequent peace? As Stanley Cavell finds in *The Claim of Reason* both "skepticism and tragedy" can issue in the refusal to own "that I am I."[31] For the Unnamable, as Cavell puts it, "the alternative to my acknowledgement" of a besieged and vulnerable self "is not my ignorance of him but my avoidance of him, call it my denial of him."[32]

Misleadingly, the Unnamable initially presents the recovery of his first-person perspective as his aim. Our speaker at first behaves as if he has mislaid his memories, rather than actively repudiated them. His preoccupation at first appears to be the reestablishment of identity: "I. Who might that be?"[33] He refers to himself as disembodied, or as a head only, and reiterates that his insatiable desire, his determinative compulsion, is to materialize more fully and speak his way to greater self-understanding.[34] Indeed, he tells us that a chorus of insinuating voices insists that he certify his past and person once and for all. His supposed desire is to gratify them: to articulate self and surroundings satisfactorily, and in this way find relief from further questing speech. He says optimistically, "I do not despair of one day sparing me, without going silent" – that is, he does not despair of finishing his investigation by suitably voicing his backstory to these listeners.[35] His opening pretense is that he, too, hopes one day to possess the information expected of a narrator:

> And that day, I don't know why, I shall be able to go silent, and make an end, I know it.... Then it would be a life worth having, a life at last. My speech-parched voice at rest would fill with spittle, I'd let it flow over and over, happy at last, dribbling with life, my pensum ended, in the silence.... I was given a pensum, at birth perhaps, as a punishment for having been born perhaps.... Strange task, which consists in speaking of oneself.[36]

Here he entertains the notion that were he to affix his "I" to the character and story that a "master" provides for him, "whose burden is roughly to the effect that I am alive," he would at last be contented.[37] He would "dribble with life," his identity confirmed and further narration superfluous. This would be comedic closure: narrating himself into a man "happy at last," his pensum completed.

But the Unnamable also avers with ferocity that these invasive voices expect the impossible. To behave as they command, he would be obliged to evince the following:

> Warmth, ease, conviction, the right manner, as if it were my own voice, pronouncing my own words, words pronouncing me alive, since that's how they want me to be, I don't know why, with their billions of quick, there trillions of dead, that's not enough for them, I too must contribute my little convulsion, mewl, howl, gasp and rattle, loving my neighbour and blessed

> with a reason.... The same old sour teachings I can't change a tithe of.
> A parrot, that's what they're up against, a parrot.... [I must] look as if
> I mean what I'm saying.[38]

The Unnamable rebels against this "same old sour" identity formation. This
pedagogy, were he to parrot it, would bless him with a reason to live, to die,
to act – a comprehensive characterological rulebook – but he claims that to
adopt it would be self-perjury. To overflow with ebullient life would be a
sham. He does not, in fact, believe in such counter-tragic vitality, he says;
life is suffering, not satisfaction. Life must be avoided, not accepted.

Although he grants that his lava of words could cease if this pantomime
were to seem to him credible – such is the tempting bargain – he
ultimately lambasts the voices' socially regulatory coercion:

> the madness of having to speak and not being able to, except of things that
> don't concern me, that don't count, that I don't believe, that they have
> crammed me full of ... Ah a nice state they have me in, but still I'm not
> their creature, not quite, not yet.... It's a poor trick that consists in
> ramming a set of words down your gullet on the principle that you can't
> bring them up without being branded as belonging to their breed. But I'll
> fix their gibberish for them. I never understood a word of it in any case, not
> a word of the stories it spews, like gobbets in a vomit.[39]

He cannot lastingly imagine and does not want full inscription within a
supposedly intelligible narrative. He does not want to belong to the species
possessed of "their gibberish" and its stories – "their breed." He is now
incensed by the expectation that he will eventually speak in a manner
pleasing to these voices: "having to speak" of "who I am, where I am" on
their terms.[40] He finds himself "not being able to," never deploying words
that feel to him representative and right – indeed, the requisite words, he
asserts, only prevent communication of his condition (pain) and his true
desire (to be rid of it). He vows that "[n]othing will remain of all the lies
they have glutted me with."[41]

He mounts an insurrection against their false promise of happiness, as
he now sees it. He will not pretend to coincide with the character assigned
him, called "Mahood" – that nearly recognizable man, that nearly human
specimen, as close to normative manhood as they can push him. If the
pensum allotted to him at birth is to accept the role of Mahood – to own,
explain, and endorse this role in the customary manner – he will not do it.
He comes to assert that only the silence of a voiceless void will save him
from these intrusive fabricators. The Unnamable passes from an inclination to mollify the voices, to play along with them, to a commitment to
exterminate them, to refuse their definition of personhood:

I'll scatter them, and their miscreated puppets.... Do they consider me so plastered with their rubbish that I can never extricate myself, never make a gesture but their cast must come to life? But within, motionless, I can live, and utter me, for no ears but my own. They loaded me down with their trappings and stoned me through the carnival. I'll sham dead now, whom they couldn't bring to life, and my monster's carapace will rot off me. But it's entirely a matter of voices, no other metaphor is appropriate. They've blown me up with their voices, like a balloon, and even as I collapse it's them I hear. Who, them?... Ah but the little murmur of unconsenting man, to murmur what it is their humanity stifles, the little gasp of the condemned to life, rotting in his dungeon garroted and racked, to gasp what it is to have to celebrate banishment, beware.[42]

This "little murmur" and "little gasp" are the Unnamable's "unconsenting" mutiny: he feels "condemned" to life and will not pretend otherwise. "To murmur" that "their humanity stifles" him is now his duty; he is obliged "to gasp" what it is to "have to" rally around "banishment" from their ilk. His exile from "their" world is transformed into a dissident's threat: "beware."

The Unnamable's patent commitment to nay-saying, in Theodor Adorno's view, is a political statement unto itself. If contemporary thought is de facto collaboration in atrocity, a mixture of witting and hapless complicity (as Clamence fears), then wholesale renunciation of such a world *is* moral action. In Adorno's reading, the novel rightly says "no" to all that currently exists – such that readers might hunger for wholly new praxis. For Adorno, Beckett razes the social world so that readers might reconceive it. To denounce the entirety of the current state of affairs is to compel us to dream another – and to abstain from whitewashing status quo horrors. For Adorno, morally motivated antagonism to society is the first step to rebuilding it. Simon Critchley describes the Adornian defense of cleansing negation as follows:

the most common and banal accusation levelled at Beckett's work is that it is apolitical and nihilistic because it lacks any of the critical social content evident, say, in the theatre of Brecht or Sartre. Yet, Adorno shockingly suggests that Beckett's work is the *only* appropriate response to the Holocaust, more so than direct witness accounts, precisely because it is not part of the manifest content of Beckett's work, as if it were subject to a *Bilderverbot* [image ban]. What is being alluded to here ... is Adorno's belief that the best modernist artworks, like Beckett's, in their aesthetic autonomy and their refusal of meaning (hence the superficial accusation of nihilism) function as determinate negations of contemporary society and can give the formal semblance of a society free from domination. Beckett's

work successfully negotiates the dialectic between the necessary autonomy
of modernist art and the function of social criticism *not* by raising its voice
against society or protesting against the obvious injustice of the Holocaust,
but rather by *elevating social criticism to the level of form*. This means that
Beckett's work, in its steadfast refusal to mean something – a refusal of
meaning that is still achieved by way of dramatic or novelistic form –
exhibits an autonomy that, far from conspiring with apolitical decadence
or "nihilism," gives an indication of the transformative political praxis from
which it abstains, namely "the production of a right or just life.". . . . [A]s
Adorno astutely points out, what seems like Stoicism on Beckett's part
("I can't go on, I'll go on") is "a legacy of action" that "silently screams that
things should be otherwise. Such nihilism implies the opposite of an
identification with the Nothing."[43]

Adorno lauds Beckett's characters for their dissent, treating it as a potent
call to action – a call for desperately needed and wholly new politics that
has yet to materialize. The Unnamable's wanting connection to the world
might make us miss it, crave it, feel its needfulness, provided that the
"same old sour teachings" do not govern social relations – do not produce
more parrots force-fed stories, identical men cast in plaster, balloon-people
inflated with the ubiquitous voices' hot air. Adorno sees this ethical
provocation in Beckett's sweeping evacuation of social content from his
narrators' speech. Beckett unleashes a gaping negativity that screams for
something else, something better.

Beckett's nonconforming narrator, however, passes beyond social critique. He aims to negate even the consciousness – his own – that performs
such abstention from contemporary history. Swallowing and regurgitating
social content, argues the Unnamable, precludes his putting an end to the
voices' promptings in the only way that he can tolerate: ceasing to be
altogether. To "put an end to it" means to exempt himself from their
kind – their social *and* biological kind.[44] It means not "dribbling with life"
on any terms.[45] Having eschewed social indoctrination, the Unnamable
still confronts a "worstward" fate, laid bare, that he feels compelled to keep
at bay: "And but suppose, instead of suffering less than the first day, or no
less, [one] suffers more and more, as time flies.... Eh?"[46] It is the
accumulation of time and the pain that time uncovers that appalls him:
"the question may be asked, off the record, why time doesn't pass, doesn't
pass from you, why it piles up all about you, instant on instant, on all sides,
deeper and deeper, thicker and thicker, your time, others' time, the time of
the ancient dead and the dead yet unborn, why it buries you grain by
grain."[47] The Unnamable not only sides against the voices championing
Mahood but forms common cause with a rival figment who counsels him

to gain "quittance" of time entirely, by committing suicide: "Come come, a little cooperation please, finish dying, it's the least you might do."[48] Picture yourself buried alive by time in order to motivate and precipitate self-destruction, whispers this other advisor. The Unnamable praises and gravitates toward this "other voice, of him who does not share this passion for the animal kingdom."[49] The Unnamable's rejection of the "wrong" words – in Adorno's view, the language of fascism, of the concentration-ary – passes into a rejection of all symbolic representation. The Unnamable comes to want all possible experience "out of sight and mind."[50] Having disavowed a certain normative identity, its hubris and its dogmas of supremacy – "Pupil Mahood, repeat after me, Man is a higher mammal. I couldn't" – the Unnamable tries to disavow sentient being per se ("the animal kingdom").[51]

Philosopher Emil Cioran, Beckett's admirer and contemporary, articulates this same renunciation in *On the Heights of Despair* (1934): "As far as I am concerned, I resign from humanity. I no longer want to be, nor can still be, a man."[52] To object to playing Mahood, Cioran recognizes, is to enter a tragic universe: one devoid of Mahood's "higher" purposes and privileges. Here the heights are of despair. Such lucidity, Cioran sees, may issue in the desire for diminished consciousness, for not being. Rather than Camusian revolt that finds a new basis for going on, those small nonnarrative happinesses that nourish tragic subjects, a truly nihilistic anti-Mahood will pose Cioran's question: "When all the current reasons – moral, esthetic, religious, social, and so on – no longer guide one's life, how can one sustain life without succumbing to nothingness?"[53] Cioran, too, sides against self-recognition in the absence of these traditional crutches: "Nobody would dare look at himself in the mirror, because a grotesque, tragic image would mix in the contours of his face with stains and traces of blood, wounds which cannot be healed, and unstoppable streams of tears."[54] "What meaning," Cioran asks, "is there in the tragic suffering of a man for whom everything is ultimately nothing and whose only law in this world is agony?"[55] For the Unnamable, too, terror gives rise to thought and thought fails to subdue the terror that prompted it: "I only think, if that is the name for this vertiginous panic as of hornets smoked out of their nest, once a certain degree of terror has been exceeded," says the Unnamable.[56] He therefore prefers feats of imagination that aim to extinguish rather than intensify sensation: "For sometimes I confuse myself with my shadow.... And often I went on looking without flinching until, ceasing to be, I ceased to see."[57] At sunset, he imagines himself a shadow; when the light is gone, then so is "he." Yet he views the situation in a backward and dissociative manner. It is not "ceasing to be" that occasions his no longer seeing. It is his projection of his person onto the shadow, and his ceasing to behold it, that affords him the pleasing illusion of disappearance.

Losing Species: From Mahood to Worm

Toward the end of *The Unnamable*, Beckett's speaker entertains another fantasy of quelled consciousness. He introduces his vegetative test subject, Worm, who has neither sensation nor emotion nor insight. A kind of primal oblivion envelops Worm and anesthetizes him against suffering. The Unnamable describes Worm as "[o]ne alone turned towards the all-impotent, all-nescient," adopting Hardy's term.[58] "Before Life and After" (1909) is Hardy's own exploration of insentience, of "nescience":

> A time there was – as one may guess
> And as, indeed, earth's testimonies tell –
> Before the birth of consciousness,
>   When all went well.
>
> None suffered sickness, love, or loss,
> None knew regret, starved hope, or heart-burnings;
> None cared whatever crash or cross
>   Brought wrack to things.
>
> If something ceased, no tongue bewailed,
> If something winced and waned, no heart was wrung;
> If brightness dimmed, and dark prevailed,
>   No sense was stung.
>
> But the disease of feeling germed,
> And primal rightness took the tinct of wrong;
> Ere nescience shall be reaffirmed
>   How long, how long?[59]

Worm is turned toward – or returned to – this "primal rightness" and lies motionless and passive. The "disease of feeling" has not yet "germed" in him. Worm has not yet entered any germline as a feeling creature. Instead, the Unnamable has "reaffirmed" nescience, a vision of the organism "before the birth of consciousness," as "earth's testimonies tell," when nothing near to manhood adorned the tree of life.

Such a creature as Worm is powerless, but this want of agency cannot trouble him. "Before Mahood," the Unnamable theorizes, "there were others like him, of the same breed and creed, armed with the same prong.

But Worm is the first of his kind."[60] Worm is envisaged as an alternative, creedless species, set apart from the familiar, stock variety whose distinguishing feature is its sadistically administered dogmas. Worm is valorized, set above spurned Mahood. Worm emerges as the most enviable of entities. Imagined devolution to unconscious form – before life or after – is presented here as a fresh mode of dubiously realizable being.

Critically, however, the Unnamable imagines that even Worm will be hammered into human shape against his will. The Unnamable admits that Worm, too, will be molested by insinuating voices. Like his inventor, Worm will be coerced irrevocably into self-awareness – will face extreme pressure to become Mahood. Despite the coma-like tranquility of his den, Worm will be expected to take on flesh, to perceive, navigate, and contemplate the larger world, to live and to die in the common way. Even he will not be "spared by the mad need to speak, to think, to know where one is, where one was, during the wild dream, up above, under the skies, venturing forth at night."[61] Unsolicited demands from without will force upon him this defining "transit . . . from darkness to light."[62] The slightest notice of a whispering sound, the barest recognition of the external world, promises the end of Worm's slumber, his exodus from the primordial pit, and an onslaught of troubles. Incipient perception is the first damning marker of one "condemned to life."[63] In the Unnamable's imagining, cries and flickers bruise Worm's inchoate sensibility, and when raw sound fills his head, some irreversible chemistry occurs, generating emotive responses; next comes receptivity to language. Worm will evolve through stages of sensation and self-consciousness at lightning speed. Worm will develop into one who thinks about his physical and metaphysical anguish, and his sorrows will ravage and absorb him.

Worm's doom is inaugurated by his body, by his senses on alert. Once Worm cocks an ear, his "life-warrant" is issued.[64] His inadvertent failing is this unsought attainment of some degree of mind. In the early stages:

> [Worm] merely hears, and suffers, uncomprehending, that must be possible. A head has grown out of his ear, the better to enrage him, that must be it. The head is there, glued to the ear, and in it nothing but rage, that's all that matters, for the time being. It's a transformer in which sound is turned, without the help of reason, to rage and terror, that's all that is required, for the moment. The circumvolutionisation will be seen too later.[65]

The ear proves a dolorous conduit. It makes for "nerves torn from the heart of insentience, with the appertaining terror and the cerebellum on fire."[66] It later allows for the racket of the indefatigable voices to madden the listener. Even before Worm comprehends these voices, they assault and frighten him. The shattering of Worm's silence inaugurates a host of further violations:

> he suffers more and more, as time flies, and the metamorphosis is accomplished . . . But for the moment let him toss and turn at least, roll on the ground, damn it all, since there's no other remedy, anything at all, to relieve the monotony, damn it all, look at the burnt alive, they don't have to be told, when not lashed to the stake, to rush about in every direction, without method, crackling, in search of a little cool, there are even those whose sang-froid is such that they throw themselves out of the window. No one asks [Worm] to go to those lengths. But simply to discover, without further assistance from without, the alleviations of flight from self, that's all, he won't go far, he needn't go far. Simply to find within himself a palliative for what he is, through no fault of his own.[67]

This palliative needn't be suicide (going to "those lengths"), but it must be something inside Worm that can help him to forget his condition. Here we have the Unnamable's own strategy. Once brute emotion has robbed Worm of equanimity – Plato's charge against tragedy – the Unnamable recommends that Worm do his utmost, imaginatively, to reenter his former, nescient state. Wolosky would see in this "not a reduction to essence, but mere reduction."[68] Wolosky characterizes such moves as "apocalyptic negation."[69] The alternative to embodiment and "language here is not transcendence. It is utter annihilation of both word and world."[70] Worm would be "left then not with nothing as truth, but with truly nothing."[71]

The problem with this thought experiment, from the Unnamable's point of view, is that Worm as he was, undisturbed Worm, is irrecoverable. Prebirth, prehuman paradise is, in the Unnamable's account, definitively lost. The Unnamable obsessively rehearses and recapitulates Worm's fall:

> Feeling nothing, knowing nothing, capable of nothing, wanting nothing. Until the instant he hears the sound that will never stop. Then it's the end, Worm no longer is. We know it, but we don't say it, we say it's the awakening, the beginning of Worm, for now we must speak, and speak of Worm. It's no longer he, but let us proceed as if it were still he, he at last, who hears, and trembles, and is delivered over, to affliction and the struggle to withstand it, the starting eye, the labouring mind. Yes, let us call that thing Worm, so as to exclaim, the sleight of hand accomplished.[72]

"Affliction and the struggle to withstand it" prove the culmination of Worm's "delivery." He is "delivered over to" pain, not from it. Worm begins "without the help of reason," but his development of a "labouring mind" does nothing to comfort him.[73] The only means of withstanding this induction into consciousness, in the Unnamable's view, is to elude it, is flight.

In a telling formulation, however, this awakened Worm has no eyelid to close, in order not to see. He can only weep in response to his nascent, inexplicable, and life-demarcating suffering:

> Tears gush from [Worm's eye] practically without ceasing, why is not known, nothing is known, whether it's with rage, or whether it's with grief, the fact is there, perhaps it's the voice that makes it weep, with rage, or some other passion, or at having to see, from time to time, some sight or other, perhaps that's it, perhaps he weeps in order not to see, though it seems difficult to credit him with an initiative of this complexity. The rascal, he's getting humanized.[74]

Having no "way out," Worm comes to "regret being a man, under such conditions, that is to say a head abandoned to its ancient solitary resources," sensory and intellectual resources that do him little good.[75] For the Unnamable, then, to weep unconsolably, with grief or rage or some other passion, is to join the ranks of humanity.

Our narrator finishes this strange parable of forced and irreversible humanization by turning its lesson upon himself: "when I have failed to be Worm I'll be Mahood, automatically, on the rebound?... Worm proving to be Mahood the moment one is he?"[76] Having imagined a character stripped of consciousness, the Unnamable now sees that he cannot atavistically become him, "be Worm." If he were to *know* himself Worm, he, too, would be on his way to playing Mahood after all. The Unnamable crystallizes his lament, still analyzing Worm's case: "others conceive him and say, Worm is, since we conceive him, as if there could be no being but being conceived."[77] The Unnamable balks at this necessity, "being conceived," in others' beds and in others' minds, and in his own mind. Neither the voices' propagandistic version of manhood nor his own tragic sense of it can be borne. He cannot grin and bear the roles conceived for Mahood, torturer or tortured. He cannot pretend that these parts delight rather than agonize him. And Mahood's doleful script fails to occlude the grief, rage, and terror – the tragic substrate – of living per se (being conceived, being born). That is why the Unnamable wants being that is nescient. Made to speak in the voice of outsiders, dissenting in a voice that he would also like to relinquish, senselessly suffering and beset by weeping – what resources of the head, what conceptions of the imagination, can remedy this condition? Insofar as he would like to

suppress every painful manifestation of it, the Unnamable seems to epitomize a nihilistic, counter-tragic mania – demanding the cancellation of
his humanity.

But because even his beloved Worm is bound for internal soliloquizing,
cast in a drama not of his choosing, it at last dawns on the Unnamable that
he has shown total evasion of existence to be impossible. He acknowledges,
fleetingly, that the incessant voices that hound him are manifestations of
"the life that's on every tongue, the only possible!"[78] These voices, he
admits, are his projections from within and make him no candidate for
dormant Wormhood at all:

> it's I am talking, thirsting, starving, let it stand ... I'm in words, made of
> words, others' words, what others, the place too, the air, the walls, the floor,
> the ceiling, all words, the whole world is here with me, I'm the air, the
> walls, the walled-in one, everything yields, opens, ebbs, flows, like flakes,
> I'm all these flakes, meeting, mingling, falling asunder, wherever I go I find
> me, leave me, go towards me, come from me, nothing ever but me, a
> particle of me, retrieved, lost, gone astray, I'm all these words, all these
> strangers, this dust of words.[79]

He, too, finds that an external world permeates his subjectivity. At last, he
accepts that his living tongue devises these others, these supposed
strangers. Yet he quickly returns to maintaining his preferred illusion: that
he has no voice, has banished all voices, and that silence can be his.
Nothingness of character, we see, is his greatest and most laborious fiction.
It is the nihilistic antidote to human fate, imagined for Worm but
rescinded as a real and viable possibility – the fantasy of "he the famished
one, and who, having nothing human, has nothing else, has nothing, is
nothing."[80] Even this much-desired panacea is tinged with sadness –
Worm, after all, is "famished," starved for life. For the Unnamable, it is
a no-win situation. If Worm exchanges his "unchanging stare" for livelier,
quickened existence – if he does have something human – alas "[h]e who
seeks his true countenance, let him be of good cheer, he'll find it,
convulsed with anguish, the eyes out on stalks."[81]

Beckett's Oedipus and Lispector's Mystic

According to the Unnamable, self-recognition issues in anguished self-
blinding. The Unnamable is Beckett's nihilistic Oedipus, who does not
want to see and who demands exile from his community. Both the
Unnamable and Oedipus fixate on the ill luck of birth itself: "That
dreadful mark – I've had it from the cradle," says Oedipus.[82] Initially,

he, too, professes, "I must see my origins face-to face," but like the Unnamable he comes to loathe what there is to uncover: "for all your power / Time, all-seeing Time has dragged you to the light," says the chorus, and light is never gentle in its illuminations.[83] Oedipus experiences painful lucidity:

> O god –
> all come true, all burst to light!
> O light – now let me look my last on you!
> I stand revealed at last –
> cursed in my birth, cursed in marriage,
> cursed in the lives I cut down with these hands![84]

Oedipus eschews the light of life, of the sun – the dual meaning that the word carries – and the shepherd who features in Oedipus' scene of recognition names the congenital sentence that the Unnamable, too, seeks to elude: "you were born for pain."[85]

Oedipus' first act of self-assertion, postrecognition, is to recoil from the character to which he has been awakened. His response to knowledge, his acknowledgment of it, is his refusal to see:

> Apollo, friends, Apollo –
> he ordained my agonies – these, my pains on pains!
> But the hand that struck my eyes was mine,
> mine alone – no one else –
> I did it all myself!
> What good were eyes to me?
> Nothing I could see could bring me joy.[86]

Oedipus distinguishes between hurt ordained from birth, about which he can do nothing, and this his own response to it. The messenger echoes: "terrible things, and none done blindly now, / all done with a will."[87] Following this apex of suffering, Oedipus pronounces the Unnamable's very credo:

> No, if I could just block off my ears,
> the springs of hearing, I would stop at nothing –
> I'd wall up my loathsome body like a prison,
> blind to the sound of life, not just the sight.
> Oblivion – what a blessing . . .
> for the mind to dwell a world away from pain.[88]

Like the Unnamable, he now wants his "loathsome body" to be spared reminders of life, auditory or visual. At the end of *Oedipus Tyrannus*, it is this disgust-laden sentiment that fuels the tragic hero's denunciation of the world. Oedipus comes to embody the nihilistic "wisdom of Silenus" that the chorus speaks in *Oedipus at Colonus*:

> Not to be born is best
> when all is reckoned in, but once a man has seen the light
> the next best thing, by far, is to go back
> back where he came from, quickly as he can.
> For once his youth slips by, light on the wing
> Lightheaded . . . what mortal blows can he escape
> what griefs won't stalk his days?[89]

Here is the Sophoclean chorus's apology for nescience. Even in this later play, Oedipus has not made peace with his fate – although he does go on by way of his daughters' guiding hands – and he repeatedly professes his total innocence. As tragic hero engaged in retrospection, he refuses the idea of a rotten nature responsible for his destiny, an original guiltiness.[90] Like the Unnamable, he claims that he is dealt an unearned, a chance fate. An unwanted identity has been foisted on him. Like Worm, he assumes it unwittingly. Even contesting it, he continues to suffer. If any explanation is to be found for his persecution, it lies in the constitution of his "race from ages past," not in "something criminal deep inside me."[91] Both the Unnamable and Oedipus refuse to share the chorus's nearly Christian hope for justice for the wronged and tortured tragic hero: "Numberless agonies / blind and senseless, came his way in life – / now let some power / some justice grant him glory!"[92]

The Unnamable would like to resign from life; he does not anticipate deliverance from harm. This is the difference between Beckett's narrator and Clarice Lispector's in *The Passion According to G.H.* (1964). Both characters take issue with language, but the Unnamable's lonesome, futile speech acts in pursuit of self-erasure bear little resemblance to G.H.'s rapt ascension to wordless and communal existence. She embraces "the radiating center of a neutral love in Hertzian waves."[93] "I only have that ecstasy," she elaborates, "which also is no longer what we called ecstasy, since it is not a peak," not a climax.[94] This neutral love, she clarifies, is joy without *telos*; the neutral is undelimited, nonlinguistic, flavorless, atonal, and amoral.

In contrast to the Unnamable, G.H. experiences this Nietzschean, Dionysiac self-dissolution. Her "living root" takes "ferocious joy" in it.[95] What is illicit and excruciating, from her usual individuated viewpoint, proves delicious. Her desire for this conversion is strictly Nietzschean: "The world would only cease to terrify me if I became the world. If I were the world, I wouldn't be afraid."[96] On one hand, she is "a murderer of myself"; on the other, she is "plankton and pneuma and pabulum vitae."[97] This is what Deleuze and Guattari call the "*nonhuman becomings of man.*"[98] Renouncing her human qualms and quailing stomach, G.H. asks: "What was I afraid of? becoming unclean with what? Becoming unclean with joy."[99] G.H. is Nietzsche novelized. She is beyond good, evil, disgust, fear, and pity. She is beyond hope in other worlds. She grows oracular: "We shall be inhuman.... I was banished from paradise when I became human. And the true prayer is the mute inhuman oratorio."[100]

The Unnamable, too, pines for the mute and the inhuman, but he will never wax poetic about it as G.H. does – not because it is ineffable, but because to him it is unattainable. He and Worm are humanized and there is no help for that, save ceasing to be. Beneath the "monster's carapace" of social indoctrination, the Unnamable finds only the anguish of mortal life. Beneath G.H.'s conventional façade is delectable liberation. It is G.H. who can experience and voice boundless, painless being:

> the life in me does not bear my name ... Language is my human effort.... But – I return with the unsayable. The unsayable can only be given to me through the failure of my language. Only when the construction fails, can I obtain what it could not achieve.... Finally, finally, my casing had really broken and without limit I was.[101]

This is the testimony of ebullient transcendence – transcendence of language and embodiment – that Beckett's narrator cannot deliver. He believes in no supersensible realm, beyond time and space. Nor is this immanent fusion with all life possible for him. He does not cultivate, either, those moments of reprieve that Hardy's, Woolf's, and Camus's tragic characters do.

Nihilism and Recoil from Nihilism

Whether his is the determinate negation of contemporary society or the determined negation of human being, his pointed withdrawal from an existence pervaded by suffering is the ethical crux of the novel. Nevertheless, the novel does not let tragedy go unnamed or eluded. It dispenses with the idea of curative peace, and it also thwarts the Unnamable's own aim, the eclipse of all sentiment and sentience. Beckett may flout Lukács's prohibition on "anti-realism" and "anti-humanism," but if he pens defeated and self-defeating minds, as Lukács would say, these are incitements to distinguish our own urges from his characters'.[102] Beckett's modernist case studies, revealing aggrieved exile from everyday reality, may impel us to protest that we might like to grapple differently with sensation, grief, rage, and unconscionable history – aware that each runs the risk of becoming so intolerable that we, too, could defect to this life-negating position.

Martha Nussbaum, however, understands Beckettian characters' refusal to make any aspect of earthly life the basis for sturdy and practicable ethics to be the nihilistic impasse that the novels fail to overcome. Her diagnostic interpretation in "Narrative Emotions: Beckett's Genealogy of Love" shows us routes to life's affirmation that such characters broach, only to retreat from them into stymied and stagnant negation. But it is this pronounced negativity that might provoke readers to travel other paths – precisely because these nihilistic procedures do not serve their purpose. They do not quiet suffering. In tracking characters' forays into nihilism, that is, Nussbaum shows us the capacious Beckettian "no" that cries out for spots of "yes."

Nussbaum first identifies what, in her view, Beckett's characters do aim to achieve in the trilogy (*Molloy, Malone Dies, The Unnamable*): freedom from Christian teachings that train them to spurn a fallen world and a corrupt human body. Nussbaum reads Beckett's *Molloy* in particular as the staging of this endeavor to renounce self-hatred. Yet she finds that such attempted reeducation pivots back into self-loathing – never constructs ethics on new grounds. She concludes that neither Molloy, the Unnamable, nor Beckett himself can abandon the notion that terrestrial life is too imperfect to be accepted:

> It is as if Beckett believes that the finite and frail can only inspire our disgust and loathing.... And this is because, as we said, mortality in Beckett's world is seen not as our neutral and natural condition but as our punishment for original sin. The complete absence in this writing of any joy in the limited and finite indicates to us that the narrative as a whole is an expression of a religious view of life. Lucretius and Nietzsche stand apart from what they condemn [a religious view of life]. They have a separate and uncorrupted sense of pleasure and of value; and because of this they can see how a finite life can have its own peculiar splendor. Beckett's narrative does not see this.[103]

For Nussbaum, Beckett's speakers' aversion to physical and sexual life binds them to the religiously based fear and degradation they seek to eschew. It is continuing to view the mortal, "frail body" as Christian punishment, Nussbaum suggests, that leads characters "from a perception of human limits to a loathing of the limited, from grief to disgust and hatred."[104] Of signal importance is that Nussbaum expects not only characters' Camusian embrace of love within limits but a love *of* "neutral and natural" mortality.

But even those unencumbered by "[r]eligious teleological patterns of desire" might not awaken to the "peculiar splendor" of "finite life."[105] Simon Critchley describes Nietzsche's explanation of nihilism as Nussbaum does – as the direct issue of Christianity – but also acknowledges a non-Christian barrier to forging ethics anew:

> For Nietzsche, the cause of nihilism cannot be explained socially, politically, epistemologically, or even physiologically (i.e. decline of the species), but is rather rooted in a specific interpretation of the world: *Christianity*. For Nietzsche, the "Christian–Moral" interpretation of the world had the distinct advantage of being an antidote to nihilism by granting the world meaning, granting human beings value, and preventing despair (WM 10–11/WP 9–10).... Christian metaphysics turns on the belief in a true world that is opposed to the false world of becoming that we inhabit here below. However, with the consciousness of the death of God, the true world is revealed to be a fable. Thus, and this is the antinomy, the will for a moral interpretation or valuation of the world now appears to be a will to untruth. Christianity, like ancient tragedy, does not so much die as commit suicide. And yet – here's the rub – a belief in a world of truth is required simply in order to live because we cannot *endure* this world of becoming.[106]

Beckett's narrators epitomize outrage at this "true" and unendurable "world of becoming." This is the painful terrestrial world that Nietzsche is determined wholly to revalue in order to overcome nihilism, to end all "loathing of the limited," as Nussbaum calls it. Yet Critchley finds in Beckett a laudable refusal to make a virtue of finitude. Critchley finds in Beckett "[a] response to nihilism and its crisis of meaning [that does] not consist in the restoration of a new totality of meaning derived from the datum of finitude: a new thesis on Being, the creation of new values, the achievement of philosophy as revolutionary praxis, or whatever."[107] Whereas Nussbaum determines that Beckettian characters are still beholden to the hope for salvation – that they evince a "second-order longing (for a redemption from the longing for redemption)," and persist in this desire which they can neither fulfill nor relinquish – Critchley sees Beckettian characters truly forgo "the rose-tinted spectacles of any narrative of redemption."[108] He sees their "radical de-creation of these salvific narratives ... a redemption from redemption."[109] Contra Nussbaum and Nietzsche, the Unnamable might echo Critchley's own conclusion in *Very Little ... Almost Nothing*: "Can I assume my finitude affirmatively as a source of meaning in the absence of God?... 'I cannot.'"[110] Limited time will not be the grounds for the Unnamable's post-Christian attachment to life. It will be what he labors to unknow. In Critchley's case, affirmation is possible on other grounds, because finitude (even loathing for finitude) and happiness are not incompatible. Very little, almost nothing, can still be a sustaining portion. Not so for the Unnamable. Eluding all experience is his nihilistic *telos*. That is his response not just to the notion, abhorrent to him, of a Christian fall into sinfulness, but to atheistic suffering without reason or remission.

That is perhaps why, as Nussbaum observes, he recoils from both tragic and nontragic ethical systems. Tragedy is true and unbearable; its Pollyannaish opposites are false and unbearable. In the latter category are ancient Stoicism and Epicureanism and their modern descendants. "Beckett is a member of this therapeutic company," Nussbaum determines, but "his pessimism (or that of his voices) denies a possibility that they [Lucretius and Nietzsche] hold open," that of joyful and affirmative existence.[111] Beckett critiques these schools and his narrators decline membership in them. Stoicism, that is, as Nussbaum demonstrates, proffers a methodology for eradicating the belief that external powers and unsolicited fates largely rule our lives, compromise our well-being, and curtail our self-determination. The Stoics dispute our caring about what befalls us and how our plans turn out; they teach that only what is under our control, our thoughts in response to what takes place and our plans themselves, matter. The Epicureans also, in their way, dismiss human vulnerability to harm. Epicurus in his famed letter to Menoeceus instructs his disciple that whatever produces anxiety and grief is rooted in false belief; naturalistic explanation of the cosmos is in fact the treatment prescribed to relieve this needless suffering.[112] Epicurus' empiricist's vision does not inaugurate its own host of fears – because he has dispensed with the myth of a nightmarish afterlife and has shown all other reasons for mortal fear to be spurious.[113] His followers can resemble the Epicurean gods, who themselves forgo commerce with our messy Earth and know permanent peace; his followers can be tranquil and self-sufficient, as impervious to loss as Nietzsche's supermen. Lucretius similarly maintains that poetry is the soundest means of dispensing this restorative medicine to humankind, of curing our unnecessary angst.[114] Lucretius disputes the necessity of "furious laments" altogether.[115]

The Unnamable's rejection of both Christianity and these philosophical remedies bespeaks his tragic worldview. Unlike these philosophers, he claims no access to knowledge conducive to human happiness. He experiences the world as the unintelligible crucible of his absurd and ignoble condition. He can surmise that – in truth – it is not a repository of pleasing order, available to him were he to think or to act in the proper manner.

The Unnamable's resultant turn to nihilism, however, could act on readers as reverse, rehumanizing psychology. This could be Beckettian purging, Beckettian catharsis – not of painful feeling but of a suicidal response to it. This purgative course would be predicated on our entering wholeheartedly into the anguish of this character, only to feel extreme relief that we are not him. Beckett's novel does not, then, model an ethics of tragedy, like that of Camusian revolt. But contrary to the Unnamable's own agenda and to Nussbaum's interpretation, the novel might fire audiences to live tragically rather than evasively.

Beckett's Ancient Philosophy

Beckett is exceedingly well versed in Greek philosophy. Nussbaum does not capriciously compare his narrators' strategies to those of the Stoics and Epicureans. Yet Beckett himself is drawn to philosophical schools that embrace the irrational, the uncontrollable, the tragic. To Platonism and Pythagoreanism – rationality and cataphatic mysticism – Beckett prefers Democritus' materialism, Heraclitus' ceaseless mutability, and the Sophists' refusal of reigning transcendental truths. Sophism, Plato's nemesis, is the philosophy most concordant with tragedy. Sophism refuses a given fate predetermined and fixed meaning, legible within a single conceptual schema. Gorgias, the master Sophist, takes up this interpretive uncertainty in his "Encomium of Helen," for instance, revisiting a central figure of myth – whose guilt is presumed to be indubitable – in order to argue for her blamelessness. Gorgias rereads Helen's story in multiple lights, affording her defection four separate points of origin, each of which reveals her to be innocent, a victim of insuperable circumstance. What Beckett then tests in his own fiction are the most extreme psychological responses to Gorgias's tragic universe – the most radical unmooring of besieged subjectivity.

In David Addyman and Michael Feldman's work on Beckett's "Philosophy Notes" – notebooks in which Beckett tracked his intensive private studies from 1932 to 1933 – we see clear evidence of Beckett's partiality to the Sophists.[116] While Beckett's principal source for the ancients, as Addyman and Feldman write, is Wilhelm Windelband's *A History of Philosophy*, which champions Platonism and its rationally ordered universe, Beckett gravitates toward the very positions Windelband finds objectionable. Addyman and Feldman show, for example, that when Beckett recopies passages from *A History of Philosophy*, seemingly verbatim, he omits Windelband's negative framing of Sophism. Windelband himself writes the following condemnation of Sophism:

But as they [Sophists] considered what they practised and taught – viz. the skill to carry through any proposition whatsoever – the *relativity* of human ideas and purposes presented itself to their consciousness so clearly and with such overwhelming force that they disowned inquiry as to the existence of a universally valid truth in the theoretical, as well as in the practical sphere, and so fell into a scepticism which was at first a genuine scientific theory and then became frivolous. With their self-complacent, pettifogging advocacy, the Sophists made themselves the mouth-piece of all the unbridled tendencies which were undermining the order of public life.[117]

Beckett retains only the following, however, beginning, as Addyman and Feldman note, by dropping the "but" which for Windelband signals the advent of criticism:

As the Sophists considered what they practised and taught – viz. the skill to carry through any proposition whatsoever – the relativity of human ideas and purposes struck them with such overwhelming force that they disowned inquiry as to the existence of a universally valid [*sic*] in both theory and practice, and so fell into a scepticism which was at first genuine scientific theory and then became frivolous.[118]

Doubt, incessant reframing, and the undermining of dominant, ostensibly unassailable narratives can certainly be counted among the Unnamable's tactics, taken to the extreme. Whereas Windelband, as Addyman and Feldman explain, defends the discipline of philosophy as that which uncovers and articulates the norms governing all other disciplines, in order to prove not the relativism of belief systems but the immutable laws that permit their operation, Beckett prefers the Sophists' admission of interpretive instability. Addyman and Feldman write: "Windelband again devalues the Sophists, contrasting their 'pettifogging' with 'the plain, sound sense, and the pure and noble personality' of Socrates; again, Beckett omits this phrase."[119] Whereas Windelband seeks the truths contained within "normativity," hewing to ancient realism, Beckett argues for the nominalism of human perspectives, for the uniqueness of individual sensations.[120] While Windelband disparages Protagoras's "*sensualism*," Beckett praises Protagoras.[121] Reading Archibald Alexander's *A Short History of Philosophy*, Beckett records that Protagoras is the "first *great* individualist, relativist & agnostic."[122] Beckett makes Sophism's philosophical linchpins – perspectivalism and agnosticism – foundational features of his fictional universes. Although Windelband condemns Sophism for going too far, for veering into hyperbolic doubt, Beckett allows his own narrators to do just that – presenting the excesses of their antirationalist positions. As Addyman and Feldman contend in relation to *Murphy* (1938), Beckett depicts its protagonist's approval of absolutely untethered interiority, but the novel as a whole suggests that such a descent into solitude is deleterious to those who live it.[123] Total denial of the material world, in Beckett, is not salutary or saving.

Beckett's works retreat from absolutes, from both unbounded inwardness and singular extrahuman truth. Anthony Cordingley writes of Windelband, too, as the champion of those fixed belief systems from which Beckett formatively distances himself: "Windelband's enthusiasm for the virtues of a Greek education (*paideia*) and the assimilation of Aristotelian ethics into Christian morality is exemplary of the teleological current of intellectual and artistic history against which Beckett's own oeuvre stands."[124] Cordingley contends that in *How It Is* (1961), for instance, Beckett now takes aim not at untenable subjectivism but at its opposite: all too ferocious protestations of a knowable a priori rational and moral order. On Cordingley's reading, Beckett creates a main character hounded by an "ancient voice" that insists that all be made intelligible, indubitable.[125] Cordingley finds in *How It Is* "Beckett's parody of philosophical ratiocination," in which Beckett's "English translation – 'ancient voice' – accentuates an underlying discourse with the ancients, for the transferal of voice and its learning finds its allegory in principles of Pythagorean and Platonic education."[126] The speaker of *How It Is*, argues Cordingley, cannot bear that others should remind him of irrationality, and so is sadistically bent on converting the sophistical Pim:

> Like a surd, the irrational number *pi* cannot be expressed as a fraction of two rational numbers, and *Pim*'s prelinguistic emergence out of unformed chaos is an affront to the Pythagoreanism of the "I," provoking his most violent effort to inscribe Pim within the *Logos*. Commenting on the irrational in Beckett's work, David Hesla observes that Latin translations of Euclid use the term *surdus* (deaf) for *alogos*, which was an irrational or "deaf root" (7). Pim is also deaf and his absurdity must be hammered into order until his "song ascends in the present" (81; 2.80). In the eye of the narrator/narrated, Pim's song is stripped of the pure absurdity of its primary being, for Pim has been coerced into a prevailing "tropism towards" the mysterious "deity" of the "I," his "other above in the light."[127]

Such is the "transit ... from darkness to light" that the Unnamable holds to be Worm's lamentable fate. Like one of the Unnamable's insatiable, creed-mongering voices, "the narrator/narrated" of *How It is*, as Cordingley describes him, "conceives of his universe through a willful blindness to the irrational" and holds language to be an instrument of reason and indoctrination (393). Cordingley concludes that this character then fails in his Platonic suppression of chaos. This disciplinarian finds that Pim's "breath will never be refined into *Logos* or imitate the breath of Christ, the Christian *Logos*, for it is fundamentally 'ill-heard ill-captured ill-murmured' and thus 'ill-said.'"[128] His demand, that words capture supersensible Reality, goes unanswered. As Wolosky claims, in Beckett's work it is a mistake, as Nietzsche saw, to posit an immaterial domain of truth in the first place:

> Nietzsche first identifies nihilism not with the denial of metaphysical categories, but with their invention. Nihilism in this has two stages: first as the false investment of value in a "totality," a "universal" that leads to devaluation and reduction of meaning in this present world; and then as the recognition of its falsehood, withdrawing the categories "which we used to project some value into the world . . . so that the world looks valueless."[129]

Cordingley, in complementary fashion, contends that in *How It Is* "Plato's *eidos* or Soul-as-Form," "translated as Species," is presumed to be ultimate reality.[130] But even the text's rigidly rationalist "narrator/narrated eventually laments his 'loss of species,'" his failure to demonstrate a realm of Ideas and a clearly reasoning human essence.[131] Cordingley therefore claims that this character's "species," understood as soul, never manifests a transcendental form. It is also true that this character's biological species is never fully shed:

> I hear me again murmur me in the mud and am again
>
> the journey I made in the dark the mud straight line sack tied to my neck never quite fallen from my species and I made that journey.[132]

It is Beckett's Unnamable who cultivates species loss, because neither immaterial Platonic Form nor biological form attracts him.[133] He refuses the rationalist education that Pim, like Worm, experiences as a lie and a brutalization. He resists fictions and philosophies that promise to make sense of his pains, as well as the tormenting irrationality of the pains themselves. But signatures of terrestrial life – evolved verbal and physical markers of species – remain.

No Counter-Tragic Calm

"How many times, since I've known Beckett," writes Cioran in his reminiscences in *Anathemas and Admirations* (1986), "have I wondered (an obsessive and rather stupid interrogation) about his relation to his characters. What do they share? Who could conceive of a more radical disparity?"[134] How, asks Cioran, can the flesh-and-blood Beckett whom he knows and so keenly admires resemble these haunted husks? Reading Beckett, Cioran tells us that he has "[t]he sensation of entering into a posthumous universe, some geography dreamed by a demon released from everything, even his own malediction."[135] Cioran's words capture the Unnamable's wish: if only he could have a posthumous life – a contradiction in terms – released from everything, even his own self-loathing, he might become a happy ghost. If he could exist before or beyond or beneath his humanity – assume a prehuman or posthuman character – without subjectivity, not an "I," he should be released from everything, especially his own maledictions. He should be, paradoxically, protected and extinct.

Yet rather than contend with the eeriness of Beckettian characters as Cioran does, much Beckett scholarship pursues the philosophical moral of Beckett's story, the lesson it is presumed to teach. As Joshua Landy remarks: "Many critics appear to assume, as though it goes without saying, that Beckett is simply trying to *inform* us of something: that free will is an illusion, for example, that the self is in language, that Descartes is wrong, or that there is no ground for epistemological certainty."[136] Cioran's contrary mode of reading supposes characters who exist along a continuum of shared humanity with readers and writer but who become fantastically distorted – such that a "radical disparity" seems to exist between real and fictional persons. Landy, too, treats Beckett's characters as fellow sufferers; yet he finds that readers can in fact share in their habits and might indeed resemble them. Landy argues that Beckett's character studies do present readers with a cure for a disease of the mind – the disease of ceaseless rumination, of philosophy itself. In Landy's view of Beckett the experimental doctor, the Unnamable labors to achieve post-philosophical peace and succeeds.[137] Beckett's trilogy becomes a practicum in the banishing of unease, in Landy's reading, that meets its objective, whereas Nussbaum had argued for its want of tenable ethics.

For Landy, Beckett's trilogy does afford its characters a viable calmative strategy, one that readers may emulate:

> readers of Beckett are suffering from the same disease as Beckett's characters, in search of the same recovered health, and eager to undergo the same treatment. ... Now health here, let me add, means peace of mind; the disease, here, is philosophy; and the treatment, here, is nothing other than the trilogy itself.[138]

Now the ailment is not grief at mortal life, but the very philosophy, perhaps, that tries and fails to subdue such feeling (Platonism, Aristotelianism, Stoicism, Epicureanism). Landy contends that Beckett's narrators instead practice Pyrrhonian skepticism, an extreme form of skepticism, that effectively dissolves the agitations of cognition into *ataraxia* (peace of mind, freedom from rumination).

While Hegelian philosophy synthesizes opposites, Pyrrhonian skepticism dissipates philosophical disquiet into mental blankness. Landy cites Molloy's contention that "[t]o know nothing is nothing, not to want to know anything likewise, but to be beyond knowing anything, to know you are beyond knowing anything, that is where peace enters in."[139] Landy affirms:

> Molloy could not be any clearer: the ultimate *telos* of the Beckettian quest, whether or not such a *telos* may in practice ever be attained, is *peace*. And this means that Molloy, like most of Beckett's heroes, is not just a skeptic but an *ancient* skeptic, indeed a *Pyrrhonian* skeptic. For him, that is, epistemological questions, questions about what can and cannot be known, and with what degree of certainty, are *secondary*, merely instrumental to the primary goal, which is *ataraxia*, freedom from disturbance, enduring peace of mind.[140]

Landy outlines a methodology of intellectual cancellation – let no thesis or antithesis prevail or combine – that nullifies certainty on all points. Audrey Wasser, following Deleuze, argues for a similar (Deleuzian) logic in Beckett's prose: a logic of "exhaustion," in which every epistemological permutation or possibility is tried and discarded, spent and rejected, until nothing remains. One is not weary afterward (exhausted as in fatigued); one is simply empty.[141]

Landy celebrates as curative this Pyrrhonian flight from tragic lament and philosophical reasoning. Here skepticism is both counter-tragic (will curtail all feeling) *and* counter-philosophical (will curtail all thinking):

> *There is no way to make an end-run around intellect*: once we are started on the game of ruminating, we cannot simply will ourselves to stop.... The sole remaining solution, at this point, is to convince the intellect to abdicate (as Proust would say) of its own accord, out of sheer despair. It must somehow be convinced not only that it *does* not know, but also that it *cannot* know; it must be convinced, as Molloy puts it, that it is "beyond knowing anything." And in order to bring about this blissful condition, one must bring before it *opposite hypotheses* in answer to every question that arises, the equal plausibility of which is sure to leave the intellect in the appropriate state of *epoché* (suspension of judgment). Silence and resignation are not givens, but require to be *made*; nothingness is not a state that pre-exists objects and beliefs but is, instead, a state that results from their mutual cancellation....
>
> All this, of course, is straight out of the skeptical playbook. "Skepticism," writes Sextus Empiricus, "is an ability ... which opposes appearances to

judgments in any way whatsoever, with the result that, owing to the equipollence of the objects and reasons thus opposed, we are brought firstly to a state of mental suspense and next to a state of 'unperturbedness' or quietude." *Antilogoi, epoché, ataraxia*; in Beckettian terms, "find again, lose again, seek in vain, seek no more."[142]

Landy suggests that for both Pyrrhonian skeptics and Beckettian characters "[t]he intellect refuses to take orders from the intuition and the emotions," and can cease and desist only once it has practiced this art of "mutual cancellation," convinced itself that no answers to its myriad questions are possible.[143]

But it would seem that the intellect's crisis in *The Unnamable* is that it cannot silence these instigators to thought (emotion and intuition), cannot satisfy their craving for an end to pain and thereby ensure peacefulness. As Critchley puts it:

> Our difference with antiquity, for good or ill, is that there is little sense of philosophy as a calmative or consoling influence that prepares the individual stoically for his passage on to either nothingness or eternal bliss. Beckett's Murphy strapped into his chair has replaced the Garden of Epicurus as an image of the philosopher in late modernity.[144]

Landy concludes, nonetheless, that while "[w]e do not begin from nothing," we can "*end* there, if we are lucky. (Emotional) nothingness is not a given; it is something that needs to be made."[145] Landy evokes the Flaubertian "goal of 'loving nothing,' the goal of being at last outside of desire" to describe the aim of Beckett's voluble speakers.[146] Indeed, throughout *The Unnamable*, nothingness – epistemological and, in particular, emotional nothingness – is the narrator's "[s]trange hope, turned towards silence and peace."[147] Even so, the Unnamable's incessant excoriation of self and world seems to betray the impossibility of achieving this end, and the inefficacy of the therapy in question. Such an emotionally purgative course seems to do the Unnamable more harm than good – to leave him in a state of partial animation, of living death, his desires more warring than becalmed. He is akin to Oedipus, who is still tormented in his darkness by an "unspeakable" fate. Oedipus cries:

> Dark, horror of darkness
> *my* darkness, drowning, swirling around me
> crashing wave on wave – unspeakable, irresistible
>   headwind, fatal harbor! Oh again,
> the misery, all at once, over and over
> the stabbing daggers, stabs of memory
> raking me insane.[148]

The Unnamable is tortured by prods to fully revive and he is tortured by prods to "finish dying."[149] Certain practices of ancient philosophy, like certain practices of modern psychology, would aim to rid him of his anxieties. They are to no avail in the novel. Beckett's fiction rejects the proposition that we can banish mental agitation by means of either Platonic, Epicurean, or Stoic reasoning or via this Skeptical abdication of intellectual foment. It likewise eschews Christian or historical redemption. Beckett's fiction denies that we can either love or escape all of "natural" life, foregoing lamentation at its pains. Beckett's fiction, however, opens onto another possibility: that we might live with grief. "Not to be cured, but to live with one's ailments" is Camus's formulation of this course of action in *The Myth of Sisyphus.*[150]

To speak of Beckett and Camus in tandem is not fortuitous. In a letter of January 21, 1985, Beckett writes to Aldo Tagliaferri in Milan: "Yes, Camus' *Mythe de Sysyphe* was in my mind," composing the trilogy.[151] "Tagliaferri," explains the accompanying note, "had asked whether Albert Camus's essay *Le Mythe de Sisyphe* (*The Myth of Sisyphus*) had had an influence on SB's writing of *Molloy, Malone meurt,* and *L'Innommable.*"[152] As Ann Banfield remarks of the exchange: "[Beckett's] affirmative answer is striking, given that in a letter of 27 April, 1984 to Lawrence Shainberg he had written 'No, I got nothing from W. [Wittgenstein] Indeed I begin belatedly to wonder if I ever got anything from anybody, so stupid was I.'"[153] It is *The Myth of Sisyphus* that advances an ethics of tragedy and that insists on the irrationality of natural history. It elaborates "[a] horde of irrationals [that] has sprung up and surrounds" human beings.[154] It is also Camus's study of suicide, a subject to which he returns in *The Rebel* (1951). Camus reiterates there that "[a]bsolute negation is therefore not consummated by suicide."[155] What he means is that the denial of all value is not the cause of suicide; the sheer inexistence of value should issue in indifference. Instead, Camus determines, suicide reveals our failure to acquire or keep hold of some cherished value. A wish for suicide attests to a character's powerlessness to attain or to retrieve what might, had it been found or restored to him, have furnished him with reason to live. Perhaps this is why nihilism in *The Unnamable,* like the call to suicide, is perennially pained: its "no" (to emotion, to reason) is the expression of a thwarted "yes."

Camus's Sisyphus, however, models a strategy for surviving the inordinate and undue pains of tragedy. While he cannot evade "the torment of which he will never know the end," he finds that "all is not, has not been, exhausted."[156] Camus is determined to read Oedipus, too, as the rebel who affirms in the full, harsh light of the tragic dawn. Camus's Oedipus and Sisyphus are in possession of renewed attachment, on recalibrated grounds, to tragic existence. While each "concludes" that "higher destiny ... is inevitable and despicable," both find "a breathing-space which returns as surely as his suffering."[157] "One must imagine Sisyphus happy," writes Camus.[158] One is hard-pressed to imagine the Unnamable happy. The Unnamable's closing words – "you must go on, I can't go on, I'll go on" – evince a tormented perseverance. Adorno is right that these words ring with protest rather than acceptance. Beckett's original publication of the novel in French in 1953 had only the two clauses: "il faut continuer, je vais continuer" (you must go on, I'll go on).[159] Translating the novel into English in 1958, Beckett added the dissention: "I can't go on."[160] He then revised the French edition to include it: "il faut continuer, je ne peux pas continuer, je vais continuer," reads the 1971 text.[161] This racked going on does not join pain and its remittance as Camus's account of Sisyphus does:

> If this myth [of Sisyphus] is tragic, that is because its hero is conscious. Where would his torture be, indeed, if at every step the hope of succeeding upheld him? The workman of today works every day in his life at the same tasks, and this fate is no less absurd. But it is tragic only at the rare moments when it becomes conscious. Sisyphus, proletarian of the gods, powerless and rebellious, knows the whole extent of his wretched condition: it is what he thinks of during his descent. The lucidity that was to constitute his torture at the same time crowns his victory. There is no fate that cannot be surmounted by scorn.[162]

The Unnamable is lucid. He is wretched. He is scornful. But he has not countered his subjection with intermittent joys, those afforded by the "breathing-space" of "descent." "One always finds one's burden again," writes Camus, and so it is for the Unnamable.[163] But he discovers no counterweight to this baleful necessity. He despairs of that respite, that fully conscious, rebellious interval of thought, that Camus comes to believe is common and makes for solidarity. Rather than modeling such sustaining reprieve and common cause, *The Unnamable* drives us to desire it – precisely by withholding it. Beckett's *Company* begins to outline its realization.

Company: "That was I. That was I then."

It is the narrator of Beckett's *Company* who reproduces the Unnamable's self-negating logic only to renounce it. He emerges from the dark via stabs of memory that, like a mnemonic touch of the hand, reattach him to the light of the living. Whereas the Unnamable had said, "Bah, any old pronoun will do, provided one sees through it" – meaning that one recognize the complicity of all pronouns in toxic identity formation and in consciousness per se – the main character of *Company* comes to "see through" his "hes" and "yous" to the governing "I" beneath.[164] Exactly the schema the Unnamable devises to cast doubt on his "I," calling all pronouns misleading, the narrator of *Company* foregrounds and questions: he investigates the source of these voices who appear to come from outside and who convey intimate information to one "alone on his back in the dark" who is not certain such information pertains to him.[165] *Company* capitalizes on novelistic form, relays the musings of an unnamed "he," akin to the Unnamable in his habitat and predicament. But this "he" does not prove, as we read on, a traditional character; his thoughts are not rendered in free indirect discourse or reported via impersonal narration. Instead, "he" proves the transposition of a submerged "I" who tells of himself. This retracted first person projects his own circumstances onto a third-person pronoun, as if this posture will help "he" to materialize, to puzzle out self and surroundings – as if "he" will grow more real when summoned forth and addressed as a character.

As a "devised deviser" – posing as an omniscient narrator – this undercover "I" is empowered to range across extrahuman and human time with greater confidence.[166] As Percy Lubbock wrote of such a third-person advantage in *The Craft of Fiction*:

> For now, while the point of view is still fixed in space, still assigned to the man in the book, it is free in *time*; there are no longer stretches, between the narrator and the events of which he speaks, a certain tract of time, across which the past must appear in a more or less distant perspective. All the variety obtainable by a shifting relation to the story in time is thus in the author's hand.[167]

Company's protagonist begins by adopting this stance that affords certainty, immediacy in relation to his "character's" past – that overrides temporal distance, that is never skeptical. From there, he moves to the more intimate addresser-addressee relation of second-person narration. To "he," become "you," more proximate second-person narration also whispers incontestable memories – those not "held in a more or less distant perspective." He fabricates this rapport with a character who is himself. He fictionalizes, that is, a narrator's third-person omniscient, then second-person and intimate, command over his character in order to recover his own personhood.

One might counter that such projection is only a sign of inhibited self-reference. It does attest to our storyteller's reluctance to fully appear as the hero of his own life. Nonetheless, *Company*'s narrator intuits and discloses his substitution of "he" for "I." Whereas the Unnamable shuns identity under any guise, *Company*'s speaker finds his identity's conferral on made-up characters problematic, and so is one step nearer to resuscitating it. While the Unnamable insists that his "I" is mendacious because it is *not* his, the creator of *Company* confesses that all his characters and voices (including that of narrator) are dubious because they *are* facets of a long-lost first person. The Unnamable will credit no imaginings that, thanks to his imagining, seem to come from without, and claims that no speech originates in him; only fleetingly, gaspingly, does he glimpse his agency and admit to his self-denial. *Company* recognizes, more schematically, more calmly, that externalized voices, and their appeals to imagine, are misleading because they do come from within, indicate identity, and evidence both an imagining "I" and an external world.

Lyrical passages, moments of being, intersperse *Company*'s third-person tale: quite beautifully worded memory infiltrates dimmed third-person prose. These forays into various pasts and places come addressed to the unnamed "you," in the second person. For instance: "Kneeling at your bedside you included it the hedgehog in your detailed prayer to God to bless all you loved."[168] Nor does "he" accuse this voice of sophistry, as the Unnamable would. "He" does not comment at all on these moments of resurgent memory; they appear involuntary and testify to some still existent rapport with a lovely, anguishing, outside world. Indeed, the voice of second-person address proclaims: "You first saw the light on such and such a day and now you are on your back in the dark."[169] In the next sentence the narrator editorializes: "A device perhaps from the incontrovertibility of the one to win credence for the other."[170] So a known sensation, "you are on your back," paired with the evocation of a birthday ("you first saw the light"), may attach past and present with some credibility, just as the Unnamable had feared. Were our unacknowledged "I" to admit that he generates this narrator and character, this recollecting voice and its addressee, and these images of a young and old man, he could embrace these stories and presences as his own, become *one* "on his back in the dark." Despite his dissociative tactics, the narrator comprehends this underlying desire: "As if willing him by this dint to make [these infusions of life] his. To confess, Yes I remember. Perhaps even to have a voice. To murmur, Yes I remember. What an addition to company that would be! A voice in the first person singular. Murmuring now and then, Yes

I remember."[171] Given the Unnamable's aversion to voices, he caustically treats "assistance from without" as an oxymoron; his methods are subtractive.[172] Meanwhile, *Company*'s speaker applauds "an addition to company" and orchestrates this fiction of choral consciousness and mutual understanding.

Our character in *Company* hasn't the rage of the Unnamable. Sunk into doubt and darkness, as desolate as his predecessor, he finds his situation not disgusting but lonesome, dreary, and unfulfilling: "If he were to utter after all? However feebly. What an addition to company that would be! You are on your back in the dark and one day you will utter again. One day! In the end. In the end you will utter again. Yes I remember. That was I. That was I then."[173] This effaced storyteller has passed from a third to a second to a first person in these few lines. Initially, he invokes "he," proceeds intimately to address him as "you," and then conjures up an "I" for remembering and affirmation. He glimpses the extent of his fictionalizing, understands that his narratorial practice is that of a "[d]evised deviser devising it all for company," "[d]evising figments to temper his nothingness."[174] He understands that some real first person must animate a "devised deviser," a narrator. Our supine figure is on the verge of granting his authorial status, admitting to autobiography. But he pulls back in a panic. Still, the Unnamable's ranting, multipage tirades against fearsome *anagnorisis* – his elaborate "alleviations of flight from self" – become *Company*'s crisp and pared-down self-admonishment, "Quick leave him."[175]

This narrator, in rushing from direct self-knowledge, seems to choose unreal company over an embodied "I" bound to real others. But as he abdicates his first person, it splinters into these other pronouns, and "lying" in both senses, his splinters pain him; he is troubled by this solipsistic companionship in a perennially suspect world. So he does establish an indirect procedure for remembering and, as a result, for owning his "I." Populating his lonesome outpost with remembered persons and pasts, his imagination hardly lies dormant; it satisfies a veritable hunger for human connection, for others' acknowledgment of him. As Wayne Booth remarks: "What a joy it is to find [Beckett], in *Company*, daring to imagine once again, 'from naught anew,' a life, even though another bleak one."[176] Booth himself envisions another version of this tale, in which we might "learn the full story of why the 'you' is 'numb with the woes of your kind.' Indeed, even in this brief version we know enough about 'him' in the end – about what he loves, what he fears, what he longs for – to imply a novel richer than most."[177] This character who knows woe is not numb after all. He is not bent on numbing himself to grief or on exiling himself from his "kind."

Booth sums up *Company* as a "metaphoric evocation of 'how it is' to be alone and old and lacking all faith, unable to believe even in the effort to tell your story but still determined to exercise your failing powers of reason and wit as best you can: making something, imagining something."[178] Guaranteeing no supremely gratifying result, Beckett does make "imagining something" – rather than nothingness – seem noble, humanizing, and unavoidable. Booth in particular mentions *Company*'s moments of "meaning in the meaningless dark ... moments when the light breaks through into the book," "as deceptive miracle."[179] Here is Lily Briscoe's realization that "[t]he great revelation perhaps never did come. Instead there were little daily miracles, illuminations, matches struck unexpectedly in the dark."[180] And these moments that burst upon the speaker of *Company* – that haunt and return to him, that attest to the passage of time, that do present his human "I" as something others may register and conceive – represent all that the Unnamable wishes to deconstruct and to resist. The more an evocative lyricism washes over *Company*'s "you," the more he is vulnerable to the pain that attaches to remembrance, but he comes to recapture, in Camus's words, "those two or three great and simple images in whose presence his heart first opened."[181]

Palliative Moments

The Unnamable harbors no Platonic hopes of human flourishing in a moral universe, in which justice and happiness walk hand in hand. Nor does he aim to create his own modest happiness, as Tess's narrator, Jude, Mrs. Ramsay, Bernard, Sisyphus, Janine, Jessica, and Jacques do. He is another tragic hero *manqué*, so sickened by what he has seen that no moments of being can attract and sustain him. Innocent, he will not take Sue's "burden of badness" on himself to explain his condition. Instead, he denounces the species that could envision such rationalizations. He will not think in such a way, either, so as to have an Epicurean emotional life, immune to harm. He cannot think in such a way as to have a Stoic emotional life – entirely in command of his feelings. He may attempt to think skeptically, a further ploy to have neither emotion nor knowledge – the most radical departure from a tragic worldview – but he does not achieve such calm. No Platonic, Epicurean, Stoic, or Skeptic cure, it seems, can eliminate tragedy without eliminating much of the patient. This is Zeno's realization, following his own Freudian treatment, in Italo

Svevo's *Zeno's Conscience*: "Unlike other sicknesses, life is always fatal. It doesn't tolerate therapies. It would be like stopping the holes that we have in our bodies, believing them wounds. We would die of strangulation the moment we were treated."[182] The Unnamable tries to stop up his senses, to stop life, to become unmolested Worm, to abolish weeping, to imagine imagination dead. Yet he cannot put an end to the two great "diseases" that assail him: tragedy and philosophy. Like the Sophist Gorgias, he finds that tragic fate has no absolute meaning. It is a problem he cannot solve. Like Clamence and like Oedipus in the act of blinding himself, the Unnamable is despairingly drawn to insensibility. But the Unnamable's ailments continue to hound him; the world is not so pliable that he can imagine them away. He cannot reconcile himself to his pains, and he cannot elude them. He can neither master his fate philosophically nor accept the sufferings that attend tragedy. His revolted consciousness tries and fails to produce a self-annihilating "no." Only *Company* begins to generate antibodies, momentary affirmations. To *Company's* narrator, dreaming of companionship on his back in the dark, no glaring floodlights reveal the totality of his woes, or any remedy for them, in one bright flash. But he does not seek the blanket oblivion of not being either. Perhaps he uncovers what the Unnamable obscurely craves, speaking of Worm: a "palliative for what he is, through no fault of his own."[183]

Notes

Chapter 1

1 Lucas, *Tragedy*, 44.
2 Critchley, *ABC*, 23.
3 Woolf, *Waves*, 278.
4 See Lukács, "Realism in the Balance" and "The Ideology of Modernism."
5 Woolf, "Novels of Thomas Hardy," 254, 246.
6 Woolf, "Novels of Thomas Hardy," 257.
7 Woolf, "On Not Knowing Greek," 38.
8 Camus, "Future of Tragedy," 306.
9 See Horkheimer and Adorno, *Dialectic of Enlightenment*.
10 Beckett, *Proust*, 67.
11 Beckett summarizes Anaximander: "Definite individual existence constitutes an injustice & must be atoned for by extinction"; Peter Fifield locates Beckett's source for this note in Friedrich Ueberweg's 1871 *History of Philosophy: From Thales to the Present Time*. See Fifield, "Beckett and Early Greek Philosophy," 135. Schopenhauer writes in *The World as Will and Representation*, vol. 1: "The true sense of tragedy is the deeper insight that the hero does not atone for his particular sins, but for original sin instead, i.e. the guilt of existence itself" (281). David Tucker draws our attention to this related passage, another that Beckett copies down, from Arnold Geulincx's *Ethics* (1675): "Thrust into a body as if into a prison, am I paying the penalties that I have deserved, and among others this grave one, that I am oblivious of the offence that I am expiating?" (quoted in Tucker, "Beckett's 'Guignol' Worlds," 247). Erik Tonning writes of Beckett: "Furthermore, Beckett's biographer James Knowlson suggests that his acute sensitivity to suffering, and in particular his outrage at any attempt to justify suffering as potentially redemptive in terms of a larger cosmic scheme, may have been decisive in his eventual rejection of Christian faith"; see Tonning, "Beckett and Schopenhauer," 83.
12 Carson, preface to *Grief Lessons*, 7.
13 Beckett, *Unnamable*, 318, 353.
14 Beckett, *Three Novels*, 353.

15 Karen Zumhagen-Yekplé and Michael LeMahieu write in *Wittgenstein and Modernism* (2017): "The latter term, modernism, reflects the processes of social modernization and cultural modernity even as it signifies a critique of those processes" (4). David Scott explicitly proposes writers' recourse to tragedy as an alternative to modernity's triumphalist narratives in *Conscripts of Modernity.*

16 Blanton, *Epic Negation*, 5.

17 Blanton, *Epic Negation*, 8.

18 Camus, *Plague*, 253.

19 Saint-Amour, *Tense Future*, 38.

20 See Clayton, "Modern Synthesis," 875–96. Cf. John Plotz, "Speculative Naturalism."

21 Lukács, *Soul and Form*, 194; Krutch, "Tragic Fallacy," 85–97; Woolf, *Lighthouse*, 16; Woolf, *Waves*, 277.

22 Honig, "Antigone's Two Laws," 6; Leonard, *Tragic Modernities*, 126.

23 Honig, "Antigone's Two Laws," 9.

24 Watkin, *Difficult Atheism*, 6.

25 Watkin, *Difficult Atheism*, 4.

26 Watkin, *Difficult Atheism*, 134.

27 Today classical scholars have come to suggest that catharsis in Aristotle's *Poetics* is neither purgation nor purification of the emotions (two long-standing interpretations), because spectators' fear and pity are neither pathological nor impure, are in need of neither removal nor cleansing. Critics instead debate catharsis in terms of Aristotle's position on the educative or pleasure-inducing ends of tragedy. Martha Nussbaum prefers the "cognitivist" view in which tragedy fosters learning and moral improvement – in her reading, it is a school for sympathy. Jonathan Lear argues, on the contrary, that tragedy's special pleasure lies in the very relief that audiences derive from its fictionality (as Hume, following Fontenelle, also suggested). See these discussions in Lear, "Katharsis," and Nussbaum, *Fragility of Goodness.*

28 Eagleton, *Sweet Violence*, 14.

29 Nietzsche, *Birth of Tragedy*, 23; Nietzsche, *Daybreak*, 80.

30 Nietzsche, *Birth of Tragedy*, 46.

31 Nietzsche, *Birth of Tragedy*, 23, 24.

32 Nietzsche, *Birth of Tragedy*, 40.

33 Nietzsche, *Birth of Tragedy*, 18.

34 Nietzsche, *Birth of Tragedy*, 81.

35 Nietzsche, *Birth of Tragedy*, 52–3.

36 Nietzsche, *Will to Power*, 536–7.

37 Eliot, "*Ulysses*, Order, and Myth," 177.

38 Harrison, *Themis*, xii.

39 Newton, *Modern Literature*, 2, 4.

40 Though it is a philosopher, Max Scheler, who defines tragedy via a reading of Icarus' fall. Writing on the genre in 1923, Scheler identifies this tragic

structure: the closer Icarus' wings bear him to the sun, what he values most, the more his wings melt and he is doomed to fall ("On the Tragic," 10).

41 Halliwell, "Plato and Aristotle on the Denial of Tragedy"; Cascardi, "Tragedy and Philosophy"; Lear, "Katharsis"; Harris, *Reason's Grief*; Lurie, "Facing up to Tragedy"; Nussbaum, "Tragedy and Self-Sufficiency"; Critchley, *Tragedy, the Greeks, and Us.*
42 Jones, *Racial Discourses*, 92.
43 Peirce, *Writings*, 189.
44 Peirce, *Writings*, 185.
45 Peirce, *Writings*, 185.
46 Whitehead, *Science*, 72.
47 Whitehead, *Science*, 10.
48 Whitehead, *Science*, 11.
49 Hartshorne, "Metaphysics of Evolution," 62.
50 Eighteenth-century physiologist Albrecht von Haller, in analogous debates about embryological development, captured the prevailing concern: such development from formlessness to form "needs a force which has foresight, which can make a choice, which has a goal, which, against all the laws of blind combination, always and unfailingly brings about the same end" (quoted in Mensch, *Kant's Organicism*, 5).
51 Darwin Correspondence Project, Letter 2814 (Darwin to Asa Gray, May 22, 1860).
52 Newton, *Modern Literature*, 64–5, final ellipsis in original.
53 Bowler, *Evolution*, 224–73.
54 Morton, *Vital Science*, 18–35.
55 Provine, "England," 330.
56 Quoted in Rensch, "Neo-Darwinism," 289
57 Boesiger, "Evolutionary Biology in France," 315.
58 Boesiger, "Evolutionary Biology in France," 317.
59 Boesiger, "Evolutionary Biology in France," 317.
60 Hardy, "Apology," 561.
61 Russell, *Mysticism and Logic*, 62.
62 Clayton, "Modern Synthesis," 880.
63 Monod, *Chance and Necessity*, 44.
64 Shepherd-Barr, *Theater and Evolution*, 260.
65 Shepherd-Barr, *Theater and Evolution*, 253.
66 Van Hulle, "'Eff it,'" 283.
67 Van Hulle, "'Eff it,'" 284.
68 Burstein, *Cold Modernism*, 2.
69 Burstein, *Cold Modernism*, 28.
70 Russell, *Problems of Philosophy*, 52–8.
71 Burstein, *Cold Modernism*, 28.
72 Burstein, *Cold Modernism*, 28, 2.
73 Meillassoux, *After Finitude*, 112.

74 Beckett, *Disjecta*, 152. See also Murphy, "Beckett's Critique of Kant," 277, and Furlani, "The Contradictions of Samuel Beckett," 461.
75 Feldman, "Samuel Beckett," 183.
76 Quoted in Murphy, "Beckett's Critique of Kant," 264.
77 Feldman, "Samuel Beckett," 181.
78 Quoted in Rabaté, *Think, Pig!*, 109, second ellipsis in original.
79 Meillassoux, *After Finitude*, 63. Meillassoux writes: "We can now claim to have passed through the correlationist circle – or at least to have broken through the wall erected by the latter, which separated thought from the great outdoors, the eternal in-itself, whose being is indifferent to whether or not it is thought" (63). And again: "For it could be that contemporary philosophers have lost the great outdoors, the absolute outside of pre-critical thinkers: that outside which was not relative to us, and which was given as indifferent to its own givenness to be what it is, existing in itself regardless of whether we are thinking of it or not; that outside which thought could explore with the legitimate feeling of being on foreign territory – of being entirely elsewhere" (7).
80 Russell, "My Mental Development," 15–16.
81 Quoted in Feldman, "Samuel Beckett," 162.
82 Camus, "Myth of Sisyphus," 121, 122.
83 Conrad, *Letters Vol. 1*, 425.
84 Conrad, *Letters Vol. 2*, 16.
85 Conrad, *Letters Vol. 2*, 30.
86 Hardy, *Jude*, 17.
87 Hardy, *Two on a Tower*, 31.
88 Woolf, *Waves*, 287.
89 Woolf, *Lighthouse*, 64.
90 Woolf, *Lighthouse*, 16.
91 Woolf, *Lighthouse*, 135.
92 Unamuno, *Tragic Sense of Life*, 47.
93 Nietzsche, *Will to Power*, 545.
94 Critchley, *Very Little … Almost Nothing*, 8.
95 Nussbaum, "Narrative Emotions," 249.
96 Critchley, *Notes on Suicide*, 72.
97 This short text, *The Education of the Stoic*, is compiled from Pessoa's manuscript fragments, those signed by the Baron himself. Pessoa wrote under a multiplicity of so-called heteronyms, each with his own personality and history. The Baron's pieces were not collected and published all together in Portuguese until 1999. An English translation and presentation of the Baron's materials was published in 2005. Pessoa wrote to his future biographer, Gaspar Simões, of heteronyms "yet to appear" in 1932; the Baron is most likely one of these, as translator and editor Ricard Zenith comments (ix). The Baron kills himself, according to Pessoa's fictional newspaper report, on July 11, 1920.
98 Conrad, *Letters Vol. 2*, 30.
99 Schopenhauer, *World as Will and Representation Vol. 2*, 433.

100 Unamuno, *Tragic Sense of Life*, 36.
101 Cioran, *Heights of Despair*, 43.
102 Lawrence, *Women in Love*, 253, 383, 384.
103 Lispector, *Passion*, 78.
104 Lispector, *Passion*, 145, 104.
105 Deleuze and Guattari, *What Is Philosophy?*, 169.
106 Beckett, *Unnamable*, 340.
107 Rabaté, *Think, Pig!*, 8.
108 See Sartre, *Being and Nothingness*, 98, 131–3, 208.
109 See Furlani, *Beckett after Wittgenstein*. Furlani writes that language, in Wittgenstein's view, has its "enabling circulation within the congruent behaviors comprising a 'form of life' (*Lebensform*) – that is, the sum of those largely unarticulated agreements . . . in our communal activities" (23). Again: "Paramount in Wittgenstein's later work is the ascendancy of the particular (sensation, gesture, expression) over generality; the tangible conditions of a specific form of life, he stresses, determine all paradigms" (18). Furlani also defines this ground as both bereft of justification and inalterable, citing Wittgenstein: "If I have exhausted the justifications I have now reached bedrock, and my spade is turned. I am then inclined to say, 'this is just how I go about it'" (210).
110 Woolf, *Waves*, 64, 205.
111 Pessoa, "On a terribly," 15, 12.
112 Pessoa, "Today," 9–10, 25–6.
113 Pessoa, "I'd give anything," 1, 10, final ellipsis in original.
114 Pessoa, "The four songs," 18, 3–4, ellipsis in original.
115 Pessoa, "The four songs," 16.
116 Pessoa, "The four songs," 20.
117 Dienstag, *Pessimism*, 168.
118 Lukács, "Ideology of Modernism," 25.
119 Camus, "Almond Trees," 136.
120 Quoted in Büttner, *Samuel Beckett's Novel "Watt,"* 30.
121 Stewart, "Signing Off"; Gottschall, *The Storytelling Animal*; Robbe-Grillet, "Nature, Humanism, Tragedy"; Sheehan, *Modernism, Narrative, and Humanism*.
122 Woolf, *Lighthouse*, 97.
123 Dimock, "After Troy," 67.
124 DuBois, "Toppling the Hero," 142.

Chapter 2

1 See also White's "Notes on Externalizing Problems," in *Introducing Narrative Therapy*, eds. White and Denborough, 219–24.
2 Jameson, *Antinomies of Realism*, 10. While Jameson's "affect" is largely collective and impersonal, Hardy favors subjective and intersubjective feeling as plot's antithesis.

3 Woolf, "Novels of Thomas Hardy," 256–7, 247.
4 Moretti, *Way of the World*, 19.
5 Lukács, *Theory*, 41.
6 Lukács, "Ideology of Modernism," 17, 32, 34.
7 See Camus, "Future of Tragedy," and Scott, *Conscripts of Modernity*.
8 Hardy, *Tess*, 193.
9 Vernant, "Intimations of the Will," 63.
10 Sophocles, *Oedipus the King* 1516, 1529.
11 Sophocles, *Oedipus at Colonus* 288–9, 292–5.
12 Sophocles, *Oedipus at Colonus* 615–16.
13 Sophocles, *Oedipus at Colonus* 1098–105.
14 Hardy, *Jude*, 269.
15 See Maura Nolan and Willard Farnham on medieval tragedy and its legacies. Medieval English conceptions of the genre were generated by authors who had no direct access to the Greek plays; they did not read Greek. Medieval theories of tragedy were based on indirect paraphrases and limited Latin commentaries; see Mary Marshall, "Theatre in the Middle Ages." A certain freedom attached to medieval notions of tragic fate; the Middle Ages in fact developed two understandings of tragedy's causality. One model pictured human agency within a providential universe – great men who are punished for their vices. The other model evoked a pagan contingency outside providential narrative. This fundamental duality laid the groundwork for the ensuing Renaissance, neoclassical, Enlightenment, German Idealist, Victorian, and twentieth-century battles over the interpretation of the Greeks. In this regard, see Michael Lurie's "Facing up to Tragedy." Lurie contrasts Renaissance thinkers Joachim Camerarius's and Francesco Robortello's theories of Aristotle and Sophocles – in which Greek characters' sufferings are undeserved and do not testify to divine justice – with a concerted Christianization of the genre. Philippe Melanchthon and André Dacier, for instance, insist that Attic drama does represent divine providence: plots that punish the wicked and characters whose own vices occasion their downfalls. As Lurie shows, even during the late seventeenth- and eighteenth-century backlash against Renaissance and neoclassical interpretations' Christianizing of Aristotle and tragedy, when thinkers such as Saint-Évremond, Fontenelle, and the Abbé Terrasson argued for a decidedly non-Christian Attic worldview, they did so in order to disparage this Greek outlook and to profess the superiority of a modern tragedy that could perform moral work (Lurie, "Facing up to Tragedy," 448–9). In their bid to distinguish modern-day reason and justice from a Greek impiety alien to God's providence, these Enlightenment thinkers gave voice to the very view of the cosmos that Hardy understands as Greek and espouses as his own. For Hardy, however, to dramatize cosmic amorality is not to encourage immoral behavior. See also Simon Goldhill on German Idealism's conflation of tragedy and theodicy.
16 Peter Morton, for instance, argues that Tess is impulsive and incautious by birth; she is free of culpability for a nature she did not choose, but doomed

from within to act in self-destructive ways. See also Dale Kramer and Jeannette King, who discuss Victorian tragedy's apology for innocent suffering. Hardy, I would contend, rejects the notion that such suffering hallows heroines and confirms their virtue; unwarranted pain, in his fiction, distorts rather than consummates character and is a spur to ameliorative ethical action. Pamela Gossin argues, as I do, that Hardy instead adopts a "neo-Greek" view of the cosmos, in which blameless characters are subject to externally wrought misfortune (at the hands of both chance and men, as the Greeks had it).

17 When William Dean Howells and Havelock Ellis defend *Jude* in 1895 and 1896, respectively – taking the minority position at the time – they still regret that a "capricious troll" at times holds the reins of his plot (Howells, Review of *Jude the Obscure*, 1156; Ellis, "Concerning *Jude the Obscure*," 42). T. S. Eliot and E. M. Forster complain similarly of Hardy's narrative structure (*After Strange Gods*, 54–8; *Aspects of the Novel*, 140–2).

18 Woolf, "Mr. Bennett," 749.

19 Little attention has been given to Tess's narrator as a significant contributor to the form of Hardy's novel. I see him as a replacement for the Greek tragic chorus, an onlooker who not only laments but refuses the plot at hand. Yet Hardy's narrator in *Tess*, if discussed at all, is often viewed as the mouthpiece for an overly intrusive author and as an awkward and self-contradictory spokesman. See R. P. Draper's collection *Hardy: The Tragic Novels*, in particular, David Lodge's "Tess, Nature, and the Voices of Hardy."

20 Nietzsche, *Gay Science*, 170, 157.

21 Hardy, *Tess*, 31,

22 Hardy, *Jude*, 315.

23 Hardy, *Tess*, 30–1.

24 Hardy, *Jude*, 279.

25 Halliwell, "Plato and Aristotle," 52.

26 Aristotle, *Poetics* 1.9.1452a6–9. All Greek citations refer to the Loeb Classical Library edition of the *Poetics*. English translations come from Stephen Halliwell's *The "Poetics" of Aristotle: Translation and Commentary*.

27 See Stephen Halliwell, with whom I agree, in *Aristotle's "Poetics"* for a full discussion of this "secularization" of tragedy (e.g., 208, 232–4).

28 Aristotle, *Poetics* 1.24.1460a26–29.

29 Nussbaum, *Fragility of Goodness*, 283.

30 Vernant, "Intimations of the Will," 59–60, 67–9.

31 Lear, "Katharsis," 325.

32 Aristotle, *Poetics* 1.25.1461b22–24.

33 Nussbaum, "Tragedy and Self-Sufficiency," 278.

34 Lucas, *Tragedy*, 102.

35 Lucas, *Tragedy*, 14.

36 Halliwell, "Plato and Aristotle," 67.

37 Cascardi, "Tragedy and Philosophy," 171.

38 See Cascardi, Critchley, Halliwell, Harris, and Lear.

39 Hardy, *Tess*, 179, 265.

40 Hardy, *Tess*, 267.
41 Hardy, *Tess*, 224–5.
42 Hardy, *Tess*, 202.
43 Hardy, *Tess*, 30.
44 Hardy, *Tess*, 57.
45 Hardy, *Tess*, 57.
46 1 Kings 18:29.
47 Hardy, "Hap," 13.
48 Hardy, "A Sign-Seeker," 7.
49 See Catherine Gallagher on Hardy's anthropological method and Victorian anthropology's new vision of sexual and sacrificial primitive ritual. See also Nicole Loraux's *Tragic Ways of Killing a Woman* on the sacrifice of virgins and the suicide of wives in ancient tragedy.
50 Hardy, *Tess*, 62.
51 Hardy, *Tess*, 62.
52 Hardy, *Tess*, 62.
53 Hardy, *Tess*, 63.
54 Hardy, *Tess*, 71.
55 Hardy, *Tess*, 71.
56 Hardy, *Tess*, 71.
57 Hardy, *Tess*, 82.
58 Hardy, *Tess*, 67.
59 Hardy, *Tess*, 139.
60 Hardy, *Tess*, 72.
61 Hardy, *Tess*, 75.
62 Hardy, *Tess*, 99.
63 Hardy, *Tess*, 71.
64 Hardy, *Tess*, 116, 78.
65 Hardy, *Tess*, 78, 79.
66 Hardy, *Tess*, 81.
67 Hardy, *Tess*, 115.
68 Johnson, "Argument," 391.
69 Hardy, *Tess*, 314.
70 Hardy, *Tess*, 77.
71 Hardy, *Tess*, 98.
72 Hardy, *Tess*, 240.
73 Hardy, *Tess*, 151.
74 Hardy, *Tess*, 153.
75 Hardy, *Tess*, 240.
76 Hardy, *Tess*, 236, 219.
77 Hardy, *Tess*, 40.
78 Hardy, *Tess*, 261.
79 Hardy, *Tess*, 189.
80 Hardy, *Tess*, 190.
81 Hardy, *Tess*, 282.

82 Hardy, *Tess*, 304, 300, 301.
83 Hardy, *Tess*, 299.
84 Hardy, *Tess*, 312.
85 Hardy, *Tess*, 124; Hardy, *Jude*, 7.
86 Hardy, *Jude*, 270.
87 Hardy, *Tess*, 243.
88 Hardy, *Jude*, 275, 210.
89 Hardy, *Jude*, 283, 277.
90 Hardy, *Jude*, 275, 276, 283.
91 Hardy, *Jude*, 171.
92 Hardy, *Jude*, 285.
93 Hardy, *Jude*, 270.
94 Hardy, *Jude*, 170, second ellipsis in original.
95 Hardy, *Jude*, 168.
96 Hardy, *Jude*, 111.
97 In Hardy's manuscript only, Jude exclaims: "When men of a later age look back upon the barbarism, cruelty, and superstition of the times in which we have the unhappiness to live, it will appear more clearly to them than it does to us that the irksomeness of life is less owing to its natural conditions, though they are bad enough, than to those artificial compulsions arranged for our well-being, which have no root in the nature of things!" (415). See Patricia Ingham's "Explanatory Notes" in the Oxford World's Classics edition of *Jude* for such textual variants.
98 Hardy, *Jude*, 264.
99 Hardy, *Jude*, 264.
100 Hardy, *Jude*, 266.
101 Hardy, *Jude*, 270, 266, 270.
102 Hardy, *Jude*, 307, 306, 271.
103 Hardy, *Tess*, 218.
104 Hardy, *Tess*, 179, 199.
105 Hardy, *Jude*, 289.
106 Hardy, *Jude*, 290.
107 Carson, "Gender of Sound," 126.
108 Carson, "Gender of Sound," 127.
109 Carson, "Gender of Sound," 126.
110 Carson, "Gender of Sound," 133.
111 Carson, "Gender of Sound," 132.
112 Carson, "Gender of Sound," 132–3.
113 Vernant, "Ambiguity and Reversal," 133–5; Vidal-Naquet, "Oedipus between Two Cities," 326.
114 Vernant, "Oedipus without the Complex," 106.
115 Carson, "Gender of Sound," 133–4.
116 Carson, "Gender of Sound," 134.
117 Coles, "Borderline Personality Disorder."
118 Berger, "Power, Selfhood, and Identity," 1.

119 Berger, "Power, Selfhood, and Identity," 2.
120 Berger, "Power, Selfhood, and Identity," 3.
121 Shaw and Proctor, "Women at the Margins," 487.
122 Shaw and Proctor, "Women at the Margins," 488.
123 Nussbaum, *Fragility of Goodness*, 400; Euripides, *Hekabe* 767–70. Nussbaum translates these lines as follows: "The gods are strong, and so is convention (*nomos*) which rules over them. For it is by *nomos* that we recognize the gods and live our lives, making our distinctions between injustice and justice" (400).
124 Euripides, *Hekabe* 820.
125 Euripides, *Hekabe* 225, 230–3, emphasis in original.
126 Euripides, *Hekabe* 360–1.
127 Euripides, *Hekabe* 375, 389.
128 Euripides, *Hekabe* 552–3.
129 Euripides, *Hekabe* 265–6.
130 Euripides, *Hekabe* 341.
131 Euripides, *Hekabe* 111.
132 Euripides, *Hekabe* 223.
133 Euripides, *Hekabe* 705.
134 Euripides, *Hekabe* 607.
135 Euripides, *Hekabe* 662–3; Nussbaum, *Fragility of Goodness*, 409.
136 Euripides, *Hekabe* 1136.
137 Hardy, *Jude*, 14.
138 Hardy, *Jude*, 17.
139 Hardy, *Jude*, 14, 15, 17.
140 Hardy, *Jude*, 15.
141 Hardy, *Jude*, 14.
142 Hardy, *Jude*, 15–16.
143 Hardy, *Two on a Tower*, xvii.
144 Hardy, *Two on a Tower*, 29.
145 Hardy, *Two on a Tower*, 30.
146 Hardy, *Two on a Tower*, 29.
147 Hardy, *Two on a Tower*, 28.
148 Hardy, *Two on a Tower*, 57–8.
149 Arnold, "On the Modern," 464.
150 Arnold, "On the Modern," 471.
151 Arnold, "On the Modern," 464; Hardy, *Two on a Tower*, 31.
152 Hardy, *Letters Vol. 3*, 5.
153 These are Hardy's words to William Archer; see Archer, *Real Conversations*, 45.
154 Hardy, *Letters Vol. 5*, 51.
155 Hardy, *Letters Vol. 5*, 50.
156 Hardy, *Letters Vol. 5*, 84.
157 Hardy, *Letters Vol. 5*, 84.
158 Hardy, "In Tenebris II," 5.

159 Hardy, "In Tenebris II," 14.
160 Lawrence, *Study*, 29.
161 Lawrence, *Study*, 29.
162 Lawrence, *Study*, 29–30.
163 Woolf, "Novels of Thomas Hardy," 255.
164 Kelly, "Schopenhauer's Influence," 232, 241.
165 Archer, *Real Conversations*, 47.
166 Hardy, *Tess*, 62. Rachel Ablow's chapter on Hardy in *Victorian Pain* (2017) notes a number of critics who read *Tess* and *Jude* as instances of Hardy's "ethical turn" toward a more "humanitarian" and "instrumental" depiction of pain: representing pain as a means of consciousness-raising in readers (116, 121). Ablow, however, emphasizes Hardy's continued representation of "existential suffering" in *Tess* and addresses suffering, across Hardy's oeuvre, that does not appear social in origin – and therefore does not appear susceptible to remediation (121).
167 Hardy, "Apology," 557.
168 Hardy, "Apology," 557.
169 Hardy, "Apology," 558.
170 Archer, *Real Conversations*, 46–7.

Chapter 3

1 Woolf, *Lighthouse*, 128.
2 Woolf, "On Not Knowing Greek," 38.
3 Woolf, *Waves*, 24–5.
4 Aeschylus, *Seven against Thebes*, 675–6.
5 Woolf herself recounts a nearly identical experience in her autobiographical "A Sketch of the Past," penned over a decade after *The Waves*: "I overheard my father or my mother say that Mr Valpy had killed himself. The next thing I remember is being in the garden at night and walking on the path by the apple tree. It seemed to me that the apple tree was connected with the horror of Mr Valpy's suicide. I could not pass it. I stood there looking at the grey-green creases of the bark – it was a moonlit night – in a trance of horror. I seemed to be dragged down, hopelessly, into some pit of absolute despair from which I could not escape. My body seemed paralysed" (*Moments of Being*, 71).
6 Woolf, "Novels of Thomas Hardy," 254.
7 Woolf, "Novels of Thomas Hardy," 255.
8 Woolf, "Novels of Thomas Hardy," 246; Hardy, "A Sign-Seeker," 7.
9 Hardy, "A Sign-Seeker," 36, 37–40.
10 Hardy, "A Sign-Seeker," 41.
11 Hardy, *Jude*, 269.
12 Woolf, *Essays Vol. 4*, 592.
13 Woolf, "Novels of Thomas Hardy," 257.
14 Woolf, "Novels of Thomas Hardy," 246.

15 Woolf, *Lighthouse*, 134.
16 Woolf, *Lighthouse*, 135.
17 Harrison, *Themis*, 477.
18 Plato, *Republic* 604c.
19 Mills, "Goddesses and Ghosts," 108.
20 Mills, "Goddesses and Ghosts," 105.
21 Barr, "Divine Politics," 129, 132–3; Fowler, "Moments and Metamorpho-
    ses," 228, 230, 233; Wyatt, "The Celebration of Eros," 160, 162–3, 165.
22 E.g., Carpentier, *Ritual, Myth, and the Modernist Text*, 171–88.
23 Dalgarno, *Visible World*, 174.
24 Lucas, *Euripides*, 15.
25 See Prins, *Ladies' Greek* for more on Case, Woolf, and Harrison, among
    others.
26 Woolf, "On Not Knowing Greek," 31. Woolf of course did know Greek. She
    began classes at age fifteen and studied privately with Clara Pater and Janet
    Case. Throughout her life, Woolf turned and returned to the Greeks. She
    documented her early reading of the tragedians in her diaries and letters (what
    pride and pleasure she took in it), confided her childhood sexual abuse to
    Case, and composed her own reviews and essays that treated Homer, the
    tragedians, and Plato ("On Not Knowing Greek," "The Perfect Language").
    Woolf read and admired Harrison's scholarship, and traveled to Greece in
    1906 and 1932. She analyzed contemporary English translations of the Greek
    tragedians and performed her own translation work: pasted the Greek text of
    Aeschylus' *Agamemnon* into a notebook in which she made a "complete
    edition, text, translation, & notes of my own – mostly copied from Verrall;
    but carefully gone into by me" (*Diary 2*, 215). Woolf kept two such note-
    books on Aeschylus: on *Choephori* (1907) and on *Agamemnon* (1922). For
    analyses of these notebooks and for commentary on Woolf's learning of
    Greek, Greek and Latin in nineteenth- and early twentieth-century education
    and culture, and the gender politics of studying the classics, see Prins,
    "OTOTOTOI: Virginia Woolf and 'The Naked Cry' of Cassandra"; Mills,
    Virginia Woolf, Jane Ellen Harrison, and the Spirit of Modernist Classicism;
    McCoskey and Corbett, "Virginia Woolf, Richard Jebb, and Sophocles'
    Antigone"; Koulouris, *Hellenism and Loss in the Work of Virginia Woolf*;
    Dalgarno, *Virginia Woolf and the Visible World*.
27 Plato, *Republic* 604c.
28 Carson, "Gender of Sound," 127–8.
29 Carson, "Gender of Sound," 128.
30 Carson, "Gender of Sound," 133.
31 Woolf, "Time Passes," Holograph ms (first page of draft). See Woolf Online,
    Berg Materials, Folios 27 and 149, page 198, www.woolfonline.com/?node=
    content/text/transcriptions&project=1&parent=6&taxa=25. Strikethrough in
    original.
32 Camus, "Future of Tragedy," 305.
33 Woolf, *Lighthouse*, 63, 62.

34 Woolf, *Lighthouse*, 63.
35 Woolf, *Lighthouse*, 54.
36 Woolf, *Lighthouse*, 192.
37 Woolf, *Lighthouse*, 160.
38 Woolf, *Moments of Being*, 142.
39 Woolf, *Moments of Being*, 71.
40 Woolf, *Moments of Being*, 72.
41 Levy, "Woolf's Metaphysics," 116.
42 Banfield, "Tragic Time," 61–2, 64–5, 67.
43 Halliwell, "Plato and Aristotle," 64.
44 For more on Aristotle's conceptions of chance and probability, see *Probabilities, Hypotheticals, and Counterfactuals in Ancient Greek Thought*, particularly Victoria Wohl's essay "Play of the Improbable: Euripides' Unlikely *Helen*."
45 Euripides, *Alkestis* 835–7, 845–9.
46 Sophocles, *Women of Trachis* 1266–70.
47 Euripides, *Hippolytos* 1572; Euripides, *Herakles* 487.
48 Lucas, *Tragedy*, 101.
49 Darwin Correspondence Project, Letter 2713 (Darwin to Asa Gray, February 24, 1860).
50 Darwin Correspondence Project, Letter 5395 (Darwin to J. D. Hooker, February 8, 1867).
51 For more on Darwin and chance, see Johnson, *Darwin's Dice*. Johnson clarifies that one can predict, probabilistically, the fitness of a given phenotype within a given environment; however, genetic variations, as well as their phenotypic effects, may be in theory unpredictable. Darwin routinely discussed chance in both of these ways. Theorists today also recognize that migration (gene flow) and genetic drift (the spreading of certain genes purely by luck, not because of any benefit they might confer on organisms) can greatly affect the gene pool of a species. In which environments certain variations occur is also a matter of chance. Modernist geneticists, too, grappled with the role of chance in extinction (see Lewontin on Sewall Wright), the fact that phenotypes are the luck of the hereditary draw (see Allen on Thomas Hunt Morgan), and the fact that de novo mutations may occur contingently and be unforeseeable in principle. Geneticist Jacques Monod argued in *Chance and Necessity* that life itself came about by chance. For a general survey of the rise of chance in the nineteenth century, see Hacking, *The Taming of Chance*; for the scientific milieu in which modernists lived, see Thiher, *Fiction Refracts Science*. For an introduction to Darwin and literary studies, see Greenberg. For Darwinian tenets and anxieties in fiction, see Beer, *Darwin's Plots*; Ebbatson; Glendening; Knight; and Richter. For Darwinian legacies in modernism, see Waugh and Rohman. For thoroughly nontragic Darwinian inheritances in literature and culture, see Beer, "Darwin and the Uses of Extinction"; Levine; and Grosz.
52 Darwin, *Variation Vol. 2*, 321.
53 Reprinted in Gray, *Darwiniana*, 70.

54 Gray, *Darwiniana*, 28–9.
55 Darwin Correspondence Project, Letter 13299 (Darwin to T. H. Farrer, August 28, 1881); Wallace, *World of Life*, 259. Hans Driesch's late nineteenth-century vitalism was also explicitly a corrective to Darwin's "apotheosis of chance," as reviewer Francis Sumner names the object of Driesch's critique (105). Driesch insisted that immaterial spirit directed evolution.
56 Wallace, *World of Life*, 401.
57 Wallace, *Darwinism*, 477.
58 Darwin Correspondence Project, Letter 2998 (Darwin to Asa Gray, November 26, 1860).
59 Darwin Correspondence Project, Letter 2855 (Darwin to Asa Gray, July 3, 1860).
60 Darwin Correspondence Project, Letter 2814 (Darwin to Asa Gray, May 22, 1860).
61 Russell, *Mysticism and Logic*, 58.
62 Russell, *Mysticism and Logic*, 72.
63 Russell, *Mysticism and Logic*, 72.
64 Williams, *Shame and Necessity*, 163, 166. Thanks to Simon Critchley for alerting me to these passages. Cf. Critchley, *Tragedy, the Greeks, and Us*, 66–70.
65 Mills, *Virginia Woolf*, 7.
66 Harrison, *Themis*, 472.
67 Harrison, *Themis*, 472.
68 Harrison, *Themis*, 48.
69 Harrison, *Themis*, 339.
70 Harrison, *Themis*, xi.
71 Harrison, *Themis*, 334, italics in original.
72 Harrison, *Themis*, 443.
73 Harrison, *Themis*, 476.
74 Harrison, *Themis*, 468.
75 Harrison, *Themis*, 490.
76 Harrison, *Themis*, 478.
77 Murray, "Excursus," 342.
78 Murray, "Excursus," 342–3.
79 Murray, "Excursus," 344.
80 Murray, "Excursus," 343.
81 Murray, "Excursus," 344.
82 Dienstag, *Pessimism*, 169.
83 Dienstag, *Pessimism*, 169–70.
84 Reginster, *Affirmation of Life*, 248.
85 Nietzsche, *Birth of Tragedy*, 124.
86 Nietzsche, *Gay Science*, 169.
87 Nietzsche, *Gay Science*, 170.
88 Nietzsche, *Gay Science*, 157.
89 Nietzsche, *Will to Power*, 452; Nussbaum, "Transfigurations," 99.

90 Nussbaum, "Transfigurations," 99.
91 Nussbaum, "Transfigurations," 99.
92 Nehamas, *Nietzsche*, 89, 166.
93 Reginster, *Affirmation of Life*, 220.
94 Dienstag, *Pessimism*, 169; second ellipsis in original.
95 Nietzsche, *Daybreak*, 80.
96 Nietzsche, *Daybreak*, 80.
97 Hacking, *Taming of Chance*, 147–8; ellipsis in original.
98 Nietzsche, *Daybreak*, 81.
99 Nietzsche, *Daybreak*, 81.
100 Nietzsche, *Gay Science*, 104; Nietzsche, *Will to Power*, 536.
101 Reginster, *Affirmation of Life*, 159–62.
102 Reginster, *Affirmation of Life*, 126.
103 Reginster, *Affirmation of Life*, 246–8.
104 Nietzsche, *Birth of Tragedy*, 12.
105 Woolf, "On Not Knowing Greek," 26.
106 Woolf, "On Not Knowing Greek," 26.
107 Woolf, "On Not Knowing Greek," 26.
108 Plato, *Republic* 604c; Hardy, "Hap," 12.
109 For Woolf, Russell, and Cambridge philosophy, see Ann Banfield, *The Phantom Table* and "Time Passes: Virginia Woolf, Post-Impressionism, and Cambridge Time."
110 Banfield, "Tragic Time," 66.
111 Banfield, "Tragic Time," 66.
112 Woolf, *Waves*, 251.
113 Banfield, *Phantom Table*, 83–5.
114 Russell, *Problems of Philosophy*, 57.
115 Russell, *Problems of Philosophy*, 56, 58, 59.
116 Russell, *Problems of Philosophy*, 25, 48.
117 Russell, *Problems of Philosophy*, 28.
118 Banfield, *Phantom Table*, 13.
119 Banfield, *Phantom Table*, 59–107, 165.
120 Russell, *Mysticism and Logic*, 180.
121 Banfield, *Phantom Table*, 194.
122 Banfield, *Phantom Table*, 148–54, 190.
123 Woolf, *Waves*, 249.
124 Woolf, *Night and Day*, 331; quoted in Banfield, *Phantom Table*, 121.
125 Woolf, *Night and Day*, 196–7; quoted in Banfield, *Phantom* Table, 122.
126 Woolf, *Waves*, 130.
127 Woolf, *Waves*, 21.
128 Woolf, *Waves*, 285.
129 Woolf, *Waves*, 189.
130 Woolf, *Waves*, 238–9.
131 Woolf, *Waves*, 272.
132 Woolf, *Waves*, 283.

133 Woolf, *Waves*, 257.
134 Woolf, *Waves*, 262.
135 Woolf, *Waves*, 271.
136 Woolf, *Waves*, 287, 285.
137 Woolf, *Waves*, 295.
138 Woolf, *Waves*, 295.
139 Woolf, *Waves*, 283.
140 Woolf, *Waves*, 257, 255.
141 Woolf, *Waves*, 285, 287.
142 Woolf, *Waves*, 146.
143 Woolf, *Waves*, 24.
144 Woolf, *Waves*, 145.
145 Woolf, *Waves*, 278.
146 Woolf, *Waves*, 138.
147 Woolf, *Waves*, 143.
148 Woolf, *Waves*, 142.
149 Woolf, *Waves*, 145, 143.
150 Woolf, *Waves*, 278.
151 Woolf, *Waves*, 278.
152 Woolf, *Waves*, 279.
153 Woolf, *Waves*, 52.
154 Woolf, *Waves*, 266.
155 Fletcher and Bradbury read Woolf in this light in "The Introverted Novel." For those who refute this stance and argue that Woolf is centrally concerned with more than psychological interiority and Bergsonian time, see Banfield, *The Phantom Table*; Hornby, "The Cameraless Optic"; Hussey, *The Singing of the Real World*; Rosenbaum, "The Philosophical Realism of Virginia Woolf"; Sim, *Virginia Woolf: The Patterns of Ordinary Experience*; and Sumner, *A Route to Modernism*.
156 Woolf, *Waves*, 280.
157 Woolf, *Lighthouse*, 134.
158 Woolf, *Lighthouse*, 134.
159 Woolf, *Waves*, 269.
160 Woolf, *Waves*, 275.
161 Woolf, *Waves*, 269, 270.
162 Woolf, *Lighthouse*, 16.
163 Woolf, *Lighthouse*, 16, 63, 62.
164 Woolf, *Lighthouse*, 62.
165 Woolf, *Lighthouse*, 62.
166 Woolf, *Lighthouse*, 59.
167 Woolf, *Lighthouse*, 63.
168 Woolf, *Lighthouse*, 63.
169 Woolf, *Lighthouse*, 64.
170 Woolf, *Lighthouse*, 63.
171 Woolf, *Lighthouse*, 64.

172 Woolf, *Lighthouse*, 65.
173 Woolf, *Lighthouse*, 65.
174 Woolf, *Lighthouse*, 65.
175 Woolf, *Lighthouse*, 65.
176 Lewis, *Men without Art*, 160.
177 Woolf, *Lighthouse*, 44, 59, 60.
178 Woolf, *Lighthouse*, 83, 64.
179 Woolf, *Lighthouse*, 15, 207.
180 Woolf, *Diary 3*, 13.
181 Woolf, *Lighthouse*, 97.
182 Woolf, *Lighthouse*, 105.
183 Woolf, *Lighthouse*, 112.
184 Woolf, *Waves*, 277.
185 Woolf, *Waves*, 169, 128.
186 Woolf, *Waves*, 277–8.
187 Woolf, *Lighthouse*, 126.
188 Woolf, *Lighthouse*, 125.
189 Peirce, *Writings*, 125.
190 Euripides, *Hippolytos* 1197–200.
191 Woolf, *Lighthouse*, 134, 135.
192 Banfield, "Tragic Time," 49.
193 Woolf, *Lighthouse*, 128.
194 Woolf, *Lighthouse*, 132.
195 Woolf, *Lighthouse*, 109.
196 Woolf, *Lighthouse*, 133.
197 Woolf, *Lighthouse*, 129.
198 Woolf, *Lighthouse*, 129.
199 Woolf, *Lighthouse*, 129.
200 Woolf, *Lighthouse*, 129.
201 Woolf, *Lighthouse*, 135.
202 Exodus 3:13–14.
203 Woolf, *Lighthouse*, 138.
204 Worman, *Virginia Woolf's Greek Tragedy*, 59.
205 Woolf, "On Not Knowing Greek," 30.
206 Woolf, *Waves*, 285.
207 Woolf, "On Not Knowing Greek," 31. For more on Woolf and translation (the ways in which Woolf construed and intervened in British debates about "knowing" Greek, participated in and indicted racist perspectives on Greece, and registered the difference that one's subject position makes to interpretation), see Dalgarno, *Virginia Woolf and the Migrations of Language* and "Virginia Woolf: Translation and 'Iterability'"; Spiropoulou, "'On Not Knowing Greek': Virginia Woolf's Spatial Critique of Authority"; and Worman, *Virginia Woolf's Greek Tragedy*.
208 Woolf, "On Not Knowing Greek," 30.
209 Worman, *Virginia Woolf's Greek Tragedy*, 60.

210 Worman, *Virginia Woolf's Greek Tragedy*, 59–60.
211 Woolf, "Agamemnon" Notebook. Woolf's notebook is housed in the New York Public Library's Berg Collection. Woolf's translation of this passage faces the corresponding Greek lines 376–86 in the notebook. From the *Thesaurus Linguae Graecae* online database the Greek is as follows and comes from D. L. Page, ed., *Aeschyli Septem Quae Supersunt Tragoedias* (Oxford: Clarendon Press, 1972):

πόθωι δ' ὑπερποντίας
φάσμα δόξει δόμων ἀνάσσειν·
εὐμόρφων δὲ κολοσσῶν
ἔχθεται χάρις ἀνδρί,
ὀμμάτων δ' ἐν ἀχηνίαις
ἔρρει πᾶσ' Ἀφροδίτα.
ὀνειρόφαντοι δὲ πενθήμονες
πάρεισι δόξαι φέρου-
σαι χάριν ματαίαν·
μάταν γάρ, εὖτ' ἂν ἐσθλά τις δοκοῦνθ' ὁρᾶι,
παραλλάξασα διὰ
χερῶν βέβακεν ὄψις, οὐ μεθύστερον
πτεροῖς ὀπαδοῦσ' ὕπνου κελεύθοις.

(414–26)

212 Verrall, *"Agamemnon" of Aeschylus*, 52–3, bold in original.
213 Woolf, "On Not Knowing Greek," 30.
214 Aeschylus, *Agamemnon*, trans. Carson, 304–5.
215 Aeschylus, *Agamemnon*, trans. Lattimore, 418–19.
216 Aeschylus, *Agamemnon*, trans. Fagles, 417.
217 Beckett, *Unnamable*, 340.
218 Woolf, *Mrs. Dalloway*, 86, 88.
219 Woolf, *Lighthouse*, 134.
220 Woolf, *Lighthouse*, 131, 133.
221 Woolf, *Lighthouse*, 133, 134.
222 Woolf, "Agamemnon" Notebook. Woolf's translation faces Greek lines 387–8 in the notebook. The Greek reads "τὰ μὲν κατ' οἴκους ἐφ' ἑστίας ἄχη / τάδ' ἐστὶ καὶ τῶνδ' ὑπερβατώτερα" (427–8) in Page, *Aeschyli Septem Quae Supersunt Tragoedias*.
223 Woolf, "Agamemnon" Notebook. Woolf's translation faces Greek line 394 in the notebook. The Greek reads "τεύχη καὶ σποδός" (435) in Page, *Aeschyli Septem Quae Supersunt Tragoedias*.
224 Worman, *Virginia Woolf's Greek Tragedy*, 42.
225 Woolf, *Lighthouse*, 161.
226 Carpentier, *Ritual, Myth, and the Modernist Text*, 187.
227 Woolf, *Lighthouse*, 79.
228 Woolf, *Lighthouse*, 161.
229 Woolf, *Lighthouse*, 180.
230 Woolf, *Waves*, 297. Fowler notes that "[i]t will be left to Bernard, the unheroic, to fling himself against oblivion with Ajax's words ὦ Θάνατε

Θάνατε: 'O Death!' (Sophocles, *Ajax*, 1.854; *The Waves* 297)" ("Moments and Metamorphosis," 233).
231 Woolf, *Waves*, 297.

Chapter 4

1 Camus, "Future of Tragedy," 306.
2 Camus, "Helen's Exile," 149.
3 Camus, "Future of Tragedy," 306.
4 Camus, "Helen's Exile," 150.
5 Fanon, *Wretched of the Earth*, 312.
6 Sharpe, "Restoring Camus," 409.
7 Camus, "Future of Tragedy," 297.
8 Camus, "Future of Tragedy," 304.
9 Camus, "Future of Tragedy," 305, 297–8.
10 Camus, "Future of Tragedy," 302, 306.
11 Camus, "Future of Tragedy," 301.
12 Camus, "Future of Tragedy," 302.
13 Camus, "Future of Tragedy," 302.
14 Camus, "Future of Tragedy," 302, 304.
15 Camus, "Future of Tragedy," 306, 307.
16 Camus, "Future of Tragedy," 303–4.
17 Camus, *Myth of Sisyphus*, 119, 120, 122.
18 Camus, *Myth of Sisyphus*, 122; Camus, "Future of Tragedy," 305.
19 Camus, *Myth of Sisyphus*, 122.
20 Camus, *Myth of Sisyphus*, 122.
21 Camus, *Myth of Sisyphus*, 123.
22 Woolf, *Lighthouse*, 59.
23 Camus, *Myth of Sisyphus*, 123, 121.
24 Camus, "Future of Tragedy," 304.
25 Camus, *Myth of Sisyphus*, 21.
26 Camus, "Future of Tragedy," 305.
27 Camus, "Future of Tragedy," 305.
28 Camus, *Rebel*, 303.
29 Camus, "Create Dangerously," 265.
30 Camus, "Future of Tragedy," 308.
31 Camus, *Plague*, 127.
32 Camus, "William Faulkner," 313.
33 Camus, "Future of Tragedy," 306.
34 Camus, *Rebel*, 221–2.
35 Camus, *Rebel*, 30.
36 Sharpe, *Camus, Philosophe*, 314.
37 For Camus's and Monod's friendship, exchange of ideas, and mutual knowledge of one another's work, see Carroll, *Brave Genius*.

38 Monod, *Chance and Necessity*, 112–13.
39 Monod, *Chance and Necessity*, 166, italics in original.
40 Monod, *Chance and Necessity*, 170.
41 Monod, *Chance and Necessity*, 171.
42 Monod, *Chance and Necessity*, 180.
43 In *The Rebel* Camus criticizes Epicurus and Lucretius for their impulse to wall themselves off from pain and proclaim invulnerability to harm: "But what a strange form of enjoyment! It consists in sealing up the walls of the citadel, of making sure of a supply of bread and water and of living in darkness and silence.... Epicurus, in order to escape from destiny, destroys sensibility.... [For Lucretius] [t]he walled citadel becomes an armed camp. *Moenia mundi*, the ramparts of the world, is one of the key expressions of Lucretius' rhetoric" (28–9, 30).
44 Woolf, *Lighthouse*, 62.
45 Camus, *Notebooks 1935–1942*, 9.
46 Woolf, *Lighthouse*, 63; Camus, *Notebooks 1935–1942*, 9.
47 Catherine Camus published *Albert Camus: solitaire et solidaire*.
48 Gaspari, "Écrire contre soi-même," 52.
49 Gaspari, "Écrire contre soi-même," 52.
50 Gaspari, "Écrire contre soi-même," 54, 65–6.
51 Gaspari, "Écrire contre soi-même," 52, 54, 65.
52 Gaspari, "Écrire contre soi-même," 66–7.
53 Camus, "Preface," 17.
54 Camus, "Preface," 13–14, 6.
55 Woolf, *Waves*, 278; Woolf, *Lighthouse*, 65. See Prouteau, *Albert Camus ou le présent impérissable* (2008) for further discussion of the moment throughout Camus's writings. Prouteau argues that Camus's initiatory, ecstatic moments dilate time but do not abolish it; the point is not to move beyond the material world or to exchange time for timelessness (225–8, 255–7). Prouteau distinguishes Camus's moments of plenitude from Jean Grenier's: both authors are interested in indelible, foundational moments that seem, simultaneously, to be unexpected visitations from without, communions with the natural world, and bearers of self-knowledge. But Camus finds these epiphanic moments quintessentially human, earthy, and bodily, while Grenier finds them mystical, aesthetic, so many signs of divinity (72–7). Camus's moments are not, that is, instances of the Kantian sublime, of terror and transcendence, but secular moments of joy.
56 Beauvoir, *Ethics*, 44.
57 Beauvoir, *Ethics*, 34.
58 Dienstag, *Pessimism*, 129.
59 Corbic, *Camus*, 173–4, my translation.
60 Jeanson, "Albert Camus," 2074, my translation.
61 Jeanson, "Albert Camus," 2076, my translation.
62 Jeanson, "Albert Camus," 2084, my translation.
63 Sartre, "Réponse," 346.
64 My translation.
65 Foley, *Albert Camus*, 119.

66 Camus, *Rebel*, 136–7, 223.

67 Hayden, *Camus*, 118.

68 Hayden, *Camus*, 17–18, 99–100.

69 Hayden, *Camus*, 70–1 and 89–90nn1–2 on Sartre's evolving sense of the role of violence in history and revolution.

70 Hayden, *Camus*, 64.

71 Hayden, *Camus*, 72–5.

72 Hayden, *Camus*, 73.

73 Sartre, "Réponse," 346, my translation. Sartre refers to the following lines from Camus's 1939 essay "The Minotaur, or Stopping in Oran": "At certain times, though, how tempted one feels in this town to defect to the enemy! How tempting to merge oneself with these stones, to mingle with this burning, impassive universe that challenges history and its agitations! A vain temptation, no doubt.... Nothingness lies within our grasp no more than does the absolute" (130, 131). Camus insists on a natural history that exceeds human history, but its hot, stony "challenge" to human affairs throws into relief their human meaning.

74 Camus, "Adulterous Wife," 25.

75 Camus, "Adulterous Wife," 4.

76 Camus, "Adulterous Wife," 4.

77 Camus, "Adulterous Wife," 27.

78 Camus, "Adulterous Wife," 28.

79 Camus, "Adulterous Wife," 23.

80 Camus, "Adulterous Wife," 24.

81 Camus, "Adulterous Wife," 24.

82 Woolf, *Lighthouse*, 161.

83 Camus, "Adulterous Wife," 24.

84 Camus, "Adulterous Wife," 25.

85 Camus, 29–30, first ellipsis in original.

86 Woolf, *Lighthouse*, 105.

87 Camus, "Adulterous Wife," 31.

88 Camus, "Adulterous Wife," 32–3.

89 Camus, "Adulterous Wife," 32.

90 Camus, "Adulterous Wife," 32.

91 Camus, "Adulterous Wife," 32, 33.

92 Woolf, *Lighthouse*, 65.

93 Toura, *Quête*, 95–116.

94 Sharpe, *Camus, Philosophe*, 314n1348.

95 Camus, "The Desert," 102.

96 Camus, "Nuptials at Tipasa," 66–8.

97 Camus, "The Desert," 102.

98 Camus, "The Wind at Djemila," 77–9.

99 Toura, *Quête*, 100–1.

100 Toura, *Quête*, 102, my translation.

101 Camus, *Algerian Chronicles*, 152.

102 Sartre, "Colonialism Is a System," 36.
103 Sartre, "Colonialism Is a System," 36.
104 Conor Cruise O'Brien in "Camus, Algeria, and 'The Fall'" (1969) cites Camus's comment to a reporter in Sweden, after he has received the Nobel Prize: "I have always condemned terror. I must also condemn a terrorism which operates blindly, in the streets of Algiers for example, and which one day may strike my mother or my family. I believe in justice but I will defend my mother before justice" (172). "Terrorism which operates blindly" echoes Camus's characterization of tragic fate itself – to which he will not accord justice.
105 Sartre, "Colonialism Is a System," 45.
106 Camus, *Algerian Chronicles*, 102, 104.
107 Camus, 108, Camus's italics.
108 Sartre, "A Victory," 67.
109 Camus, "Three Interviews," 348.
110 Carroll, "An Interview," https://cup.columbia.edu/author-interviews/carroll-camus-algerian.
111 Camus, "Helen's Exile," 150, 151, 154.
112 Dienstag, *Pessimism*, 141.
113 Dienstag, *Pessimism*, 141.
114 Todd, *Albert Camus*, 405.
115 Camus, *First Man*, 283, 284.
116 Camus, *First Man*, 26.
117 Spiquel, "*Premier Homme*," 18. All translations mine.
118 Spiquel, "*Premier Homme*," 23.
119 Camus, *First Man*, 282–3.
120 Quoted in Spiquel, "*Premier Homme*," 24.
121 Quoted in Spiquel, "*Premier Homme*," 20–1.
122 Quoted in Spiquel, "*Premier Homme*," 24.
123 Quoted in Spiquel, "*Premier Homme*," 24.
124 Quoted in Spiquel, "*Premier Homme*," 30.
125 Quoted in Spiquel, "*Premier Homme*," 31; Camus, *Notebooks 1942–1951*, 248.
126 Camus, "Adulterous Wife," 33.
127 Camus, "Three Interviews," 364.
128 Sharpe, *Camus, Philosophe*, 127.
129 Sharpe, *Camus, Philosophe*, 200–1.
130 Camus, *Rebel*, 101–2.
131 Srigley, *Critique of Modernity*, 71.
132 Srigley, *Critique of Modernity*, 80.
133 Srigley, *Critique of Modernity*, 75–6, 80.
134 Sartre, "Explication," 121.
135 Camus, *Stranger*, 59.
136 Camus, *Stranger*, 59.
137 Camus, *Stranger*, 121.
138 Robbe-Grillet, "Nature, Humanism, Tragedy," 73.

139 Robbe-Grillet, "Nature, Humanism, Tragedy," 63–4.
140 Williams, *Modern Tragedy*, 176, 175.
141 Robbe-Grillet, "Nature, Humanism, Tragedy," 59.
142 For postcolonial criticism of Camus, see Edward Said, "Camus and the French Imperial Experience," in *Culture and Imperialism* (1993), and Conor Cruise O'Brien, *Albert Camus of Europe and Africa* (1970). David Carroll, in *Camus the Algerian* (2008), reads Meursault as both Arab colonial subject, his humanity denied by the French, and Jew – "In a novel published in occupied Paris in 1942, Meursault, as a hated indigenous Other, thus also dies as a Jew" (37).
143 Camus, *Stranger*, 122–3, 121.
144 Camus, *Stranger*, 123.
145 Camus, "La Nausée," 201.
146 Camus, "Three Interviews," 356, 346.
147 Camus, "Create Dangerously," 272; Sartre, *Nausea*, 62, 143, 145, 146, 150.
148 Camus writes in *The Rebel*: "As for Proust, his contribution has been to create, from an obstinate contemplation of reality, a closed world that belonged only to him and that indicated his victory over the transitoriness of things and over death" (266).
149 Camus, *Notebooks 1935–1942*, 8.
150 Camus, *Notebooks 1935–1942*, 9.
151 Terada, *Looking Away*, 136.
152 Camus, *Notebooks 1935–1942*, 6.
153 Woolf, *Lighthouse*, 16.
154 Woolf, *Lighthouse*, 60; Camus, *Rebel*, 258.
155 Camus, "Create Dangerously," 268, 264.
156 Camus, *First Man*, 277.
157 Camus, *Rebel*, 251.
158 Camus, *Rebel*, 10.
159 Woolf, *Lighthouse*, 105, 161.
160 Camus, "Create Dangerously," 264.
161 Woolf, *Lighthouse*, 105.
162 Srigley, *Critique of Modernity*, 63–5.
163 Camus, *Fall*, 39.
164 Camus, *Fall*, 40.
165 Camus, *Fall*, 42, 96.
166 Camus, *Fall*, 80.
167 Camus, *Fall*, 136.
168 Camus, *Fall*, 121.
169 Camus, *Fall*, 124.
170 Camus, *Fall*, 73.
171 Camus, *Fall*, 110.
172 Sanyal, "Broken Engagements," 38, 39, 40.
173 Srigley writes: "The other type of regime that practices this sort of elimination [of dissent] is the modern liberal or bourgeois regime. This type of regime, typified in *The Fall* by two cities – Amsterdam and Paris – does not

silence its population through mass killing, as do totalitarian regimes. But Clamence claims that it does have its own 'kind of liquidation.' In such regimes the complete rational organization on which it rests slowly nibbles away at every aspect of life – job, family, leisure time – until one is left with nothing but 'an immaculate skeleton.'. . . No strong loves, no strong hates, nothing to fear or to overcome. One is, as Clamence puts it, 'cleaned up,' which means that one is spiritually dead and thus ready for participation in the modern bourgeois regime" (*Critique of Modernity*, 102)

174 Felman, *Testimony*, 177–8, 174.
175 Camus, *Fall*, 132.
176 Sanyal, "Auschwitz as Allegory," 177–8, 174.
177 Sanyal, "Auschwitz as Allegory," 168–9.
178 Camus, *Fall*, 106.
179 Camus, *Fall*, 89.
180 Camus, *Fall*, 106.
181 Camus, *Fall*, 88, 83.
182 Camus, *Fall*, 144.
183 Camus, *Fall*, 147.
184 Camus, *Fall*, 146–7.
185 Camus, *Stranger*, 123.
186 Camus, *Stranger*, 122.

Chapter 5

1 Beckett, *Unnamable*, 341.
2 Tonning, "Beckett and Schopenhauer," 88. See also Tonning, "Fleshly, Creative and Mystical Vision."
3 Beckett, *Unnamable*, 403.
4 Ackerley, "The Ideal Real," 60.
5 Buning, "Samuel Beckett's Negative Way," 130.
6 Wolosky, *Language Mysticism*, 118, 119.
7 Wolosky, *Language Mysticism*, 105, 89.
8 Wolosky, *Language Mysticism*, 105.
9 Robinson, *Long Sonata*, 18, quoted in Wolosky, *Language Mysticism*, 83.
10 Wolosky, *Language Mysticism*, 107.
11 Wolosky, *Language Mysticism*, 107, 82.
12 Ackerley, "The Ideal Real," 61.
13 Weller, *Language and Negativity*, 107.
14 Weller, *Language and Negativity*, 29.
15 Weller, *Language and Negativity*, 16–17, 27, 59, 99.
16 Weller, *Language and Negativity*, 96.
17 Ackerley, "'Perfection,'" 40.
18 Ackerley, "'Perfection,'" 40.
19 Louise Hornby discusses modernism's surmounting of this barrier in *Still Modernism*. She addresses modernist means of capturing the world as it is

whether we name or observe it or not. "Objectivity here," she writes, "does not indicate a naive realism or the notion of a singular truth, but rather the ideal form of an unoccupied perspective" (142). These unoccupied perspectives are, à la Russell, vantage points that no subject need inhabit, that exist apart from anthropocentric language and sensation.

20 Van Hulle and Weller, *L'Innommable/The Unnamable*, 220.
21 Van Hulle and Weller, *L'Innommable/The Unnamable*, 220.
22 Ackerley, "'Perfection,'" 28.
23 Beckett, *Company*, 45.
24 Beckett, *Proust*, 67.
25 Beckett, *Proust*, 67.
26 Beckett, *Proust*, 67.
27 Nietzsche, *Birth of Tragedy*, 52–3.
28 Lear, "Katharsis," 325, 326.
29 Beckett, *Unnamable*, 285.
30 Beckett, *Unnamable*, 285.
31 Cavell, *Claim of Reason*, 389.
32 Cavell, *Claim of Reason*, 389.
33 Beckett, *Unnamable*, 330.
34 Beckett, *Unnamable*, 321.
35 Beckett, *Unnamable*, 296.
36 Beckett, *Unnamable*, 296, 304, 305.
37 Beckett, *Unnamable*, 304, 329.
38 Beckett, *Unnamable*, 329.
39 Beckett, *Unnamable*, 318.
40 Beckett, *Unnamable*, 318.
41 Beckett, *Unnamable*, 318.
42 Beckett, *Unnamable*, 319.
43 Critchley, *Very Little ... Almost Nothing*, 22, 23.
44 Beckett, *Unnamable*, 318.
45 Beckett, *Unnamable*, 304.
46 Beckett, *Unnamable*, 360.
47 Beckett, *Unnamable*, 382–3.
48 Beckett, *Unnamable*, 324, 326.
49 Beckett, *Unnamable*, 329.
50 Beckett, *Unnamable*, 328.
51 Beckett, *Unnamable*, 331.
52 Cioran, *Heights of Despair*, 43.
53 Cioran, *Heights of Despair*, 10.
54 Cioran, *Heights of Despair*, 12.
55 Cioran, *Heights of Despair*, 14.
56 Beckett, *Unnamable*, 344.
57 Beckett, *Unnamable*, 334.
58 Beckett, *Unnamable*, 340.
59 Hardy, "Before Life and After," 1–12.

60 Beckett, *Unnamable*, 331.
61 Beckett, *Unnamable*, 340.
62 Beckett, *Unnamable*, 351.
63 Beckett, *Unnamable*, 319.
64 Beckett, *Unnamable*, 351.
65 Beckett, *Unnamable*, 349.
66 Beckett, *Unnamable*, 343.
67 Beckett, *Unnamable*, 360, 361.
68 Wolosky, *Language Mysticism*, 87.
69 Wolosky, *Language Mysticism*, 129.
70 Wolosky, *Language Mysticism*, 129.
71 Wolosky, *Language Mysticism*, 128.
72 Beckett, *Unnamable*, 342.
73 Beckett, *Unnamable*, 349.
74 Beckett, *Unnamable*, 353.
75 Beckett, *Unnamable*, 355.
76 Beckett, *Unnamable*, 341.
77 Beckett, *Unnamable*, 340.
78 Beckett, *Unnamable*, 342.
79 Beckett, *Unnamable*, 379–80.
80 Beckett, *Unnamable*, 340.
81 Beckett, *Unnamable*, 340.
82 Sophocles, *Oedipus the King* 1134.
83 Sophocles, *Oedipus the King* 1185, 1340–1.
84 Sophocles, *Oedipus the King* 1305–10.
85 Sophocles, *Oedipus the King* 1305.
86 Sophocles, *Oedipus the King* 1467–73.
87 Sophocles, *Oedipus the King* 1359–60.
88 Sophocles, *Oedipus the King* 1518–23.
89 Sophocles, *Oedipus at Colonus* 1388-94.
90 Sophocles, *Oedipus at Colonus* 288–9, 292–5, 615–16, 1098–105.
91 Sophocles, *Oedipus at Colonus* 1100, 1104.
92 Sophocles, *Oedipus at Colonus* 1775-8.
93 Lispector, *Passion*, 182.
94 Lispector, *Passion*, 169.
95 Lispector, *Passion*, 91, 103.
96 Lispector, *Passion*, 90.
97 Lispector, *Passion*, 172, 173.
98 Deleuze and Guattari, *What Is Philosophy?*, 169.
99 Lispector, *Passion*, 70.
100 Lispector, *Passion*, 182, 169.
101 Lispector, *Passion*, 185, 186, 188.
102 Lukács, "Ideology of Modernism," 17, 32.
103 Nussbaum, "Narrative Emotions," 251.
104 Nussbaum, "Narrative Emotions," 251.

105 Nussbaum, "Narrative Emotions," 249.
106 Critchley, *Very Little ... Almost Nothing*, 7.
107 Critchley, *Very Little ... Almost Nothing*, 27.
108 Nussbaum, "Narrative Emotions," 246; Critchley, *Very Little ... Almost Nothing*, 27.
109 Critchley, *Very Little ... Almost Nothing*, 27.
110 Critchley, *Very Little ... Almost Nothing*, 25.
111 Nussbaum, "Narrative Emotions," 249.
112 Epicurus, "Epicurus to Menoeceus," 30–1.
113 Epicurus, "Epicurus to Menoeceus," 32–3.
114 Lucretius, *Nature of the Universe* 1.933–50, 3.521–5.
115 Lucretius, *Nature of the Universe* 6.16.
116 See also Feldman, *Beckett's Books*.
117 Addyman and Feldman, "Interwar 'Philosophy Notes,'" 764–5.
118 Addyman and Feldman, "Interwar 'Philosophy Notes,'" 765, emphasis Beckett's.
119 Addyman and Feldman, "Interwar 'Philosophy Notes,'" 765.
120 Addyman and Feldman, "Interwar 'Philosophy Notes,'" 762.
121 Addyman and Feldman, "Interwar 'Philosophy Notes,'" 764. "Sensualism" is italicized in Windelband, *History of Philosophy*, 297. Beckett retains this emphasis in his notes.
122 Addyman and Feldman, "Interwar 'Philosophy Notes,'" 764. Addyman and Feldman note their "italics added" (769n22). Alexander's *A Short History of Philosophy* reads: "Protagoras was thus the champion of individualism, the first agnostic and advocate of the relativity of knowledge" (50).
123 Addyman and Feldman, "Interwar 'Philosophy Notes,'" 767.
124 Cordingley, "Beckett's Philosophical Imagination," 385.
125 Cordingley, "Beckett's Philosophical Imagination," 385.
126 Cordingley, "Beckett's Philosophical Imagination," 385, 386.
127 Cordingley, "Beckett's Philosophical Imagination," 391.
128 Cordingley, "Beckett's Philosophical Imagination," 392.
129 Wolosky, *Language Mysticism*, 131.
130 Cordingley, "Beckett's Philosophical Imagination," 392.
131 Cordingley, "Beckett's Philosophical Imagination," 390.
132 Beckett, *How It Is*, 126.
133 For connections between Beckett's stage drama and evolution and species-being, see Shepherd-Barr, *Theatre and Evolution from Ibsen to Beckett*.
134 Cioran, *Anathemas and Admirations*, 134.
135 Cioran, *Anathemas and Admirations*, 134.
136 Landy, "Feeling Nothing," 226.
137 See also Landy, *How to Do Things with Fictions*, chapter 5, "Beckett: Antithesis and Tranquility."
138 Landy, "Feeling Nothing," 226.
139 Landy, "Feeling Nothing," 226.
140 Landy, "Feeling Nothing," 226.

141 See Wasser, "A Relentless Spinozism," 125–6, 129.
142 Landy, "Feeling Nothing," 227.
143 Landy, "Feeling Nothing," 227.
144 Critchley, *Very Little . . . Almost Nothing*, 25.
145 Landy, "Feeling Nothing," 228.
146 Landy, "Feeling Nothing," 228.
147 Beckett, *Unnamable*, 305.
148 Sophocles, *Oedipus the King* 1450–6.
149 Beckett, *Unnamable*, 326.
150 Camus, *Myth of Sisyphus*, 38.
151 Beckett, *Letters 4*, 651.
152 Beckett, *Letters 4*, 651n2.
153 Ann Banfield, email message to author, February 13, 2019.
154 Camus, *Myth of Sisyphus*, 21.
155 Camus, *Rebel*, 7.
156 Camus, *Myth of Sisyphus*, 121, 122.
157 Camus, *Myth of Sisyphus*, 123, 121.
158 Camus, *Myth of Sisyphus*, 123.
159 Van Hulle and Weller, *L'Innommable/The Unnamable*, 45.
160 Van Hulle and Weller, *L'Innommable/The Unnamable*, 45.
161 Van Hulle and Weller, *L'Innommable/The Unnamable*, 45.
162 Camus, *Myth of Sisyphus*, 121.
163 Camus, *Myth of Sisyphus*, 123.
164 Beckett, *Unnamable*, 336.
165 Beckett, *Company*, 4.
166 Beckett, *Company*, 33.
167 Lubbock, *Craft of Fiction*, 257.
168 Beckett, *Company*, 21.
169 Beckett, *Company*, 3.
170 Beckett, *Company*, 3.
171 Beckett, *Company*, 10.
172 Beckett, *Unnamable*, 361.
173 Beckett, *Company*, 14.
174 Beckett, *Company*, 33.
175 Beckett, *Company*, 33.
176 Booth, *Rhetoric of Fiction*, 444n20.
177 Booth, *Rhetoric of Fiction*, 449.
178 Booth, *Rhetoric of Fiction*, 450.
179 Booth, *Rhetoric of Fiction*, 455.
180 Woolf, *Lighthouse*, 161.
181 Camus, "Preface," 17.
182 Svevo, *Zeno's Conscience*, 435.
183 Beckett, *Unnamable*, 361.

Bibliography

Ablow, Rachel. *Victorian Pain*. Princeton: Princeton University Press, 2017.

Ackerley, Chris. "The Ideal Real: A Frustrated Impulse in Samuel Beckett's Writing." *Samuel Beckett Today/Aujourd'hui* 21 (2009): 59–72.

"'Perfection is not of this world': Samuel Beckett and Mysticism." *Mystics Quarterly* 30, nos. 1–2 (2004): 28–55.

Addyman, David, and Matthew Feldman. "Samuel Beckett, Wilhelm Windelband, and the Interwar 'Philosophy Notes.'" *Modernism/Modernity* 18, no. 4 (2011): 755–70.

Aeschylus. *Agamemnon*. Translated by Richmond Lattimore. In *The Complete Greek Tragedies, Aeschylus I*, edited by David Grene and Richmond Lattimore, 33–90. Chicago: University of Chicago Press, (1947) 1953.

Agamemnon. Translated by Robert Fagles. In *The Oresteia: Agamemnon, The Libation Bearers, The Eumenides*, 99–172. New York: Penguin, (1966) 1977.

Agamemnon. Translated by Anne Carson. In *An Oresteia: Agamemnon by Aiskhylos; Elektra by Sophokles; Orestes by Euripides*, 9–76. New York: Farrar, Straus and Giroux, 2009.

The Seven against Thebes. Translated by David Grene. In *The Complete Greek Tragedies, Aeschylus I*, 3rd ed., edited by David Grene and Richmond Lattimore, 63–111. Chicago: University of Chicago Press, 2013.

Alexander, Archibald. *A Short History of Philosophy*. Glasgow: Maclehose and Sons, 1908.

Alexander, Samuel. *Time, Space, and Deity*. Charleston: BiblioLife, (1920) 2010.

Allen, Garland E. "Morgan and Natural Selection Revisited." In Mayr and Provine, *Evolutionary Synthesis*, 356–82.

Archer, William. *Real Conversations*. London: William Heinemann, 1904.

Aristotle. *Poetics*. In *Aristotle: "Poetics"; Longinus: "On the Sublime"; Demetrius: "On Style"* (Loeb Classical Library 199), revised ed., 27–142. Cambridge, MA: Harvard University Press, 1995.

The "Poetics" of Aristotle: Translation and Commentary. Translated by Stephen Halliwell. Chapel Hill: University of North Carolina Press, 1987.

Arnold, Matthew. "On the Modern Element in Literature." In *Essays by Matthew Arnold*, 454–72. Oxford: Oxford University Press, 1914.

Banfield, Ann. *The Phantom Table: Woolf, Fry, Russell and the Epistemology of Modernism*. New York: Cambridge University Press, 2000.

"Time Passes: Virginia Woolf, Post-Impressionism, and Cambridge Time." *Poetics Today* 24, no. 3 (2003): 471–516.

"Tragic Time: The Problem of the Future in Cambridge Philosophy and *To the Lighthouse.*" *Modernism/Modernity* 7, no. 1 (2000): 43–75.

Barr, Tina. "Divine Politics: Virginia Woolf's Journey toward Eleusis in *To the Lighthouse.*" *boundary 2* 20, no. 1 (1993): 125–45.

Beauvoir, Simone de. *The Ethics of Ambiguity.* Translated by Bernard Frechtman. New York: Citadel, (1947) 1970.

Beckett, Samuel. *Company.* In *Nohow On*, 1–46. New York: Grove, 1995.

Disjecta: Miscellaneous Writings and a Dramatic Fragment. Edited by Ruby Cohn. New York: Grove, 1983.

How It Is. New York: Grove, 1964.

The Letters of Samuel Beckett, vol. 4: 1966–1989. Edited by George Craig, Martha Dow Fehsenfeld, Dan Gunn, and Lois More Overbeck. Cambridge: Cambridge University Press, 2016.

Proust and Three Dialogues. 3rd ed. London: John Calder, 1989.

The Unnamable. In *Three Novels: Molloy, Malone Dies, The Unnamable*, edited by Laura Lindgren, 283–407. New York: Grove, 2009.

Beer, Gillian. "Darwin and the Uses of Extinction." In "Darwin and the Evolution of Victorian Studies," edited by Jonathan Smith, special issue, *Victorian Studies* 51, no. 2 (2009): 321–31.

Darwin's Plots: Evolutionary Narrative in Darwin, George Eliot, and Nineteenth-Century Fiction. Cambridge: Cambridge University Press, 1983.

Berger, Bria. "Power, Selfhood, and Identity: A Feminist Critique of Borderline Personality Disorder." *Advocates' Forum* (2014): 1–8.

Blanton, C. D. *Epic Negation: The Dialectical Poetics of Late Modernism.* Oxford: Oxford University Press, 2015.

Boesiger, Ernest. "Evolutionary Biology in France at the Time of the Evolutionary Synthesis." In Mayr and Provine, *Evolutionary Synthesis*, 309–20.

Booth, Wayne. *The Rhetoric of Fiction.* 2nd ed. Chicago: University of Chicago Press, 1983.

Bowler, Peter J. *Evolution: The History of an Idea.* 3rd ed. Berkeley: University of California Press, 2003.

Buning, Marius. "Samuel Beckett's Negative Way: Intimations of the *Via Negativa* in His Late Plays." In *European Literature and Theology in the Twentieth Century*, edited by D. Jasper and C. Crowder, 129–42. New York: Palgrave, 1990.

Burstein, Jessica. *Cold Modernism: Literature, Fashion, Art.* University Park: Penn State University Press, 2012.

Büttner, Gottfried. *Samuel Beckett's Novel "Watt."* Translated by Joseph P. Dolan. Philadelphia: University of Pennsylvania Press, 1984.

Camus, Albert. "The Adulterous Wife." In *Exile and the Kingdom*, translated by Justin O'Brien, 3–33. New York: Knopf, 1958.

Algerian Chronicles. Translated by Arthur Goldhammer. Cambridge, MA: Harvard University Press, 2013.

"The Almond Trees." In *Lyrical and Critical Essays*, 134–7.

"Create Dangerously." In *Resistance, Rebellion, and Death*, Translated by Justin O'Brien, 249–72. New York: Vintage, (1957) 1995.

"The Desert." In *Lyrical and Critical Essays*, 93–106.

The First Man. Translated by David Hapgood. New York: Vintage, 1996.

"Helen's Exile." In *Lyrical and Critical Essays*, 148–53.

Lyrical and Critical Essays. Translated by Ellen Conroy Kennedy. Edited by Philip Thody. New York: Vintage, 1970.

"The Minotaur, or Stopping in Oran." In *Lyrical and Critical Essays*, 109–33.

The Myth of Sisyphus and Other Essays. Translated by Justin O'Brien. New York: Vintage, (1942) 1991.

Notebooks 1935–1942. Translated by Philip Thody. Chicago: Ivan R. Dee, 2010.

Notebooks 1942–1951. Translated by Justin O'Brien. Chicago: Ivan R. Dee, 2010.

Notebooks 1951–1959. Translated by Ryan Bloom. Chicago: Ivan R. Dee, 2010.

"Nuptials at Tipasa." In *Lyrical and Critical Essays*, 65–72.

"On the Future of Tragedy." In *Lyrical and Critical Essays*, 295–310.

"On Jean-Paul Sartre's *La Nausée*." In *Lyrical and Critical Essays*, 199–202.

The Plague. Translated by Stuart Gilbert. New York: Vintage, (1947) 1991.

"Preface, 1958." In *Lyrical and Critical Essays*, 5–17.

The Rebel: An Essay on Man in Revolt. Translated by Anthony Bower. New York: Knopf, (1951) 1956.

The Stranger. Translated by Matthew Ward. New York: Vintage, (1942) 1989.

"Three Interviews." In *Lyrical and Critical Essays*, 345–65.

"William Faulkner." In *Lyrical and Critical Essays*, 311–20.

"The Wind at Djemila." In *Lyrical and Critical Essays*, 73–9.

Camus, Catherine. *Albert Camus: solitaire et solidaire*. Neuilly-sur-Seine: Lafon, 2009.

Carpentier, Martha C. *Ritual, Myth, and the Modernist Text: The Influence of Jane Ellen Harrison on Joyce, Eliot, and Woolf*. New York: Routledge, (1998) 2013.

Carroll, David. *Camus the Algerian: Colonialism, Terrorism, Justice*. New York: Columbia University Press, 2008.

"An Interview with David Carroll." 2014. Columbia University Press, https://cup.columbia.edu/author-interviews/carroll-camus-algerian.

Carroll, Sean. *Brave Genius: A Scientist, a Philosopher, and Their Daring Adventures from the French Resistance to the Nobel Prize*. New York: Crown, 2013.

Carson, Anne. "The Gender of Sound." In *Glass, Irony and God*, 119–42. New York: New Directions, 1995.

Preface to *Grief Lessons: Four Plays by Euripides*, 7–9. New York: NYRB Classics, 2006.

Cascardi, Anthony J. "Tragedy and Philosophy." In *A Companion to the Philosophy of Literature*, edited by Garry L. Hagberg and Walter Jost, 161–74. Malden: Wiley-Blackwell, 2010.

Cavell, Stanley. *The Claim of Reason: Wittgenstein, Skepticism, Morality, and Tragedy.* Oxford: Oxford University Press, 1999.

Cioran, E. M. *Anathemas and Admirations.* Translated by Richard Howard. New York: Arcade, (1986) 1991.

On the Heights of Despair. Translated by Ilinca Zarifopol-Johnston. Chicago: University of Chicago Press, (1934) 1992.

Clayton, Jay. "The Modern Synthesis: Genetics and Dystopia in the Huxley Circle." *Modernism/Modernity* 23, no. 4 (2016): 875–96.

Coles, Steven. "Borderline Personality Disorder: Abandon the Label, Find the Person." *Discursive of Tunbridge Wells,* blogs.canterbury.ac.uk/discursive/borderline-personality-disorder-abandon-the-label-find-the-person/.

Conrad, Joseph. *The Collected Letters of Joseph Conrad, vol. 1: 1861–1897.* Edited by Frederick R. Karl and Laurence Davies. Cambridge: Cambridge University Press, 1983.

The Collected Letters of Joseph Conrad, vol. 2: 1898–1902. Edited by Frederick R. Karl and Laurence Davies. Cambridge: Cambridge University Press, 1986.

Corbic, Arnaud. *Camus et l'homme sans Dieu.* Paris: Cerf, 2007.

Cordingley, Anthony. "Beckett's Philosophical Imagination: Democritus versus Pythagoras and Plato in *Comment c'est/How It Is.*" *Comparative Literature* 65, no. 4 (2013): 383–407.

Critchley, Simon. *ABC of Impossibility.* Minneapolis: Univocal, 2015.

Notes on Suicide. London: Fitzcarraldo Editions, 2015.

Tragedy, the Greeks, and Us. New York: Pantheon, 2019.

Very Little . . . Almost Nothing: Death, Philosophy, Literature. New York: Routledge, 1997.

Dalgarno, Emily. *Virginia Woolf and the Migrations of Language.* New York: Cambridge University Press, 2011.

"Virginia Woolf: Translation and 'Iterability.'" *The Yearbook of English Studies* 36, no. 1 (2006): 145–56.

Virginia Woolf and the Visible World. New York: Cambridge University Press, 2001.

Darwin, Charles. *The Variation of Animals and Plants under Domestication,* vol. 2. New York: Echo Library, (1868) 2007.

Darwin Correspondence Project. Cambridge University, www.darwinproject.ac.uk.

Deleuze, Gilles, and Félix Guattari. *What Is Philosophy?* Translated by Hugh Tomlinson and Graham Burchell. New York: Columbia University Press, 1994.

Dienstag, Joshua Foa. *Pessimism: Philosophy, Ethic, Spirit.* Princeton: Princeton University Press, 2006.

Dimock, Wai Chee. "After Troy: Homer, Euripides, Total War." In Felski, *Rethinking Tragedy,* 66–81.

Draper, R. P., ed. *Hardy: The Tragic Novels.* New York: Macmillan, 1991.

duBois, Page. "Toppling the Hero: Polyphony in the Tragic City." In Felski, *Rethinking Tragedy,* 127–47.

Eagleton, Terry. *Sweet Violence: The Idea of the Tragic.* Oxford: Blackwell, 2003.

Ebbatson, Roger. *The Evolutionary Self: Hardy, Forster, Lawrence.* Brighton: Harvester, 1982.

Eliot, T. S. *After Strange Gods: A Primer of Modern Heresy.* New York: Harcourt, Brace, 1934.

"*Ulysses*, Order, and Myth." In *Selected Prose of T. S. Eliot*, edited by Frank Kermode, 175–78. New York: Harvest, (1923) 1975.

Ellis, Havelock. "Concerning *Jude the Obscure*." *The Savoy* 6 (1896): 35–49.

Epicurus. "Epicurus to Menoeceus." Translated by C. Bailey. In *The Stoic and Epicurean Philosophers*, edited by Whitney J. Oates, 30–3. New York: Modern Library, 1957.

Euripides. *Alkestis.* In *Grief Lessons*, 251–307.

Grief Lessons: Four Plays by Euripides. Translated by Anne Carson. New York: NYRB Classics, 2006.

Hekabe. In *Grief Lessons*, 99–159.

Herakles. In *Grief Lessons*, 19–84.

Hippolytos. In *Grief Lessons*, 171–242.

Fanon, Frantz. *The Wretched of the Earth.* Translated by Constance Farrington. New York: Grove, 1968.

Farnham, Willard. *The Medieval Heritage of Elizabethan Tragedy.* New York: Barnes and Noble, 1963.

Feldman, Matthew. *Beckett's Books: A Cultural History of the Interwar Notes.* New York: Continuum, 2006.

Feldman, Matthew. "Samuel Beckett, Wilhelm Windelband and Nominalist Philosophy." In Feldman and Mamdani, *Beckett/Philosophy*, 151–84.

Feldman, Matthew, and Karim Mamdani, eds. *Beckett/Philosophy.* Stuttgart: Ibidem, 2015.

Felman, Shoshana, and Dori Laub. *Testimony: Crises of Witnessing in Literature, Psychoanalysis, and History.* New York: Routledge, 1992.

Felski, Rita, ed. *Rethinking Tragedy.* Baltimore: Johns Hopkins University Press, 2008.

Fifield, Peter. "'Of being – or remaining': Beckett and Early Greek Philosophy." In Feldman and Mamdani, *Beckett/Philosophy*, 127–50.

Fletcher, John, and Malcolm Bradbury. "The Introverted Novel." In *Modernism: A Guide to European Literature, 1890–1930*, edited by Malcolm Bradbury and James McFarlane, 394–415. New York: Penguin, 1976.

Foley, John. *Albert Camus: from the Absurd to Revolt.* Ithaca: McGill-Queen's University Press, 2008.

Forster, E. M. *Aspects of the Novel.* New York: RosettaBooks, (1927) 2002.

Fowler, Rowena. "Moments and Metamorphoses: Virginia Woolf's Greece." *Comparative Literature* 51, no. 3 (1999): 217–42.

Furlani, Andre. *Beckett after Wittgenstein.* Evanston: Northwestern University Press, 2015.

"The Contradictions of Samuel Beckett." *Modernism/Modernity* 22, no. 3 (2015): 449–70.

Gallagher, Catherine. "*Tess of the d'Urbervilles*: Hardy's Anthropology of the Novel." In *Tess of the d'Urbervilles*, edited by John Paul Riquelme, 422–40. Boston: Bedford Books, 1998.

Gaspari, Séverine. "Écrire contre soi-même: Albert Camus ou la posture du romancier." In *Lectures d'Albert Camus*, 45–71. Avignon: Éditions A. Barthélemy, 2010.

Gillies, Mary Ann. "Virginia Woolf: Bergsonian Experiments in Representation and Consciousness." In *Henri Bergson and British Modernism*, 107–31. Montreal: McGill-Queen's University Press, 1996.

Glendening, John. *The Evolutionary Imagination in Late-Victorian Novels: An Entangled Bank*. Burlington: Ashgate, 2007.

Goldhill, Simon. "The Ends of Tragedy: Schelling, Hegel, and Oedipus." In "Tragedy," edited by Helene P. Foley and Jean E. Howard, special issue, *PMLA* 129, no. 4 (2014): 634–48.

Gossin, Pamela. *Thomas Hardy's Novel Universe: Astronomy, Cosmology, and Gender in the Post-Darwinian World*. Burlington: Ashgate, 2007.

Gottschall, Jonathan. *The Storytelling Animal: How Stories Make Us Human*. Boston: Houghton Mifflin Harcourt, 2012.

Gray, Asa. *Darwiniana: Essays and Reviews Pertaining to Darwinism*. Seattle: CreateSpace, (1876) 2016.

Greenberg, Jonathan. "Introduction: Darwin and Literary Studies." In "Darwin and Literary Studies," edited by Jonathan Greenberg, special issue, *Twentieth-Century Literature* 55, no. 4 (2009): 423–44.

Grosz, Elizabeth. *Becoming Undone: Darwinian Reflections on Life, Politics, and Art*. Durham: Duke University Press, 2011.

Hacking, Ian. *The Taming of Chance*. Cambridge: Cambridge University Press, 1990.

Hägglund, Martin. *Dying for Time: Proust, Woolf, Nabokov*. Cambridge, MA: Harvard University Press, 2012.

Halliwell, Stephen. *Aristotle's "Poetics."* London: Duckworth, 1986.

——. "Plato and Aristotle on the Denial of Tragedy." *Proceedings of the Cambridge Philological Society* 30 (1984): 49–71.

Hardy, Thomas. "Apology." In *Complete Poems*, 556–62.

——. "Before Life and After." In *Complete Poems*, 277.

——. *The Collected Letters of Thomas Hardy, vol. 3: 1902–1908*. Edited by Richard Little Purdy and Michael Millgate. Oxford: Clarendon, 1982.

——. *The Collected Letters of Thomas Hardy, vol. 5: 1914–1919*. Edited by Richard Little Purdy and Michael Millgate. Oxford: Oxford University Press, 1985.

——. *The Complete Poems*, edited by James Gibson. New York: Palgrave, 2001.

——. "Hap." In *Complete Poems*, 9.

——. "In Tenebris II." In *Complete Poems*, 168.

——. *Jude the Obscure*. 2nd ed. Edited by Norman Page. New York: Norton, 1999.

——. "A Sign-Seeker." In *Complete Poems*, 49–50.

——. *Tess of the d'Urbervilles*. 3rd ed. Edited by Scott Elledge. New York: Norton, 1991.

——. *Two on a Tower*. New York: Penguin, 1999.

Harris, George W. *Reason's Grief: An Essay on Tragedy and Value*. New York: Cambridge University Press, 2006.

Harrison, Jane Ellen. *Themis: A Study of the Social Origins of Greek Religion*. London: Merlin, (1912) 1963.

Hartshorne, Charles. "Charles Sanders Peirce's Metaphysics of Evolution." *The New England Quarterly* 14, no. 1 (1941): 49–63.

Hayden, Patrick. *Camus and the Challenge of Political Thought: Between Despair and Hope*. New York: Palgrave, 2016.

Honig, Bonnie. "Antigone's Two Laws: Greek Tragedy and the Politics of Humanism." *New Literary History* 41, no. 1 (2010): 1–33.

Horkheimer, Max, and Theodor W. Adorno. *Dialectic of Enlightenment*. Translated by Edmund Jephcott. Stanford: Stanford University Press, (1944) 2002.

Hornby, Louise. "The Cameraless Optic: Anna Atkins and Virginia Woolf." *English Language Notes* 44, no. 2 (2006): 87–100.

Still Modernism: Photography, Literature, Film. Oxford: Oxford University Press, 2017.

Howells, William Dean. Review of *Jude the Obscure*, by Thomas Hardy. *Harper's Weekly* December 7, 1895: 1156.

Hume, David. "Of Tragedy." In *The Philosophical Works of David Hume*, vol. 3, 237–47. Chestnut Hill: Adamant Media, 2007.

Hussey, Mark. *The Singing of the Real World: The Philosophy of Virginia Woolf's Fiction*. Columbus: Ohio State University Press, 1986.

Ingham, Patricia. "Explanatory Notes." In *Jude the Obscure*, 399–416. Oxford: Oxford University Press, 2002.

Jameson, Fredric. *The Antimonies of Realism*. New York: Verso, 2013.

Jeanson, Francis. "Albert Camus ou l'âme révoltée." *Les temps modernes* 79 (1952): 2070–90.

Johnson, Curtis. *Darwin's Dice: The Idea of Chance in the Thought of Charles Darwin*. Oxford: Oxford University Press, 2015.

Johnson, Lionel. "The Argument." In *Tess of the d'Urbervilles*, 3rd ed., edited by Scott Elledge, 390–400. New York: Norton, 1991.

Jones, Donna. *The Racial Discourses of Life Philosophy: Négritude, Vitalism, and Modernity*. New York: Columbia University Press, 2010.

Kelly, Mary Ann. "Schopenhauer's Influence on Hardy's *Jude the Obscure*." In *Schopenhauer: New Essays in Honor of his 200th Birthday*, edited by Eric von der Luft, 232–46. New York: Edwin Mellen, 1988.

King, Jeannette. *Tragedy in the Victorian Novel: Theory and Practice in the Novels of George Eliot, Thomas Hardy, and Henry James*. Cambridge: Cambridge University Press, 1978.

Knight, David. "The Law of Higgledy-Pigglety: Charles Darwin's Inheritance, His Legacy and the Moral Order of Nature." In *The Evolution of Literature: Legacies of Darwin in European Cultures*, edited by Nicholas Saul and Simon J. James, 19–33. New York: Rodopi, 2011.

Koulouris, Theodore. *Hellenism and Loss in the Work of Virginia Woolf*. Burlington: Ashgate, 2011.

Kramer, Dale. "Hardy: The Driftiness of Tragedy." In *The Ashgate Research Companion to Thomas Hardy*, edited by Rosemarie Morgan, 372–86. Burlington: Ashgate, 2010.

Krutch, Joseph Wood. "The Tragic Fallacy." In *The Modern Temper: A Study and a Confession*, 79–97. New York: Harcourt, (1929) 1956.

Landy, Joshua. *How to Do Things with Fictions*. Oxford: Oxford University Press, 2012.

"Passion, Counter-Passion, Catharsis: Flaubert (and Beckett) on Feeling Nothing." In *A Companion to the Philosophy of Literature*, edited by Garry L. Hagberg and Walter Jost, 218–38. Malden: Wiley-Blackwell, 2010.

Lawrence, D. H. *Study of Thomas Hardy and Other Essays*. Edited by Bruce Steele. New York: Cambridge University Press, (1914) 1985.

Women in Love. New York: Viking, (1920) 1960.

Lear, Jonathan. "Katharsis." *Phronesis* 33, no. 3 (1988): 297–326.

Leonard, Miriam. *Tragic Modernities*. Cambridge, MA: Harvard University Press, 2015.

Levine, George. *Darwin Loves You: Natural Selection and the Re-enchantment of the World*. Princeton: Princeton University Press, 2008.

Levy, Eric P. "Woolf's Metaphysics of Tragic Vision in *To the Lighthouse*." *Philological Quarterly* 75, no. 1 (1996): 109–32.

Lewis, Wyndham. *Men without Art*. London: Cassell, 1934.

Lewontin, Richard C. "Theoretical Population Genetics in the Evolutionary Synthesis." In Mayr and Provine, *Evolutionary Synthesis*, 58–68.

Lispector, Clarice. *The Passion According to G.H.* Translated by Idra Novey. New York: New Directions, (1964) 2012.

Lloyd Morgan, C. *Emergent Evolution*. London: Williams and Norgate, 1923.

Loraux, Nicole. *Tragic Ways of Killing a Woman*. Translated by Anthony Forster. Cambridge, MA: Harvard University Press, 1987.

Lubbock, Percy. *The Craft of Fiction*. New York: Viking, 1957.

Lucas, F. L. *Euripides and His Influence*. New York: Cooper Square, (1923) 1963.

Tragedy in Relation to Aristotle's "Poetics." New York: Harcourt, (1927) 1928.

Lucretius. *On the Nature of the Universe*. Translated by Ronald Melville. Oxford: Oxford University Press, 2008.

Lukács, György. "The Ideology of Modernism." In *The Meaning of Contemporary Realism*, translated by John and Necke Mander, 17–46. London: Merlin, (1958) 1969.

"Realism in the Balance." Translated by Rodney Livingstone. In *Aesthetics and Politics*, edited by Ronald Taylor, 28–59. London: Verso, (1938) 1980.

Soul and Form. Translated by Anna Bostock. New York: Columbia University Press, (1910) 2009.

The Theory of the Novel: A Historico-Philosophical Essay on the Forms of Great Epic Literature. Translated by Anna Bostock. Cambridge, MA: MIT Press, (1916) 1971.

Lurie, Michael. "Facing up to Tragedy: Toward an Intellectual History of Sophocles in Europe from Camerarius to Nietzsche." In *A Companion to Sophocles*, edited by K. Ormand, 440–61. Malden: Wiley-Blackwell, 2012.

Marcus, Jane. "*The Years* as Greek Drama, Domestic Novel, and Götterdämmerung." In *Virginia Woolf and the Languages of Patriarchy*, 36–56. Bloomington: Indiana University Press, 1987.

Marshall, Mary H. "Theatre in the Middle Ages: Evidence from Dictionaries and Glosses." *Symposium* 4 (1950): 1–89.

Mayr, Ernst, and William B. Provine, eds. *The Evolutionary Synthesis: Perspectives on the Unification of Biology*. Cambridge, MA: Harvard University Press, 1980.

McCoskey, Denise Eileen, and Mary Jean Corbett. "Virginia Woolf, Richard Jebb, and Sophocles' *Antigone*." In *A Companion to Sophocles*, edited by K. Ormand, 462–76. Malden: Wiley-Blackwell, 2012.

Meillassoux, Quentin. *After Finitude: An Essay on the Necessity of Contingency*. Translated by Ray Brassier. London: Continuum, (2006) 2008.

Mensch, Jennifer. *Kant's Organicism: Epigenesis and the Development of Critical Philosophy*. Chicago: University of Chicago Press, 2013.

Mills, Jean. "Goddesses and Ghosts: Virginia Woolf and Jane Ellen Harrison." PhD dissertation, City University of New York, 2008.

———. *Virginia Woolf, Jane Ellen Harrison, and the Spirit of Modernist Classicism*. Columbus: Ohio State University Press, 2014.

Monod, Jacques. *Chance and Necessity: An Essay on the Natural Philosophy of Modern Biology*. Translated by Austryn Wainhouse. New York: Vintage, (1970) 1972.

Moretti, Franco. *The Way of the World: The Bildungsroman in European Culture*. New York: Verso, 2000.

Morton, Peter. *The Vital Science: Biology and the Literary Imagination, 1860–1900*. London: Allen and Unwin, 1984.

Muller, Herbert J. *The Spirit of Tragedy*. New York: Random House, 1956.

Murphy, P. J. "Beckett's Critique of Kant." In Feldman and Mamdani, *Beckett/Philosophy*, 261–78.

Murray, Gilbert. "Excursus on the Ritual Forms Preserved in Greek Tragedy." In Jane Ellen Harrison, *Themis*, 341–63. London: Merlin, (1912) 1963.

Nehamas, Alexander. *Nietzsche: Life as Literature*. Cambridge, MA: Harvard University Press, 1985.

Newton, K. M. *Modern Literature and the Tragic*. Edinburgh: Edinburgh University Press, 2008.

Nietzsche, Friedrich. *The Birth of Tragedy and Other Writings*. Translated by Ronald Speirs. Edited by Raymond Geuss and Ronald Speirs. Cambridge: Cambridge University Press, (1872) 1999.

———. *Daybreak: Thoughts on the Prejudices of Morality*. Translated by H. J. Hollingdale. Cambridge: Cambridge University Press, (1881) 1997.

———. *The Gay Science*. Translated by Josefine Nauckhoff. Edited by Bernard Williams. Cambridge: Cambridge University Press, (1882) 2001.

The Will to Power. Translated and edited by Walter Kaufmann. New York: Vintage-Random, (1901) 1967.

Nolan, Maura. *John Lydgate and the Making of Public Culture*. Cambridge: Cambridge University Press, 2005.

"'Now Wo, Now Gladnesse': Ovidianism in the Fall of Princes." *ELH* 71 (2004): 532–58.

Nussbaum, Martha. *The Fragility of Goodness: Luck and Ethics in Greek Tragedy and Philosophy*. 2nd ed. New York: Cambridge University Press, 2001.

"Narrative Emotions: Beckett's Genealogy of Love." *Ethics* 98, no. 2 (1988): 225–54.

The Therapy of Desire: Theory and Practice in Hellenistic Ethics. Princeton: Princeton University Press, 1994.

"Tragedy and Self-Sufficiency: Plato and Aristotle on Fear and Pity." In *Essays on Aristotle's "Poetics,"* edited by Amélie Rorty, 261–91. Princeton: Princeton University Press, 1992.

"The Transfigurations of Intoxication: Nietzsche, Schopenhauer, and Diony-sus." *Arion: A Journal of Humanities and the Classics* 1, no. 2 (1991): 75–111.

O'Brien, Conor Cruise. *Albert Camus of Europe and Africa*. New York: Viking, 1970.

"Camus, Algeria, and 'The Fall.'" In *Conor: A Biography of Conor Cruise O'Brien, vol. II: Anthology*, edited by Donald Harman Akenson, 170–80. Montreal: McGill-Queen's University Press, (1969) 1994.

Peirce, Charles Sanders. *Writings of Charles S. Peirce: A Chronological Edition, vol. 8: 1890–1892*. Bloomington: Indiana University Press, 2009.

Pessoa, Fernando. *The Education of the Stoic*. Translated by Richard Zenith. Cambridge, MA: Exact Change, 2005.

"The four songs that follow now." In *The Keeper of Sheep*, 47.

"I'd give anything just to be the roadside dust." In *The Keeper of Sheep*, 53.

The Keeper of Sheep. Translated by Edwin Honig and Susan M. Brown. New York: Sheep Meadow Press, (1925) 1985.

"On a terribly clear day." In *The Keeper of Sheep*, 115.

"Today I read nearly two pages." In *The Keeper of Sheep*, 73.

Plato. *The "Republic" of Plato*. 2nd ed. Translated by Allan Bloom. New York: Basic Books, 1991.

Plotz, John. "Speculative Naturalism and the Problem of Scale: Richard Jefferies's *After London*, after Darwin." *Modern Language Quarterly* 76, no. 1 (2015): 31–56.

Prins, Yopie. *Ladies' Greek: Victorian Translations of Tragedy*. Princeton: Princeton University Press, 2017.

"OTOTOTOI: Virginia Woolf and 'the Naked Cry' of Cassandra." In *Aga-memnon in Performance: 458 BC to AD 2004*, edited by Fiona Macintosh, Pantelis Michelakis, Edith Hall, and Oliver Taplin, 163–86. Oxford: Oxford University Press, 2005.

Prouteau, Anne. *Albert Camus ou le présent impérissable*. Paris: Orizons, 2008.

Provine, William B. "England: Introduction." In Mayr and Provine, *Evolutionary Synthesis*, 329–34.

Rabaté, Jean-Michel. *Think, Pig! Beckett at the Limit of the Human*. New York: Fordham University Press, 2016.

Reginster, Bernard. *The Affirmation of Life: Nietzsche on Overcoming Nihilism*. Cambridge, MA: Harvard University Press, 2006.

Rensch, Bernhard. "Neo-Darwinism in Germany." In Mayr and Provine, *Evolutionary Synthesis*, 284–303.

Richter, Virginia. *Literature after Darwin: Human Beasts in Western Fiction, 1859–1939*. New York: Palgrave, 2011.

Robbe-Grillet, Alain. "Nature, Humanism, Tragedy." In *For a New Novel: Essays on Fiction*, translated by Richard Howard, 49–76. Evanston: Northwestern University Press, (1958) 1989.

Robinson, Michael. *The Long Sonata of the Dead*. New York: Grove, 1969.

Rohman, Carrie. *Stalking the Subject: Modernism and the Animal*. New York: Columbia University Press, 2009.

Rosenbaum, S. P. "The Philosophical Realism of Virginia Woolf." In *English Literature and British Philosophy: A Collection of Essays*, edited by S. P. Rosenbaum, 316–57. Chicago: University of Chicago Press, 1971.

Russell, Bertrand. "My Mental Development." In *The Basic Writings of Bertrand Russell*. Edited by Robert E. Egner and Lester E. Denonn, 9–22. New York: Routledge, 2009.

Mysticism and Logic and Other Essays. Auckland: Floating Press, (1917) 2010.

The Problems of Philosophy. Oxford: Oxford University Press, (1912) 2001.

Said, Edward. *Culture and Imperialism*. New York: Vintage, 1993.

Saint-Amour, Paul K. *Tense Future: Modernism, Total War, Encyclopedic Form*. Oxford: Oxford University Press, 2015.

Sanyal, Debarati. "Auschwitz as Allegory in *Night and Fog*." In *Concentrationary Cinema: Aesthetics as Political Resistance in Alain Resnais's "Night and Fog,"* edited by Griselda Pollock and Max Silverman, 152–82. New York: Berghahn Books, 2011.

"Broken Engagements: Sartre, Camus, and the Question of Commitment." *Yale French Studies* 98 (2000): 29–49.

Sartre, Jean-Paul. *Being and Nothingness: A Phenomenological Essay on Ontology*. Translated by Hazel E. Barnes. New York: Washington Square, (1943) 1984.

"Colonialism Is a System." In *Colonialism and Neocolonialism*, translated by Azzedine Haddour, Steve Brewer, and Terry McWilliams, 30–47. New York: Routledge, 2001.

"An Explication of *The Stranger*." In *Camus: A Collection of Critical Essays*, edited by Germaine Brée, 108–21. Englewood Cliffs: Prentice-Hall, (1943) 1962.

Nausea. Translated by Lloyd Alexander. New York: New Directions, (1938) 2007.

"Réponse à Albert Camus." *Les temps modernes* 82 (1952): 334–53.

"A Victory." In *Colonialism and Neocolonialism*, translated by Azzedine Haddour, Steve Brewer, and Terry McWilliams, 65–77. New York: Routledge, 2001.

Scheler, Max. "On the Tragic." Translated by Bernard Stambler. In *Tragedy: Vision and Form*, edited by Robert W. Corrigan, 3–18. New York: Harper, (1923) 1981.

Schopenhauer, Arthur. *The World as Will and Representation*, vol. 1. Translated and edited by Judith Norman, Alistair Welchman, and Christopher Janaway. Cambridge: Cambridge University Press, 2010.

The World as Will and Representation, vol. 2. Translated by E. F. J. Payne. New York: Dover, 1966.

Scott, David. *Conscripts of Modernity: The Tragedy of Colonial Enlightenment*. Durham: Duke University Press, 2004.

Sharpe, Matthew. *Camus, Philosophe: To Return to Our Beginnings*. Leiden: Brill, 2015.

"Restoring Camus as Philosophe: On Ronald Srigley's *Camus' Critique of Modernity*." *Critical Horizons* 13, no. 3 (2012): 400–24.

Shattuck, Sandra D. "The Stage of Scholarship: Crossing the Bridge from Harrison to Woolf." In *Virginia Woolf and Bloomsbury: A Centenary Celebration*, edited by Jane Marcus, 278–98. London: Macmillan, 1987.

Shaw, Clare, and Gillian Proctor. "Women at the Margins: A Critique of the Diagnosis of Borderline Personality Disorder." *Feminism & Psychology* 15, no. 4 (2005): 483–90.

Sheehan, Paul. *Modernism, Narrative and Humanism*. New York: Cambridge University Press, 2002.

Shepherd-Barr, Kirsten. *Theatre and Evolution from Ibsen to Beckett*. New York: Columbia University Press, 2015.

Sim, Lorraine. *Virginia Woolf: The Patterns of Ordinary Experience*. Burlington: Ashgate, 2010.

Sophocles. *Oedipus at Colonus*. In *The Three Theban Plays*, translated by Robert Fagles, 279–388. New York: Penguin, 1984.

Oedipus the King. In *The Three Theban Plays*, translated by Robert Fagles, 155–251. New York: Penguin, 1984.

Women of Trachis. Translated by Michael Jameson. In *The Complete Greek Tragedies: Sophocles II*, edited by David Grene and Richmond Lattimore, 63–119. Chicago: University of Chicago Press, 1957.

Spiquel, Agnès. "Qu'aurait été l'histoire d'amour dans la suite du *Premier Homme*?" In *Lectures d'Albert Camus*, 15–31. Avignon: Éditions A. Barthélemy, 2010.

Spiropoulou, Angeliki. "'On Not Knowing Greek': Virginia Woolf's Spatial Critique of Authority." *Interdisciplinary Literary Studies* 4, no. 1 (2002): 1–19.

Srigley, Ronald D. *Albert Camus' Critique of Modernity*. Columbia: University of Missouri Press, 2011.

Stewart, Garrett. "Signing Off: Dickens and Thackeray, Woolf and Beckett." In *Philosophical Approaches to Literature: New Essays on Nineteenth and*

Twentieth-Century Texts, edited by William E. Cain, 117–39. Lewisburg: Bucknell University Press, 1984.

Sumner, Francis B. Review of *The History and Theory of Vitalism*, by Hans Driesch. *Journal of Philosophy, Psychology, and Scientific Methods* 13, no. 4 (1916): 103–9.

Sumner, Rosemary. *A Route to Modernism: Hardy, Lawrence, Woolf.* New York: St. Martin's, 2000.

Svevo, Italo. *Zeno's Conscience.* Translated by William Weaver. New York: Everyman's Library, (1923) 2003.

Szondi, Peter. *An Essay on the Tragic.* Translated by Paul Fleming. Stanford: Stanford University Press, (1961) 2002.

Terada, Rei. *Looking Away: Phenomenality and Dissatisfaction, Kant to Adorno.* Cambridge, MA: Harvard University Press, 2009.

Thiher, Allen. *Fiction Refracts Science: Modernist Writers from Proust to Borges.* Columbia: University of Missouri Press, 2005.

Todd, Olivier. *Albert Camus: A Life.* New York: Knopf, 1997.

Tonning, Erik. "'I am not reading philosophy': Beckett and Schopenhauer." In Feldman and Mamdani, *Beckett/Philosophy*, 75–102.

Tonning, Erik. "'Nor by the eye of flesh nor by the other': Fleshly, Creative and Mystical Vision in Late Beckett." *Samuel Beckett Today/Aujourd'hui* 22 (2010): 223–39.

Toura, Hiroki. *La quête et les expressions du bonheur dans l'œuvre d'Albert Camus.* Cazaubon: Eurédit, 2004.

Tucker, David. "Beckett's 'Guignol' Worlds: Arnold Geulincx and Heinrich von Kleist." In Feldman and Mamdani, *Beckett/Philosophy*, 235–60.

Unamuno, Miguel de. *The Tragic Sense of Life in Men and Nations.* Translated by J. E. Crawford Flitch. Seattle: CreateSpace, (1913) 2014.

Van Hulle, Dirk. "'Eff it': Beckett and Linguistic Skepticism." In Feldman and Mamdani, *Beckett/Philosophy*, 279–98.

Van Hulle, Dirk, and Shane Weller. *The Making of Samuel Beckett's "L'Innommable"/"The Unnamable."* New York: Bloomsbury, 2014.

Vernant, Jean-Pierre. "Ambiguity and Reversal: On the Enigmatic Structure of *Oedipus Rex*." In Vernant and Vidal-Naquet, *Myth and Tragedy in Ancient Greece*, 113–40.

Vernant, Jean-Pierre. "Intimations of the Will in Greek Tragedy." In Vernant and Vidal-Naquet, *Myth and Tragedy in Ancient Greece*, 49–84.

Vernant, Jean-Pierre. "Oedipus without the Complex." In Vernant and Vidal-Naquet, *Myth and Tragedy in Ancient* Greece, 85–111.

Vernant, Jean-Pierre, and Pierre Vidal-Naquet, eds. *Myth and Tragedy in Ancient Greece.* Translated by Janet Lloyd. New York: Zone Books, 1988.

Verrall, A. W., ed. *The "Agamemnon" of Aeschylus, with an Introduction, Commentary, and Translation.* London: Macmillan, (1889) 1904.

Vidal-Naquet, Pierre. "Oedipus between Two Cities: An Essay on *Oedipus at Colonus*." In Vernant and Vidal-Naquet, *Myth and Tragedy in Ancient Greece*, 329–59.

Wallace, Alfred Russel. *Darwinism: An Exposition of the Theory of Natural Selection with Some of Its Applications*. London: Macmillan, (1889) 1912.

The World of Life: A Manifestation of Creative Power, Directive Mind and Ultimate Purpose. New York: Moffat, 1911.

Wasser, Audrey. "A Relentless Spinozism: Deleuze's Encounter with Beckett." *Substance* 41, no. 1 (2012): 124–36.

Watkin, Christopher. *Difficult Atheism: Post-Theological Thinking in Alain Badiou, Jean-Luc Nancy and Quentin Meillassoux*. Edinburgh: Edinburgh University Press, 2013.

Waugh, Patricia. "Mind in Modern Fiction: Literary and Philosophical Perspectives after Darwin." In *The Evolution of Literature: Legacies of Darwin in European Cultures*, edited by Nicholas Saul and Simon J. James, 125–40. New York: Rodopi, 2011.

Weller, Shane. *Language and Negativity in European Modernism*. Cambridge: Cambridge University Press, 2018.

Wells, H. G., Julian Huxley, and G. P. Wells. *The Science of Life*. New York: Doubleday, 1931.

White, Cheryl, and David Denborough, eds. *Introducing Narrative Therapy*. Adelaide: Dulwich Center Publications, 1998.

White, Michael. *Maps of Narrative Practice*. New York: Norton, 2007.

Whitehead, Alfred North. *Science and the Modern World*. New York: Free Press, (1925) 1997.

Williams, Bernard. *Shame and Necessity*. Berkeley: University of California Press, 1993.

Williams, Raymond. *Modern Tragedy*. London: Chatto and Windus, 1966.

Windelband, Wilhelm. *A History of Philosophy*, vol. 1. New York: Harper, 1958.

Wohl, Victoria, ed. *Probabilities, Hypotheticals, and Counterfactuals in Ancient Greek Thought*. New York: Cambridge University Press, 2014.

Wolosky, Shira. *Language Mysticism: The Negative Way of Language in Eliot, Beckett, and Celan*. Stanford: Stanford University Press, 1995.

Woolf, Virginia, "Agamemnon" Notebook, Virginia Woolf Collection of Papers, the Henry W. and Albert A. Berg Collection of English and American Literature, the New York Public Library, Astor, Lenox and Tilden Foundations.

The Diary of Virginia Woolf, vol. 2: 1920–1924. Edited by Ann Olivier Bell. New York: Harcourt, 1978.

The Diary of Virginia Woolf, vol. 3: 1925–1930. Edited by Anne Olivier Bell. New York: Harcourt, 1980.

Essays of Virginia Woolf, vol. 4: 1925–1928. Edited by Andrew McNeillie. Boston: Mariner, 2008.

Moments of Being. 2nd ed. Edited by Jeanne Schulkind. New York: Harcourt, (1972) 1985.

"Mr. Bennett and Mrs. Brown." In *Theory of the Novel*, edited by Michael McKeon, 745–58. Baltimore: Johns Hopkins University Press, (1924) 2000.

Mrs. Dalloway. New York: Harcourt, (1925) 1981.

Night and Day. New York: Harcourt, (1919) 1948.

"The Novels of Thomas Hardy." In *The Second Common Reader: Annotated Edition*, edited by Andrew McNeillie, 245–57. New York: Harcourt, (1928) 1986.

"On Not Knowing Greek." In *The Common Reader: First Series*, edited by Andrew McNeillie, 23–38. New York: Harcourt, (1925) 1984.

"Time Passes." Holograph ms. Berg Collection, New York Public Library. www.woolfonline.com.

To the Lighthouse. New York: Harcourt, (1927) 1981.

The Waves. New York: Harcourt, (1931) 1959.

Worman, Nancy. *Virginia Woolf's Greek Tragedy.* New York: Bloomsbury, 2018.

Wyatt, Jean. "The Celebration of Eros: Greek Concepts of Love and Beauty in *To the Lighthouse*." *Philosophy and Literature* 2, no. 2 (1978): 160–75.

Zumhagen-Yekplé, Karen, and Michael LeMahieu, eds. *Wittgenstein and Modernism.* Chicago: University of Chicago Press, 2017.

Index

Index

CPSIA information can be obtained
at www.ICGtesting.com
Printed in the USA
LVHW111629130920
665875LV00003B/7

9 781108 496025